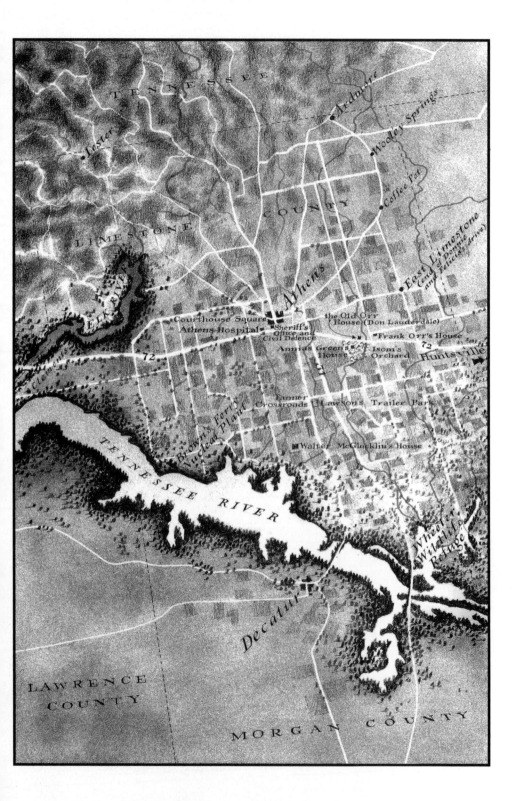

F5

DEVASTATION, SURVIVAL, AND THE MOST VIOLENT TORNADO OUTBREAK OF THE TWENTIETH CENTURY

MARK LEVINE

miramax books

NEW YORK

ISBN 1-4013-5220-0
ISBN 978-1-4013-5220-2

First Edition
10 9 8 7 6 5 4 3 2 1

*For my father, Isaac
and in memory of my mother, Evelyn*

A weary time! a weary time!
How glazed each weary eye,
When looking westward, I beheld
A something in the sky.

—Samuel Taylor Coleridge,
    "The Rime of the Ancient Mariner"

Table of Contents

Mark Levine

The People of
Limestone County, Alabama

April 3, 1974

Felica Golden, 15, Wooley Springs
Freshman, Ardmore High School.

Donnie Powers, 18, Coffee Pot
Senior, Ardmore High School.

•

Frank Orr, 23, Athens
Machinist, Monsanto Chemical Company.

Marilyn McBay, 24, Athens
Frank's sister. Homemaker.

Vergil McBay, 24, Athens
Husband of Marilyn. Machinist, 3M Company.

Jason McBay, 2, and Mark McBay, 6 days
Children of Marilyn and Vergil.

•

Spencer Black, 30, Athens
*Director, Athens-Limestone County Department of
Civil Defense.*

•

Annias Green, 34, Athens
*Assistant Manager, Laborers' International Union, Local 366;
pastor, Macedonia Primitive Baptist Church.*

Lillian Green, 31, Athens
Annias's wife. Custodian, Athens College.

Ananias ("Rabbit") Green, Jr., 11; Amos Green, 10;
and Titus Green, 7
Children of Annias and Lillian.

•

M.W. ("Buddy") Evans, 45, Athens
Limestone County sheriff.

•

Ralph Padgett, 40, Athens
Limestone County coroner.

•

Paula Marbut, 38, Lawson's Trailer Park, Tanner
Homemaker.

•

Don Lauderdale, 37, Athens
*Longtime employee, General Electric Aerospace Division;
neighbor of Frank Orr; uncle of Vergil McBay.*

•

Walter McGlocklin, 30, Tanner
Farmer; lineman for Athens Electric Department.

Ruth McGlocklin, 31, Tanner
Walter's wife. Homemaker.

Walter McGlocklin, Jr., 2; Nancy McGlocklin, 3;
Sandra McGlocklin, 5; and Grace McGlocklin, 7
Children of Walter and Ruth.

Jerry Beckham, 15
Walter's nephew.

•

Bill Dunnavant, 24, Athens
Broadcaster, WJMW-AM.

PART ONE

I t is always the same moment on this night of the calendar. Felica is in the passenger's seat. The car has stopped. The road is washed out. The faint wet glow of taillights in the distance has faded. Whatever houses there may be along the road have receded into the night. In the darkness everything is foreign. Felica is lost, nearly lost, not far from home. She doesn't know why the car is no longer moving, nor does she bother to ask. She feels hot. Her lavender dress, one of her favorites, sewn by her mother, clings to her skin. Her hair, thick and long, is damp with rain water. It is more than raining out; rain drowns every feature of the night. Felica peers out her side window. Lightning blanches the sky. The landscape, flickering into momentary view, is strange and beautiful. Oak trees in the distance lean against their roots, their canopies shrouded with silvery mist. Then, suddenly, the trees disappear. In their place a cloud comes forward, out of its element, a ground-cloud. It rides clumsily across the field, spitting dirt. It defies understanding. It looks, Felica thinks, like the spout of steam that rises from a kettle.

Lightning drains from the sky. Darkness returns, darker. Rain thrashes the roof of the car. It is hard for Felica to hear above the din. An onslaught begins. Clods of dirt are flung against the car, and scraps of wood and tin, and tree branches, and stones. The moment of impact begins to prolong itself. The eight-track tape plays dimly, as though in another *room,* Greatest Hits *by Bread. Felica's favorite song—the one she and Donnie, her boyfriend, the driver, in the seat beside her, play again and again—is called "If." Now Felica is unsure whether the song has already played and whether, in her distraction, she has missed it.* "If the world should stop revolving spinning slowly down to die," *goes the verse,* "I'd spend the end with you."

Felica seems to have been sitting in silence a long time, like a girl in a painting, placed at her lover's side but unaware of his presence. The silence builds. Then Donnie breaks from it. He turns to Felica abruptly, with vehemence. "Open the door," *he says.* "Get out."

Felica doesn't have to be here. She is here by accident. The odds against it happening to her—and she doesn't yet know what is happening, only that something is happening, is about to happen—are overwhelming. This must be happening to someone else.

It is Wednesday. It is Limestone County, the north end of northern Alabama, a speck of a world, out of the world's sight. Felica is fifteen. Her birthday was less than three weeks ago. That day, Donnie gave her a "promise ring," a wire-thin silver band set with a small diamond. She is wearing it now, on the finger where an engagement ring would be, though it promises no such thing, only that she and Donnie have progressed to some vague romantic state on the other side of "going steady." Even that seems like a lie. Felica knows she and Donnie won't be together much longer. Not after what he did last month, while he was gone on his senior class trip to Lake Winnepesaukah, an amusement park near Chattanooga. Felica could tell he was not himself when he returned. A friend called her to report that during the course of the trip Donnie had "stepped out" on her with another girl, that he had "been with" another girl. Donnie denied it at first, then faltered, confessing, then followed with a stream of apologies and pledges, and with the promise ring. But Felica has not recovered from it. She may never.

Their first date was more than a year ago. Donnie's best friend, Dwayne Cornelison, was dating Doris, Felica's older sister, and persuaded Donnie to pair with Felica on a double date. At first, Donnie protested. He had barely noticed Felica at school. She was only in eighth grade, and while she loomed over her classmates—she was a willowy five feet eight inches tall—Donnie told Dwayne she was "way too young" for his taste. He was nearly seventeen. Still, Dwayne implored him.

The two couples went to a Saturday night Sweetheart Banquet at a tiny church on a country road. By the end of the night, Donnie and Felica had stolen away from the others.

In some respects they seem an unlikely pair. At their school, Ardmore High, Felica is shy and demure, never calling attention to herself, dressing modestly and wearing little jewelry or makeup. Donnie, on the other hand, is at ease with the popular crowd. He is strikingly handsome, with a strong jaw and a chiseled brow offset by a wide, warm smile. At six feet four inches, he is the tallest boy in his class, a starter on the basketball team, and more important, one of the stars of the football team.

During games he rarely spends a moment on the sidelines. Even though, despite his best efforts, he cannot seem to add weight—he tops out at 189—he is fast and strong and can take a hit as well as he gives one. Felica is always in the stands on Friday evenings in the fall, wearing Donnie's black and gold football cardigan.

Donnie's talents have been noticed by coaches from the University of Mississippi, who offered him a scholarship to play for Ole Miss. It is a proud achievement for a small-school athlete. No one in Donnie's family has attended college. Now, with a month to go before high school graduation, he has still not made up his mind about whether to accept. His parents are encouraging him to go. He hasn't yet told Felica, but he finds himself strongly inclined toward leaving home.

For Felica's part, any future that she can imagine is uncertain. Even if she and Donnie stay together, the distance between them when he goes off to Ole Miss—as she expects he will—will surely be a strain. There will be no shortage of girls at college whom Donnie will find momentarily irresistible. Some girls, as Felica has observed, don't see anything wrong with pursuing another girl's boyfriend.

Tonight is midweek church night. Felica would go by choice, but the choice is not hers. Her father is the pastor, and has been for six years, since the family moved from Gurley. Before that, they lived in Huntsville, briefly, and before that in Gadsden, where, Felica has been told, her father was an alcoholic until he gave his life over to God. Now their home is Wooley Springs, which is barely a crossroads along the old highway to Ardmore—less a settlement than a sparse scattering of aging farmhouses and trailers. Wooley Springs Baptist is a squat brick building surrounded by fields with views of more fields beyond. Perhaps a hundred followers crowd its pews on the busiest occasions. Felica accompanies the choir on an upright piano.

Donnie started attending Wooley Springs Baptist a few months ago. It gives him the opportunity to see Felica more frequently than he would otherwise be allowed. It has also helped him to ease the suspicions of Felica's parents, who hadn't accepted him at first. They had thought he ran with a bad crowd, some of whom had long hair and drank liquor.

Felica is the youngest of five daughters, and though she is allowed to go on dates, she has to adhere to strict rules. She is permitted to see Donnie on Friday and Saturday nights, but her curfew is set for ten o'clock. Donnie is welcome to visit Felica at her home on Sundays and after church on Wednesdays, though the house is off-limits to him when a parent is not present—otherwise, neighbors might gossip—and he and Felica are forbidden from straying beyond the living room and kitchen. The prospect of holding hands within sight of Felica's parents—let alone kissing—is unthinkable to her.

Donnie's parents have no such rules. Felica has been to Donnie's house when his parents are gone, and she has seen the inside of his bedroom. She is selectively obedient to her parents' wishes. She has no interest in alcohol, and she has faithfully avoided going to movies at the Hatfield Drive-In. Anyone could see you there and tell your sisters and then you'd be in serious trouble. On the other hand, Felica has more than once flouted her parents' prohibition against "going parking" with Donnie. There are too many miles of dark gravel roads for there to be any risk of detection. When they go parking, their only company is the sound of pastured cows and crickets. Of course Felica knows above all that she must not disgrace her family, like the handful of girls in her ninth grade class who have already gotten pregnant.

Donnie picks up Felica at her house a bit before seven. The church is a quarter mile down the road. Donnie is wearing crisp blue jeans and shirt sleeves. His belt, a broad loop of white leather punched with three rows of holes, is secured by a monogrammed silver buckle. The flare at the bottom of his jeans is nearly wide enough to conceal his size thirteen shoes. His class ring, inset with Felica's birthstone, aquamarine, bulges from a finger on his left hand. Donnie has been voted Best Dressed among the forty-three boys in his graduating class, and has already posed for a yearbook photo honoring the distinction, holding hands with Donna Wales, the Best Dressed girl.

A few cold raindrops fall from the eaves of the church when Felica and Donnie enter. They go off to separate corners of the building—one for the teenage boys' youth group, one for the teenage girls'—and arrange to meet afterwards. Even inside, the air is damp, and the gray light of early evening, filtering in, has a dull finish. Steady thunder beyond.

It isn't long before there is a stirring in the church. Whispers, concerned glances. Felica is summoned from her group and told that her father has been taken from the church, dizzy and nauseated, and helped home.

This has happened before—it happens often—and Felica is never accustomed to it, never not distressed by it. Her father is only forty-four. As long as Felica can remember, he has been sick. For years doctors called his condition "side pleurisy" and told him he had to live with the pain, fatigue, and mystery of it all. Six years ago, he received a more specific diagnosis: kidney failure. He was taken to Birmingham, a hundred miles away, where he spent three months in the hospital, accompanied by Felica's mother. The children were left in Wooley Springs, mostly to take care of themselves. Several times Felica was told her father was on the verge of death, yet each time she showed up at his bedside he rallied. When he was finally allowed to go home to Wooley Springs, he was not expected to live long. The strain on Felica's mother led to a nervous breakdown; she had to leave Wooley Springs for an extended stay in a sanatorium.

Felica has to admit that Donnie, whatever his faults, has been a source of stability over the past year; she is unsure how she would cope without him. They leave the church to check on her father. The storm has gotten worse. Wind blows curtains of rain across the road.

When they reach her house, Felica is relieved to find her father awake and lucid and claiming to feel better. Then from the kitchen come the sounds of a new uproar. It is Felica's Aunt Kay, who arrived in Wooley Springs for church an hour earlier with her four children. Kay has just heard a radio announcer say that houses in her village, several miles down the road, have been battered by the evening's storm. Kay calls home but receives no answer. She has convinced herself that her husband is in danger. She paces the room like an actress playing the part of a frantic person. She insists on driving into the storm to find him.

Felica's parents plead with Kay to wait out the weather, but she won't be stopped. Then Donnie enters the clamor with a suggestion. He offers to follow Kay home to make sure she arrives safely. Felica's parents agree with the plan.

F5

Now it is Felica who steps forward. She wants to ride along with Donnie. Felica's mother refuses. It's a school night. It's storming. It's dangerous. Your father is sick.

Felica turns to her father. He has always had a hard time denying his youngest daughter anything. Felica knows this. You go on, he says. You be careful now.

Felica and Donnie follow Kay's taillights. The road, a pocked blacktop, is otherwise vacant. Felica has always liked thunderstorms. How many nights has she been eased to sleep listening to rain on the roof and windows? But she has rarely been in the midst of such a storm. The lightning display is otherworldly. It turns the sky a sequence of smudged hues—first purple, then red, then orange, then green, then yellow—trailed by percussive thunder. The car rattles. Its windows are fogged. Rain spills down the windshield in obscuring bands.

Felica is not scared. Donnie is an excellent driver. He first drove his grandfather's tractor when he was five, and at eight he got behind the wheel of his parents' Corvair. By the time he was ten, Donnie was delivering groceries from his parents' store to customers—old women, mostly— who didn't have cars of their own. They would invite him to come in and tip him with a slice of pie or a loaf of bread. When he turned sixteen he inherited the use of his family's hulking Bel Air.

He began saving for something more impressive. He took a job at the Hardee's takeout stand in town. He started at $1.20 an hour and was raised to $1.65 an hour in his senior year. He put aside $400 and borrowed another $200 from his father and showed up at home one afternoon in a '67 Mustang, ruby red inside and out. Donnie washes it and polishes it whenever he has a chance. Its front grille gleams. The only flaw in its body is a ding from bird shot, which was there when Donnie bought it. Each morning, he picks Felica up for school in the Mustang, and most of their dates involve at least a few traverses of Ardmore's strip, *from the Red Barn restaurant at one end to the Quick and Tasty Drive-In at the other. The car turns heads. Donnie loves driving it fast.*

At the moment, though, he is working hard simply to keep his tires on the road. Whenever he thinks the storm is about to let up, the sky responds with increased ferocity. Donnie has never seen anything like it. The rearview mirror reflects nothing but the rain-scoured darkness from which he and Felica have emerged and into which they are further descending.

Up ahead, Kay's lights waver dimly in and out of sight. The road is pooled with rain. Donnie shifts into low gear to try to maintain his grip on the surface. He hydroplanes. The wheels lock and kick up plumes of water. The car glides sideways. Donnie steers into the motion and regains control.

Somewhere in the darkness along the side of the road are remnants of familiarity. Donnie's house is five miles south of Wooley Springs, in an equally isolated spot called Coffee Pot. The settlement was established in the '30s by a shadowy figure from Chicago. He built a diner with a dance hall on one side, then added seven crude cabins that were rented to couples, no questions asked, and set up a boxing ring that attracted gamblers and bootleggers. When Donnie's parents bought the property, it was a derelict outpost. They opened a country grocery. They are there now, Donnie knows, closing shop.

Kay's house is only a half-dozen miles beyond Coffee Pot. Donnie thinks he should be able to get there blindfolded, but the storm has transformed the landscape beyond recognition. He and Felica could be anywhere. He grips the steering wheel with both hands and leans into the windshield. He comes to a fork in the road and veers left, slowing to a creep.

The rain is mesmerizing, assaultive. The road has vanished, no distinction between it and whatever borders it. It feels like driving through a rutted field. The car lurches and begins to stall. Donnie hammers the accelerator. The car starts moving again. By now they have lost sight of Kay entirely. Suddenly, the car skids. Water splashes underneath the floorboard. The engine begins to sputter. The car no longer responds to Donnie's instructions. It swerves, comes to a harsh stop.

Felica wonders if they are having a wreck. She has never been in a wreck before. If this is one, it doesn't seem so bad. Why, though, is the car still shuddering?

Donnie looks past Felica and into the storm. He sees a form, its out-line traced with thin light. A vast shadow against the sky. Its grains in motion. That is all it is: no substance, only motion. It sways. It ap-proaches. It wheezes like a fire sweeping through tinder. It is nothing like Donnie imagined. It is less than a moment away. This is its moment. "Open the door," *he says.* "Get out."

Forecast

Nineteen seventy-four: America was in the mood to indulge itself in swan songs—sentimental expressions of leave-taking, backwards glances at the simplicities of the past, and intimations of premature decline. For three consecutive weeks in March, "Seasons in the Sun," an adaptation by Canadian singer Terry Jacks of a poem by Rod McKuen, topped the *Billboard* pop charts. McKuen's poem derived from a raucous, mocking number called "*Le Moribund*" ("The Dying Man") by Belgian music hall star Jacques Brel, which took the form of an apparent suicide note. Something happened to Brel's song as it crossed the Atlantic and was modified for consumption over AM radio. Its anger and unease dissipated. It embraced the maudlin. "Goodbye my friend, it's hard to die," sang Jacks, in a funereal swoon, "when all the birds are singing in the sky." Brel's surly, embittered character became a sweet, if slightly troubled, free spirit, and the song an unapologetically treacly anthem for America's doomed youth. "We had joy, we had fun, / We had seasons in the sun," the waning protagonist noted, as if he were already dead. "But the wine and the song, like the seasons, / Are all gone."

"Seasons in the Sun" sold 3 million copies in its first year of release. Its success was not singular. The '70s were already flush with images of youth wasting away, like the made-for-television movies

Brian's Song, of 1971—which told the story of an interracial friendship between two football players, one of whom suffers a cruel early death—and 1973's *Sunshine*, whose exalted victim was a beautiful hippie. Indeed, on March 30, 1974, as springtime rejuvenation neared, "Sunshine (On My Shoulders)," the theme song of *Sunshine,* sung by John Denver, replaced "Seasons in the Sun" as the nation's number one hit single.

The country was coming out of a long winter. A certain collective mood disorder had set in. It was not without cause. The last U.S. forces had been brought home from Vietnam a year earlier, and the meaning of America's military failure there remained vexing. So did the enormous rifts—generational and socioeconomic and racial and regional—that the war had served to expose. There were a few attempts to tackle post-Vietnam ennui in the guise of entertainment: The most-watched television shows included, on the one hand, satires like *All in the Family* and *M*A*S*H,* and, on the other hand, pacifying and nostalgic treatments of middle America like *The Waltons* and *Happy Days.* For the most part, though, the long and unresolved conflict lingered as an irritant in the American psyche.

In the early months of 1974, the 3.4 million Americans who had served in Vietnam over the previous decade watched from afar as Cambodia fell to communists, Laos was overrun by leftist rebels, and the North Vietnamese renewed their offensive in the South. Stateside, the aftermath of the war was still unfolding. In February, a Pennsylvania Democrat named John Murtha became the first Vietnam veteran to be seated in Congress, winning a special election in a district that had been held by Republicans for a quarter-century. Three weeks later, Lieutenant William L. Calley was released on bond pending an appeal of his twenty-year sentence for leading the most notorious massacre of civilians in Vietnam, in

My Lai, in 1968. And in late March, a federal grand jury presented eight Ohio national guardsmen with indictments on charges of civil rights violations stemming from the 1970 shootings at Kent State University, which killed four students.

Even as Vietnam ebbed painfully into history, there were any number of additional signs that dreams of American ascendancy were fading. For one, the economy was in trouble. In the wake of the Yom Kippur War the previous fall, Arab members of the OPEC cartel had instituted an embargo of oil sales against supporters of Israel. OPEC would not lift its blockade of the United States until March 18, contributing to a fourfold increase in the price of oil, from $2.59 to $10.46 per barrel, in the space of six months. (The average cost of a gallon of gasoline rose from thirty-five cents in the spring of 1973, to fifty-three cents a year later.) Gasoline consumption was rationed, and long lines, reminiscent of the days of privation during World War II, formed at service stations. Americans, shocked into awareness of their dependence on foreign fuel, accepted a nationwide speed limit of 55 miles per hour. The Department of Labor blamed the energy crisis for the loss of a half million jobs—unemployment was at its highest peak in thirteen years—and the rate of inflation rose to a thirty-year high of 13.9 percent. Then, in the midst of the nation's energy woes, oil companies announced that their profits for 1973 had, curiously, increased on the order of 79 percent (Gulf) and 153 percent (Shell), which only inflamed, or confirmed, popular distrust of large corporations.

Soaring crime rates accompanied the dreary economy. In the first quarter of 1974, reports of murder, assault, rape, robbery, burglary, larceny, and auto theft rose 15 percent over the previous year; since 1960, the incidence of these crimes had increased 120 percent. Attorney General William Saxbe termed crime "America's most agonizing fact of life." Lawlessness was not only rampant in big cities; crime had also increased in the suburbs, by 21 percent, and in rural areas, by 19 percent. The most sensational crimes preyed on public fears of incipient social disorder. In San Francisco, eighteen unsuspecting white people were shot from behind by a mysterious figure, described only as a black man, or men. Twelve victims died, and authorities in the proudly progressive city devised a plan to round up young blacks for questioning. In the first week of the dragnet, 567 suspects were detained, and none arrested.

Beyond random attacks, the winter of 1974 was dominated by the attention paid to what was described as "a worldwide rash of kidnappings." The editor of the *Atlanta Constitution* was held for a ransom of $700,000; an eight-year-old Long Island boy was taken by a group of Cuban refugees; Exxon paid $14.2 million to win the release of an executive abducted in Argentina; even Britain's Princess Anne was targeted, narrowly escaping an ambush of the royal limousine near Buckingham Palace.

Most astonishing of all was the case of nineteen-year-old Patricia Hearst, daughter of newspaper publisher Randolph Hearst and granddaughter of magnate William Randolph Hearst, who was taken from the apartment she shared with her boyfriend in Berkeley, California, on February 4. Her captors, members of an upstart and hitherto unknown revolutionary group calling itself the Symbionese Liberation Army (SLA), demanded as ransom the distribution of free food to San Francisco's poor. Hearst's family obliged, donating two million dollars worth of provisions, a gesture dismissed on an audiotape released by the SLA as "throwing a few crumbs to the people." Hearst's kidnapping was widely regarded as America's first political abduction. As April approached, her whereabouts remained unknown.

Above all, the frayed state of American civic life could be traced to a single source: the Oval Office. Suspicions that President Nixon and his associates had conspired to hide the White House's role in a 1972 burglary of the Watergate offices of the Democratic National Committee were coming to a head. On February 6, the House of Representatives voted 410–4 to authorize an inquiry into the possibility of impeachment. Even some Republicans joined Democrats in calling for Nixon to resign rather than force the nation to endure such a prospect. Nixon found himself increasingly isolated. A half-dozen former aides had already been convicted on charges tangentially related to Watergate, and on March 1, 1974, a federal grand jury handed down indictments charging seven former members of Nixon's inner circle—including Chief of Staff H. R. Haldeman, Attorney General John Mitchell, and top policy advisor John Ehrlichman—with conspiracy. On March 15, Nixon was subpoenaed to appear before the House Judiciary Committee.

The spectacle took a heavy toll. In March 1974, a Gallup Poll showed that 65 percent of those surveyed disapproved of Nixon, while only 27 percent expressed approval. It was the lowest level of support ever received by a sitting president.

History and nature tell different stories. Nature is apt, most of the time, to appear as a neutral, even placid, backdrop against which human affairs run their messy course. Only rarely does nature step forward and assert itself with true ferocity. At such moments, the stories of history and of nature seem to overlap—however briefly, however irrationally. Nature captures the spirit of its times, and does so with a clarity that eludes the daily news.

That moment was coming. It would, of course, oversimplify matters to say that the astounding weather that devastated the center of the United States on April 3, 1974, had a starting point, since weather is ongoing, without origin or destination, and stays in constant flux as it circulates.

Nonetheless, one could, perhaps, begin with the sun, 93 million miles distant, which heats the earth's surface unevenly, causing the formation of blocs of air whose basic attributes—temperature, moisture, pressure—differ from those of the air with which they come into contact. The Earth's atmosphere works to negotiate these differences, making moist air drier, warm air cooler, and lowering the pressure of dense air. It is a systematic process. It can be brutal.

One could also start the story of April 3, 1974, a good deal closer to home, over the waters of the north Pacific, near Alaska's Aleutian archipelago. The Aleutians are a boundary region for weather, and boundaries—natural or man-made—can be dangerous places. Cold air from polar latitudes rides atop relatively warmer air, closer to the surface of the water, and the resulting clouds, carrying moist ocean air higher, produce storms. Steep contrasts in winter temperatures between northern and southern air cause still more turbulence along the boundary. Parcels of air passing through the area, like armies crossing a zone of active combat, gain potential for violent outbursts. Such outbursts would not be a cause of concern if air stayed in place, like flame in a fire pit. But air is anything but static, and the disturbances in the Aleutians have a way of being carried by the wind and producing stormy weather on the Pacific coast of North America. From there, the disturbances continue across the continent.

A particularly threatening storm system formed near the Aleutians in March 1974. It organized itself around a vast center of low pressure, or a "trough," fed by moisture from the ocean below, and constantly refueled itself by drawing in surrounding air. Thirty thousand feet on high, jet stream winds, which sweep along the boundary between cold and warmer air, stirred the mix. The ocean barrens above which this "Aleutian Low" hovered were draped in layers of thick clouds, and subjected to continual squalls and high winds.

Meteorologists knew the system was there. Satellite photos showed its cloud cover; buoys and ships provided readings of conditions on the ocean surface; passing planes measured the air's temperature, pressure, and moisture. Meteorologists knew, too, that even though the system could stay in place for two or three weeks, building up energy, it would, at some point, show signs of breaking down. Then the problems would begin.

The collapse started toward the end of the month, as the earth's axis pursued its ordinary springtime tilt. The system's position began to drift; its temperature and pressure became less uniform. Rogue pieces of it—"short waves," which were huge upper level agglomerations of heaving air, akin to airborne tsunamis—began to escape from their holding pattern, and migrated toward the North American coast in rapid succession.

On April 1, one such wave had made its way into the center of the United States, serving up strong thunderstorms and high winds in a region stretching from Louisiana to Ohio. Most dramatically, it gave rise to twenty tornadoes. One tornado derailed a box car in Bolivar, Mississippi, and another trashed a lumberyard in Tippecanoe, Indiana. A man died in the wreckage of his trailer near Huntsville, Alabama, and in Nashville a second hapless fellow was electrocuted by a toppled power line. Some accounts of the storm couldn't resist remarking that it had landed on April Fool's Day. Nature can be an ugly trickster.

As destructive as they were, though, the tornadoes of April 1 did not appear to be the end of the trouble for middle America. As early as March 31, satellite images detected another turbulent wave getting ready to ride out of the low pressure trough in the Aleutians.

This one, too, held the potential for serious mayhem down the line. As Allen Pearson, director of the National Severe Storms Forecast Center (NSSFC), a specialty branch of the National Weather Service, remarked, "One of the subjective rules we use is that if there are two very vigorous systems quite close together, it tends to make the second one more vigorous."

This follow-up pocket of energy left its bed high above the Pacific and broke east toward the American coastline, borne by jet stream winds blowing at more than one hundred miles per hour. It crossed onto the Pacific Northwest early on April 1 and embarked on a demonstration of the principle that the architecture of weather—unlike that of human beings—starts in the upper reaches and builds slowly down to the ground. Within the fast-moving ribbons of the jet stream were areas of even swifter winds, called "jet streaks"; air entering a jet streak would speed up, and then, leaving the streak, spread out in all directions. This "divergence" of air on high—five or six miles above ground—created a drop of pressure, leading to a chain of events, all of them tending towards storminess. Air closer to the ground, which was under higher pressure than that above, rushed towards the area of divergence. (The movement of air from a region of high pressure to one of lower pressure has a familiar name: wind.) With less air on the ground, the pressure there dropped, too, and a mix of warm and cold air was drawn to the center of the low pressure. The temperature difference between the warm and cold air near the ground led to stronger upper-level winds, and, as a result, more upper-level divergence. The cycle repeated. In this way, the upper-level disturbance and the winds near the ground inflamed each other in an intensifying loop, which weather specialists refer to as "positive feedback." For those seeking shelter from the elements there was nothing positive about it.

F5

By the evening of April 2, the system began to cross the Rocky Mountains. There, the massifs slowed down the eastward progress of cold air near the surface of the earth, while the upper level air sailed across. East of the Rockies, this created a dramatic contrast between warm surface temperatures and cold air in the higher reaches, or a "cold front aloft." In the Great Basin, the wave of cold upper-level air began tilting, orienting from northwest to southeast, a sign that the disturbance was apt to grow stronger, guided and churned by jet stream winds. Swerving sharply to the southeast, the jet stream pointed like an arrow at the Ohio Valley.

The system spilled onto the plains, extending into the Oklahoma Panhandle and Texas. Surface winds began to sweep up languid air sitting over the surrounding flat terrain, drawing, in particular, a tremendous supply of warm, moist air from the Gulf of Mexico, where the surface water temperature was 75 degrees. This was the air—sticky, seemingly stagnant, unseasonably warm—to which the broad middle of the country would wake on April 3. With temperatures and humidity much higher at the ground than at upper levels, a condition of great "instability" prevailed.

Other atmospheric ingredients, too, suggested that April 3 might bring something more than refreshing spring showers. In addition to the cold Pacific air on high, a second mass—this one highly stable, warm but dry, originating in Mexico and heated up over the desert Southwest—was also traveling deeper inland. If this warm mass, a mile or two above the ground, slid into place early in the day, it could act as a "cap," trapping the moist air from the Gulf below, and preventing the air from rising, forming clouds, and discharging its energy through precipitation. As the sun's rays heated the moist air throughout the day, surface instability, already high, would mount further.

On the ground, the instability would be invisible. The day might even appear pleasant, with cloudless skies, or a speckling of harmless cumulus clouds. It would not feel pleasant, though. As the trapped air grew warmer and moister, the day would get miserably muggy and hot. And discomfort was not the worst potential consequence. Instability at the ground could build to a fever pitch, until, at some point, the cap would be blown off by the pressure below, and pent-up unstable air would rush explosively upwards.

As April 3 approached, then, the atmosphere was preparing a pitched battle between opposing tracts of air. High up, an enormous mass of cold air was moving in. Down below, warm, moist, unstable air was accumulating. In between, a capping layer was on its way to keep the contestants apart until they were primed for engagement. But even with such features striding into place, the particular savagery of the day ahead was by no means assured.

To boost the odds of spectacularly violent weather, still other ominous factors would have to come into play on April 3, features that could trigger the air to start spinning. Instrument-bearing weather balloons, released into the skies from weather stations across the country, provided a profile of wind, temperature, and moisture at different levels of altitude, and revealed the signature attributes of what forecasters called a "Type I tornado sounding." Winds were "sheared"; like the blades on a pair of open scissors, they moved in different directions. There were, however, more than two blades: Wind at the surface blew from the southeast; at 5,000 feet, it came from the southwest; and at higher altitudes, from the west-southwest. In addition to such "directional shear," there was also evidence of substantial "speed shear," as wind velocity increased with altitude. When a thunderstorm forms in the presence of speed shear, a stream of air inside the storm can be tilted and begin spinning vertically; add some directional shear, and the stream of spinning air can become a gigantic, self-energized top.

Fearing a repetition of the tornadoes of April 1, forecasters at NSSFC took the precaution the following day of alerting radar stations operated by the National Weather Service in its Central Region to perform equipment checks. Radar, which had undergone rapid development during World War II as a means of spotting enemy aircraft and ships, had been found to provide the secondary benefit of recording the movements of areas of precipitation; since the 1950s, it had become a major tool of forecasters. Still, as NSSFC Director Allen Pearson noted, "in detecting tornadoes, the radar doesn't actually see the tornado itself. All the radar sends back is information on the cloud that surrounds it, and we have to try to infer the tornado from the general pattern."

Tornado prediction remained one of the most perplexing challenges for meteorologists, who were keenly aware of the imprecision of their craft. Into the early 1970s, a majority of tornadoes materialized without official warnings being issued, and the problem of tornado forecasting had deep historical roots. For decades, the very utterance of the word "tornado" by government forecasters was regarded as panic-inducing, and its official use had been banned in 1887, when the annual Report of the Chief Signal Officer of the Army proposed that "the harm done by such a prediction would eventually be greater than that which results from the tornado itself." It was not until 1952 that the forerunner of the National Weather Service decided, tentatively, to notify the public about the possibility of coming tornadoes. As the NSSFC's Pearson would comment, "The longer I am in the business of alerting the public, the more I am convinced that we have to be very careful not to cry wolf, and also very careful to emphasize the big outbreaks and let the rest of them fall where they may."

At 4:19 AM on April 3, the NSSFC sent its daily severe weather outlook for the 24-hour period beginning at 7:00 AM to branches of the National Weather Service. The dispatch was no model of specificity. "Scattered severe thunderstorms expected today and tonight," it noted, naming a sixteen-state area from northeast Texas to northwest Georgia. Even so, in most of the country, morning newspapers arrived on doorsteps with printed forecasts that only hinted at the possibility of trouble. In its national forecast, the *New York Times* informed readers that "fair to partly cloudy skies and mild conditions will cover . . . the Ohio Valley. Showers and thunderstorms will be scattered over the Middle and Lower Mississippi Valley, Alabama, and eastern portions of the Central Plains States."

It was reasonable to expect a typical spring day.

Limestone:
Wednesday Morning

Frank Orr was about to be warned. It was eight in the morning. Already the sun was sitting high in the east and the day was hot, even by the sultry standards of northern Alabama. Frank clocked out of his shift at the Monsanto Chemical Company, in Decatur, on the south shore of the Tennessee River, and headed home to the rural outskirts of Athens, the seat of Limestone County. It was a twenty-mile commute. He drove north, against the flow of morning traffic, and approached the bridge spanning the mile-wide river, whose current, dammed not far upstream, was sluggish and swollen by spring rain. A heavy load of silt lent the water's surface a mustard-colored sheen. Verdant spring woods lined the banks.

Frank's maroon El Camino—part muscle car, part pickup—was barely a month old, and cruising in it remained a novelty. Alabama Highway 31 went by in a haze of familiarity. The road carved a straight track through Limestone from bottom to top and had long functioned as a kind of rural Main Street for the county's 41,699 residents. It linked dozens of far-flung farming villages to the commercial hub of Athens, ferried workers to industrial Decatur—3M, Amoco, and Prestolite Spark Plug also had factories there—provided hunters and fishermen access to the swampy reaches along the river, and was dotted with a motley collection of motels, diners, auto body shops, and agricultural supply outlets. There was nightly league play at Athens Bowling Lanes, whose parking lot was a popular site for mingling, and weekend screenings at the Hatfield Drive-In, which Frank called "about the only place to take a date around here," and whose upcoming double bill of *Romeo and Juliet* and *Harold and Maude* could provide a primer in star-crossed love.

Frank passed Wheeler Wildlife Refuge. It wasn't long ago that he and his high school friends would park their cars at the Refuge and pass the night drinking beer, possession of which was outlawed in Limestone but which Frank had managed to procure, straying across county lines, since he was fifteen. Now that he was twenty-three, those days felt like another lifetime; he had, in the meantime, been to war and back. The landscape itself had changed little over the past decade. As Frank made his way toward Athens, the only structures in sight that rose higher than a barn were the looming steel frames of electrical transmission towers—power towers, as everyone called them—stretching across the terrain like science fictional scarecrows. Most of the land surrounding Highway 31 remained dedicated to cotton planting. At this time of year, the fields, not quite recovered from winter, were a bare waste. A few big antebellum houses sagged in disrepair, and here and there Frank could see a tractor creeping in the distance, or climbing onto the road and slowing down traffic. In Limestone, no one showed impatience at such obstructions. Frank drove on past a trailer park, and past a clutch of cratelike roadside churches, and past a nursery that raised houseplants and shrubs for far-off gardens.

At Tanner Crossroads, he peered left, toward his old high school, and made a right turn. Now he was driving straight into the shrill morning sun. He shielded his eyes with a forearm. He wasn't thinking about anything except getting home and going to bed.

F5

There was no part of his day, so far, that wasn't routine. He could almost have neglected to take in the sight that suddenly appeared before him.

Cows were running down the center of the road.

Frank slammed his brakes, bucked forward, and peered through his windshield.

The cows were running. Not ambling. Not standing stock-still, as if contemplating the absurdity of finding themselves on the road. They were running this way and that. Hooves clattering. Tails stiffened. Running in one direction, then stopping abruptly, with a wide-eyed, cornered hesitancy, pivoting, and taking off in the opposite direction. Running like animals that were being chased, with no pursuer in sight.

Frank did a double take. "This kind of cow just doesn't act that way," he would remark later. "These were, you know, Herefords." (He pronounced the word in a two-syllable baritone murmur: *hurfurds*.) "Normally when you go by a pasture, they won't even look up at you. They're just head down, eating. That's all they do."

He pulled over. Out in the fields, he saw more cows stampeding, kicking up clouds of dirt that nearly obscured their mottled markings. "They're running just like deer," he said, "trying to figure out how to join the other ones on the road." He noticed the gap where a barbed wire fence had been trampled. A house sat far off the road, and Frank turned toward it down a gravel lane. A group of dogs materialized alongside his car, barking wildly, and when he stopped and got out the dogs surrounded him.

A woman emerged from the house. "You, shut up," she shouted at the dogs. They did not obey. "I don't know what's gotten into them," she said.

The sky was a cloudless, bleached shade of blue. The morning was overheated. The woman's dogs looked as though they were about to pounce. None of it felt quite real. Frank pointed toward the few dozen sharp-horned cattle fleeing down the paved road.

"This is nuts," he said. He yelled past the dogs, "Ma'am, you've got cows running all over the place. They've torn a fence down."

The woman sized up Frank. He was tall and lanky; his jeans were worn and he had thick sideburns and his dirty blond hair, unkempt, fell over his ears. She said nothing. She looked beyond Frank and saw only empty fields, a farm pond, rows of fruit trees in the distance.

"Maybe they've eaten some crazy weed," Frank joked.

The woman did not laugh. She took a few steps back. "Those aren't my cows," she said, and turned away from him. The dogs followed her to the house.

Frank shook his head and returned to his car.

Spencer Black, director of the Athens–Limestone County Department of Civil Defense, showed up for work that morning expecting a quiet day. Civil Defense was run out of two cramped rooms in the basement of the sheriff's department, directly beneath the county jail, and a block from Athens's stately Greek Revival Courthouse Square. It was not typically a hive of activity. Its staff consisted of Spencer and his secretary. A ham radio enthusiast dropped by now and then to troll the airwaves for interesting transmissions. The office had two desks, a law enforcement scanner, some crates of surplus canned food, a pair of bunk beds along a cinder block wall, a pile of hard hats, and a box of official-looking armbands that had not seen much use. Spencer, who had been on the job for two and a half years, admitted, "When I started, I was as green as can be. I didn't even know what 'civil defense' was." Although he had learned a few things about emergency management since taking office, he had been little tested by experience. Among the crises that had merited his attention were an episode of flash flooding, a few drownings of fishermen, and some reports of lost children. If anybody looked fit to defend Limestone's civilians, though, it was Spencer. At age thirty, he was solidly built, weighed 250 pounds, and was aware that his presence could be intimidating. He sported sandy hair that flopped over his brow, a pair of thin scars above his left eye, and a booming voice. He could also be disarmingly affable.

At 9 AM his phone rang. The caller was H. D. Bagley, the weatherman for WHNT-TV in Huntsville, twenty-five miles east of Athens, alerting Spencer that a huge storm was on its way to the area. The news was surprising. It seemed to be a beautiful spring morning. The forecast in the local paper called for nothing beyond an ordinary mix of seasonable weather. "Variable cloudiness, windy and warmer weather is expected for the Athens area today," it read, "with a chance of thunderstorms predicted once again tonight." Nonetheless, Spencer said, "H. D. was telling me we're probably going to have some of the stormiest weather we've seen in years and years."

By 10 AM, the National Weather Service field office in Huntsville, which had responsibility for monitoring the conditions in Limestone and a handful of other counties, issued a Severe Thunderstorm Warning. Ten minutes later, a more unnerving call came in to Civil Defense: The Weather Service was announcing that a Tornado Watch was in effect until 4 PM.

Spencer pondered how seriously to take the advisory. A "watch" did not, by a long shot, mean that a tornado was on its way—only that conditions were said to be ripe for one. Such odds did not impress people in northern Alabama, who were more apt to be irritated by exaggerated weather forecasts than to be fearful of storms. There was a chance, too, that the Weather Service might be overcompensating for its failure to give adequate warning a few days earlier, on Monday, when an actual funnel had swept through parts of the county. That storm had come after dark, and by all accounts it had been sudden and terrifying. (One person was killed in a trailer in a neighboring county.) Spencer had spent the following day—just yesterday—driving around with local officials, tallying up the damage. Not far from the Tennessee River, a man named Leslie Nixon had his mobile home crushed. "I lost a lot of hard earned money here," Nixon had complained. He pointed to the rubble of his trailer. "I would rather live in my hog pen than another one of these things—at least my hog pen has a concrete floor."

The storm had continued northeast. On Lucas Ferry Road, James Vaughn had his barn roof taken off, and several pecan trees uprooted. His pickup truck, filled with soybeans, was toppled. Ten miles away, in Copeland, Hermann Vann's tractor shed was demolished, and over at Capshaw Gin the seed house lost its roof. Nearby, in Center Hill, the storm roused Wayne Hovis from sleep at 9:30. He gathered his wife and children and the family huddled together beneath a bed. "It seemed like it only lasted a minute," Hovis said, "but when it was over half of the roof was gone and my machinery shed was lying in shambles."

So it went with tornadoes.

Now, as his morning wore on, Spencer decided that the caller from the Weather Service had sounded unusually earnest on the phone. "It's about the first time I remember that they came right out and said the word 'tornado'," Spencer observed. "And they were saying it in such a way that you could just bet your life tornadoes were coming."

By the age of thirty-four, Annias Green, who had been born into dire poverty in Limestone, had become a model of middle-class respectability. He served as pastor of Macedonia Primitive Baptist

Church, down a country road on Limestone's eastern edge. He lived just outside Athens, on the grounds of a peach orchard, in a decent three-bedroom house he rented for thirty-five dollars each month from a white family, the Isoms, with whom he had a respectful, if remote, relationship. Annias would not be a tenant much longer. He had bought some land north of Athens, and the house he was building there was nearly complete; had it not been for delays in bringing electricity to the lot, he and his family—his wife, Lillian, and three sons between the ages of seven and eleven—would have moved in by now. In a county in which nearly half the black population qualified as impoverished by federal standards, and where most blacks continued to toil at manual labor, Annias was a notable exception. He had a managerial job with the Laborers' International Union of North America, Local 366, in Huntsville, the kind of position that, as Annias's oldest son realized, "only white people had ever had before." His weekly salary of $257 was more than sufficient to provide his family with the necessities that had been in chronically short supply during his own upbringing, and he was not averse to the occasional purchase of items he considered frivolous. He had, for instance, recently brought home a large Zenith color television set, even though homes in Limestone received only three TV stations, all broadcasting out of Huntsville. It didn't matter to Annias. TV was for the children. He had little use for it, himself. On those rare nights when a break in his pastoral duties allowed him to relax at home, he preferred to read the Bible or fishing magazines.

Wednesday was Annias's regular half-day at the office, and it was the closest thing he had to a day of leisure. He would arrive home while his boys were at school and his wife was at work, promptly load his twelve-foot aluminum boat in the back of his pickup, and head for the solitude of a fishing hole. He had a lifelong, intimate knowledge of the rivers, streams, creeks, and inlets that wound their way through Limestone's porous valley topography, and depending on the day, he might favor Beulah Bay, on Wheeler Lake, or Cowford Landing—wherever he had a hunch that the catfish or striped bass were biting. Annias had lost his taste for *eating* fish—growing up, he had had to subsist often enough on his catch—but he still found solace in the activity.

He fished year-round. In early spring the conditions were particularly fine. Indeed, by coincidence, today's paper—turning away from gloomy matters of national news—ran as its lead editorial a reverie called "Fishing Time": "This is the time of year blood rises in the veins of the millions of fishing Americans," the piece began. "What is it about fishing that attracts so many? One expert claims it's the natural instinct of hunting food—the basic drive to survive." The article reminded fishermen to pay close attention to the elements. "The period just before bad weather is often good," it advised. "A slight wind to ripple the water is desirable."

Annias didn't need any prodding. "I had a lot of pressures in my life," he would say, "and when I went fishing, nobody could bother me or get hold of me. I used the time for my personal benefit." Often he returned home from his outings well after nightfall. No matter what the hour, he refused to set foot in the house until he had rinsed every trace of mud from his truck and boat. "I always believed in washing that truck," he laughed. "If it was nasty, even if it had just a little dust on it, it was going to get washed." He knew he could seem fastidious. As long as he could remember, he had been called "peculiar," and he didn't dispute the tag. "Even as a child, I always liked to be by myself and to do things my own way," he said. "I never liked to run with a group of boys—I never got involved with a group of *anybody*. It always seemed that other folks wanted to start trouble, and that wasn't for me. I never drank a beer, or booze, and I never smoked a cigarette. I got my first sight of a drink and said,

'I haven't got time for that.' I was different, I got along, I tended to my own business, and I didn't bother anyone. I was a family guy. A hard worker. Life was enjoyable."

At noon, then, Annias left his office and headed home. It was breezy and muggy. A colleague had mentioned being impressed by the sight of damage from Monday night's storm, and Annias decided to take a quick detour and get a look for himself. Just over the Limestone County line, near Triana, Annias pulled his truck off the side of the road. He stood before a stand of toppled trees. It was a fascinating sight. The destruction was efficient and orderly. Roots were pried from the earth. Trunks were shaved off branches, and, in places, bark was stripped away. One of the downed trees had been cracked open near its crown. Its ripe exposed wood was bright white. It was remarkable how violent the little storm had been. But it was equally remarkable that the trees on either side of the gash in the woods stood unharmed. If he hadn't known that it was the wind's work, Annias would have thought that someone had come through with a bulldozer.

In 1805, an adventurer named John Hunt reached the Tennessee Valley and was greeted by a vision of paradisiacal plenty. "The water courses, clear as crystal, teemed with trout, bream, red horse and salmon," he effused. "Deer were abundant on our mountains, bears inhabited the canebrakes in the river bottoms; wild geese and wild ducks of a dozen varieties haunted our streams and ponds."

Limestone's first white settlers—land seekers who had been priced out of Virginia and the Carolinas—descended the hills of western Appalachia at the turn of the nineteenth century and made their way down the Tennessee River in rough-hewn flatboats. Their arrival was not welcome. The territory that included the future Limestone County had been crossed by Indians for hundreds of years—nomadic tribes had left behind mysterious grass-covered mounds of mussel shells on the riverbanks—and had, after the American Revolution, been guaranteed by treaty to the native Chickasaw. The new settlers, however, were unimpressed by treaties. Some took it on themselves to begin parceling out and selling the Indians' land. The tribal chief warned that if the interlopers were to remain, a massacre was likely. Federal troops arrived in 1809 to enforce the treaty by evicting hundreds of settler families. It was not a simple task. Each time soldiers drove them from the Indians' land, the settlers returned in short order. Soon they began to demand that their government take their side in the dispute. In a petition to President Madison, the settlers complained of being forced to suffer "merely to gratify a heathen nation who have no better right to land than we have ourselves." In 1816, the Chickasaw were cajoled into giving up their claims. Land was put up for sale. Prices started at two dollars an acre. It was a bargain. The soil, replenished by annual flooding of the river, was enormously fertile, and the climate ensured long growing seasons. The land was particularly well-suited for growing cotton, which was on its way to becoming the world's most valuable plant and the driving force of the region's plantation economy.

One hundred fifty years later, Limestone was no longer apt to be mistaken for paradise, and it had been a long time since newcomers had flocked to it in pursuit of the good life. The county had settled, instead, into the lulling rhythms of a backwater, a place that had neither kept up with the changing times, nor yet been abandoned. Its population growth was stagnant. Its people were more poor than rich (30 percent of its families had incomes under $3,000 annually), worked on farms and, increasingly, in factories more commonly than in offices, and gathered en masse most often at church and at sporting events. Blacks, a little less than a fifth of the population, kept to themselves, and were adjusting to the recent demise of legal segregation as tentatively as whites, if rather more optimistically. Even among Alabama's sixty-seven counties, Limestone remained a quiet, unremarkable spot, an island of sorts between the river and the mountains. It was not a place that made the national news. It was peopled by the abstract, and therefore unknown, entity called "ordinary Americans." In Limestone, these people, black and white alike, had a propensity for staying put, generation after generation, whether out of loyalty to their surroundings or lack of a better place to go. The outside world barely intruded on them, it seemed, and they, in turn, could be counted on to keep close to home. It was not an unpleasant arrangement. There was safety in it. It could go on.

For a young man, Frank Orr had been around danger enough to have developed a matter-of-fact stance toward it. The prospect of being sent to war had been the constant backdrop of his teenage years, and though he was hardly a gung-ho type, he couldn't see enrolling in college expressly to avoid military service. Moreover, he was under the impression that it took family connections, which he lacked, to land in the National Guard and stay stateside.

For a while it looked as though he might not be called. After graduating from high school in 1968, he hired on at Monsanto. His job was to operate the vats that produced Acrilan, a state-of-the-art synthetic fiber. When the Monsanto plant opened in Decatur in 1952, an article in *Life* celebrated Acrilan as Monsanto's "most glamorous product," and described the nine steps by which Frank and his thousand coworkers transformed acrylonitrile—a compound built on the delicate union of "explosive acetylene" and "poisonous hydrogen cyanide"—into 400-pound bales of sturdy, wrinkle-free, easy-to-clean fabric. According to the article, Monsanto was poised to realize the worst fears of farmers by making cotton a thing of the past: A 200-acre factory, the company said, could produce as much fiber as 50,000 acres of cotton. "Acrilan is warm, washable, nonshrinking, moth- and mildew-proof, and will hold permanent pleats," *Life* pointed out.

Frank took to the job well. The plant ran twenty-four hours a day, but Frank preferred the midnight shift, when there was minimal supervision and he could be mostly alone with the thrumming cylinders under his charge. The starting pay was $2.32 an hour, a figure that stuck with him because it was the same as the Athens telephone exchange. Monsanto offered its workers monthly blood tests to ensure they were not absorbing undue amounts of what Frank understood to be "poisons."

After a year at Monsanto, Frank stayed home one evening to keep an eye on the televised proceedings of the army's draft lottery. The results were not unpredictable. "Let's just say I didn't win," he offered. "But I had no choice. It was go to Vietnam or be a deserter." He was not without his misgivings. He knew that Bruce Lyle, who had gone to Athens High and who could have gotten a hardship deferment—his mother was a widow—had enlisted in the army and been killed. (Lyle was one of twenty-two residents of Limestone to die in Vietnam.) Frank also knew the unnerving story of Billy Saint, who had returned home safely from the war, only to confound his friends a short time later by leaving his pickup truck beside the railroad tracks in Tanner and sitting down in front of an oncoming freight train.

Still, Frank said, "I never questioned going."

The army determined that Frank had mechanical aptitude and offered him the chance to study helicopter maintenance. During the year he spent in training in Colorado, 9,414 American troops were killed in Vietnam, and another 53,390 were wounded. Frank deployed to Vietnam with the 101st Airborne Division in mid-1970. He was based at Camp Eagle, in the northernmost sector of operations, near the city of Da Nang. He was not yet twenty. "I was too young to be scared," he said.

Soon after he arrived, he was invited to give up his maintenance job—and the relative safety of an aircraft hangar—and to join instead a helicopter gun crew. It was one of the most dangerous tasks in Vietnam. Frank accepted the offer. "The hangar was hot," he recalled, "and there were sergeants there. Lots of supervision, lots of getting yelled at. I would see the guys on the gun crews. They were the elite bunch. There might be a line with a hundred people waiting to eat, but the gun crews could walk right in front, and nobody would say a word."

He became a door gunner in a Huey UH-1, responsible for manning the helicopter's weapons and radios. The Huey was the emblem of Vietnam's new brand of mobile, airborne warfare. Frank and others referred to it as "the flying truck." It transported infantrymen, provided cover for those on the ground, scouted enemy positions, and did whatever else was asked of it. "It was 'you call, we haul,'" he said. Despite its lumbering appearance, the Huey could approach ninety knots when pressed, and was recognizable from afar by its rotors' distinctive whooshing. Frank liked flying. He liked the freedom of being in the air. His crew often flew eight hours a day, and carried the artillery commander of the entire division, a prominent colonel, who directed his troops from the air. The mood in the helicopter could be raw. "The colonel would be sitting up front looking through his binoculars," Frank said. "Maybe the artillery was going to blow up a hill. He'd yell to our pilot, 'Drop! Drop! Drop!' The pilot would swing down, circling, cutting donuts over the hill. Gunships were going in, and troop flights were coming in, and Cobras [smaller helicopters] were escorting all of it. I had a full view behind the gun. Suddenly the hill would light up, in the middle of the night. I could hear the officers on my headset, putting troops in. I could hear them screaming, hollering, crying on the radio. They would come in with their gunships, you know, to shoot the area up, and then the troops would come in, and you could hear the soldiers crying, crying that they were getting shot up."

Frank felt secure on his helicopter—a confidence belied by the military's damage and casualty counts, which showed that nearly half of the 7,000 Hueys used in Vietnam were destroyed during the conflict, and that more than 3,000 of Frank's fellow helicopter crewmen were killed. Frank's division, the Screaming Eagles, lost 4,022 soldiers over the course of the war. "If you hear them crying like that over the radio," Frank recalled, "and you see the troops putting in, and you see a helicopter hit the ground and tumble, and disintegrate—well then, yeah, you're glad you're up there, in the sky."

He made it back to Limestone in 1971. "After all that time flying in Vietnam, I came back more than halfway around the world—Vietnam to Japan, to Alaska, to California, to New Jersey, to Atlanta—and the first time in my life I got airsick was on the last leg of it all, the forty-minute flight from Atlanta to Huntsville. I was just about home and I was so sick I couldn't get off the plane."

Spencer Black would have been the first to admit that his qualifications for the responsible-sounding job of Civil Defense director were less than obvious. "I'm dumb as grits," he liked to say. He was raised in Clements, a small community in the southwestern corner of Limestone, on a narrow thumb of land between the Elk and Tennessee rivers. The thirty-four members of his high school class of 1961 voted him "Class Clown (by far)." When he graduated, the only ambition that occurred to him was to remain on his family's

125-acre cotton farm, but his father would have none of it. "Daddy said to me, 'Farming is a thing of the past. You'll work your fingers to the bone, and you'll starve to death.'"

A long and wayward journey ensued. Spencer enrolled in a local college, but never went to classes. He joined a unit of the National Guard, based in Athens, and liked it so much that he enlisted in the army. He never got there. "I got a rupture in my left side doing some training exercise, so not only did I not get taken for the army, but the Guard released me."

He decided to study to be an electrician at a community college, but failed to complete his program. He worked as a janitor for a while, then got a job driving a cab on the grounds of Redstone Arsenal, in Huntsville, where the U.S. Army's Missile Command was located, and where NASA was building rocket boosters to propel the Apollo space mission. "It was something for a country kid to be at the Arsenal," he said. "I got to see them transporting the rockets when they were getting ready to test fire them. I loved driving a cab. If there was no one to pick up, I'd head over to the river, get under a shade tree and take a little nap. That was the first time I ever heard a two-way radio. I was resting in my cab and a voice suddenly came over. It scared the hell out of me."

Spencer's jobs rarely lasted long. He worked in a lab at Thiokol Chemical Corporation, then started his own laundry service a while later. "I just kept moving from one thing to the next. I wasn't ever contented. You might say I was the black sheep of my family." He explained, "I was getting in a lot of fights, and I was in and out of jails. I've been in jail in Alabama, and Tennessee, and Georgia. I guess I had no respect for other people back then." Drinking usually played a part in his misadventures. He frequented rough roadside bars over the state line in Tennessee, where he would have no difficulty finding trouble. "I was big and strong and very high-strung. I'd fight at the drop of a hat—especially if I saw someone being disrespectful to a woman. I never did like to hear a guy use the f-word in front of a woman. But I had all kinds of reasons for fighting. When I was twenty-one, and some sixty-year-old would confront me in a bar, that was a problem. I might have been red-neckish and backward, but that sixty-year-old in some little country bar—he was *truly* backward. I used to wear my shirt with the collar turned up and I combed my hair in a ducktail, and a lot of old guys thought that was just the weirdest thing in the world. It was enough to start a fight."

Spencer hit a low point one night in 1964. He was hanging out on Courthouse Square in Athens, and was drunk and rowdy. An officer with the Athens Police Department approached and placed him under arrest. "This cop and I knew each other," Spencer recalled. "We had drunk together on the river. But this night, he was going to prove he was a big guy. He had a little three-wheeled motorcycle that they used for giving out parking tickets, and he wanted to put me on it and carry me to jail. I told him I wasn't getting on any such thing." Punches were thrown. "I got one good lick in on him. I hit him and knocked him over his motorcycle. Then he got up and beat me pretty good with his blackjack. He almost killed me. That's how I got these scars above my eyes."

After a few more years of scrapes with the law and spotty employment, Spencer continued, "I just ran out of steam. I was pretty sure I wasn't going to live to be twenty-five. The worst of it was that I was bringing a lot of heartache to my mama and daddy." Relatives introduced him to a woman they imagined could straighten him out. Marcia was a college graduate, a teacher, and an upright Christian. "Dumb as I am," Spencer said, "it was really something for me to go with a schoolteacher. I always hated schoolteachers, and I ended up marrying one." A year later, he finally seemed to find his calling. He returned to school and studied hairstyling. "Back then, a lot of men wouldn't like to be called a 'hairdresser,' and I didn't either. But that's what I was. I was the first genuine hairstylist that ever came to Athens. I'd always been fascinated with people cutting hair. When I was a kid, we never went to the barbershop. My parents just had a pair of old clippers and cut off our hair the best they could. The first haircut I ever got in a barbershop, I thought it was pretty neat. So I went to school and learned how to do everything. I did scissors cut, and razor cut, and styling. I could primp you up."

He took a job at Bob's Barber Shop in downtown Athens. Business was good. One of his regular customers, a local named Laine Brawley, was Limestone's Civil Defense director. From what Brawley would tell him, Spencer gathered that the job was a boondoggle. "I used to tease him all the time when he came into the barbershop," Spencer said. "I'd tell him, 'If you ever give up that cushy job of yours, you let me know.'" One autumn Saturday in 1971, after Spencer had been cutting hair for about five years, Brawley sat himself down in Spencer's chair, and revealed that he was quitting. "He told me he'd met this girl down in Montgomery, and that he was leaving his old lady and running off. He said, 'If you want my job, you better get in touch with the right people.'

"The county commissioners were my friends," Spencer explained. "Back then, politicians could hire any good old boy they wanted, just because he'd voted for them, or put up signs for them during their campaign. Me, I was well known throughout the county when I got the job. I was young and energetic. I was in the public's eye a lot, cutting hair."

Spencer left Bob's Barber Shop in 1971 and moved across Courthouse Square to the Civil Defense office. His monthly pay was $425.

* * *

For Annias Green, surviving the past had been an accomplishment in itself. He was the fourth in a family of ten children. His father, Joe, had been kidnapped off the streets of New Orleans as a child and brought to Alabama by a fugitive, wanted for murder, who believed he would arouse less suspicion if he were traveling with a child. "It wasn't like it is today," Annias commented. "Nobody was able to go looking for the boy. His family didn't have money or influence with the police. My daddy just disappeared and never saw his parents again. He didn't get any education. He knew to count numbers but he couldn't sit down and read the newspaper. Much later on, I taught my daddy how to write his name."

Annias grew up barely a mile east of his current residence, on the 185-acre property of a farmer named M. Y. Dauthit. His family were sharecroppers. They lived in a typical "tenant house," which was covered with tarpaper and bits of scrap wood and tin, and lacked indoor plumbing. All of its four rooms were used for sleeping; in warm weather, some of the family would sleep on the porch. Annias shared a bed with two, and sometimes three, brothers.

As Annias explained, "Sharecropping meant you worked the fields and the man—the owner—got half of what you grew. You planted it, you worked it, you picked it, and then the man got half because he owned it." The Greens farmed forty acres. Annias described M. Y. Dauthit as a fair and decent landlord. "He had a policy. He wasn't going to call us names"—Annias was referring to racial taunts—"and he wouldn't put up with his sons calling us names, either." The Dauthits would give the Greens their sons' used clothing, which was a significant benefit at a time when Annias and his siblings would be lucky to afford a single new pair of pants each year. The terms of sharecropping, though, were unforgiving and one-sided, and there were times during the fifties when the family of twelve sometimes scraped by on as little as $250 for the year.

"That's just the way it was," Annias said. "The master had total control."

Annias began working in the cotton fields when he was six years old. "I woke up at four in the morning and worked all day. Nobody in my family lay in bed past five o'clock if they weren't sick." By the middle of March, land would be plowed in preparation for planting. Seed was laid and fertilizer spread. The crop required continual weeding and chopping back of overgrowth. From late August until Thanksgiving, the cotton was ready to be harvested, and Annias and his family remained in the fields from dawn until evening. "I could pick the good stuff," Annias said. "Just with my hands, no machines. Pick it off, put it in a cotton sack, pick a sack full, then go back and do it again. I could pick five hundred pounds in a day." He was tall and lean and strong. "How are you going to get fat when you're working all the time? We had a garden, a watermelon patch, a pea patch. My mother did a lot of canning, because we didn't have a refrigerator. About the only thing we bought was flour. We grew corn and put it out for our hogs. We had a milk cow. We didn't eat luxuriously. We would have a chicken on the odd day, maybe once a week. We ate a lot of beans."

Inevitably, his education suffered. "As a black child," Annias observed, "you were always being taken out of school to work. Once cotton planting began, it didn't matter whether there was school or not. If it was raining, you'd go to school, but not otherwise. Then, once you got big enough to haul a hundred-pound sack of fertilizer, you were likely to be done with school for good." At the time, public education for blacks in Limestone County, which was provided only through the eighth grade, was rudimentary. At least two dozen of the county's black schools were in makeshift lodgings in rural churches; sometimes the space would be divided into "classrooms" by draping a sheet on a line. Textbooks were in short supply and consisted of those that had been discarded by white schools. Most of the black children were provided no transportation; Annias had to walk three miles to his first school, Pleasant Grove. After sixth grade, he moved on to Dogwood Flat, which was considered among the best of the county's black schools. There, students drew water from a well, and boys would be sent to gather kindling to provide heat. The school's basketball team hosted other black schools, holding the games on a dirt court. Teachers in Limestone's black elementary schools earned less than half the annual salary of those who taught Athens's white children. "The schools of our white brothers," Annias commented drily, "were somewhat better. I noticed that when they integrated [beginning in 1968] they closed down the black schools, not the white ones."

Annias attended school sporadically until he was sixteen. He was not particularly uneducated by local standards. In 1974, 40 percent of Limestone's residents, blacks and whites, had less than an eighth grade education. Only thirty-seven percent had graduated from high school.

For the next six years, until he turned twenty-two, Annias had a job tending chickens for his family's landlord. Dauthit had 4,000 hens, and Annias would rise before dawn to collect the eggs, wash them, crate them, and clean out the chicken house. By eight o'clock he went off to work on his family's share of land. In the afternoon he returned to the chicken farm to feed the birds and sort through and grade the eggs. He worked every day. "Chickens don't take any days off," he remarked. Dauthit paid him $35 a week. By 1960, Annias had managed to save $375 to buy a 1952 Chevrolet, and he was more than ready to move on with his life. "There was no way I was going to continue at farm labor," he said. "My parents never did own their own home, and they were always at someone else's mercy.

F5

When you're in a low-rent situation, it's easy to stay that way. I always wanted a better life. I wanted some freedom."

John Tanner, a five-time mayor of early Athens, recalled in his 1876 memoirs that the Baptist church to which he belonged, built in 1820, had suffered the fate of being "blown down by a storm," and was "subsequently converted into a cotton gin house." Limestone had never been unacquainted with destructive winds. Its springtime weather was particularly volatile. Alabama's southern tip extended to the Gulf of Mexico, and moist air from the Gulf habitually parked over the state's flat band of farmland, awaiting collision with cooler air masses from northern latitudes. Some weather observers spoke of Dixie Tornado Alley, extending from Louisiana through Tennessee, with Alabama as its epicenter. With the fourth highest number of killer tornadoes among American states, Alabama could lay claim to a dubious place of pride in tornado lore. April was its month of highest tornado frequency.

In April 1936, a tornado rode through Limestone in the dead of night, flattening a pair of farmhouses and a sharecropper's shack, and killing five. The fatalities attracted little attention. Tornadoes were regarded as an inevitable hazard of rural life, like drownings and snakebites. Moreover, the 1936 storm produced more newsworthy effects elsewhere. Twenty minutes before Limestone was struck, a tornado touched down in Yalobusha County, Mississippi, and made a path for Tupelo. More than two hundred homes in Tupelo's affluent districts were destroyed, along with an uncounted number of what were described as "poorly constructed homes" housing the families of laborers, servants, and field hands. At least 216 people were killed, with hundreds more seriously injured. A Tupelo resident named Elvis Presley, fifteen months of age, made it through the storm unharmed.

Then, at around 8:30 the following morning, a pair of tornadoes trod a seven-mile path toward Gainesville, Georgia, converging, as if by prior arrangement, on the edge of the town's central business district. The workday was just getting under way. The Cooper Pants factory, located in a cavernous masonry structure, collapsed and caught fire, killing seventy workers. Outside, a crowd of pedestrians, including many high school students, spotted the approaching funnel and fled to shelter at Newnan's Department Store. The store caved in, burying twenty people. A one-ton cast-iron bell, suspended above the courthouse, was said to have been flung a quarter mile. Two hundred and three deaths were reported—bodies were collected in the town's three largest cotton mills—though rubble filled the streets to depths of ten feet and made a thorough accounting of casualties impossible.

Limestone had never suffered storm damage on such a scale. Its tornado history was modest, if steady. On average, one had crossed the county every five years or so during the first seventy-four years of the twentieth century. The deadliest had occurred on May 26, 1924, when a family of eight tenant farmers was struck in the midst of sleep about five miles from Athens. Their house was "completely swept away. Fragments of the bodies were hurled up to ¾ mile. . . . All eight were buried in a common grave." In 1939, a woman was killed in a tornado in Tanner, and in 1958 a pair of twisters hit the county on a single night. Even when Limestone had a tornado-free year, there was often havoc to report nearby. In March 1932, fifteen tornadoes, including ten of notable destructiveness, descended on central Alabama in a single day. Hundreds were killed—in their beds, in their barns, in school, killed running for cover beneath trees, killed by bricks flung from falling chimneys, killed on hilltops and on the sides of streams. In Tuscaloosa, bodies were piled in the center of town. The outbreak targeted places with names like

Plantersville, Gantt's Quarry, Piney Grove, and Sylacauga. Debris from Paint Rock, where three workers were killed in a hosiery mill, reached Athens, 105 miles away, like a mordant greeting.

It wasn't yet 9:00 AM when Frank pulled up to his house. As he stepped from the car, the humidity was staggering. "It's like you're pushing against a wall," he said. "Just like in the tropics." He paused to consider his encounter with the stray cows. He wasn't apt to take it seriously. Still, he reflected, "An animal being afraid means something. It's not some kind of a religious thing. It's not a prophecy. It's more like a prediction. If you watch animals, they give you a warning."

Frank still lived with his parents. After returning from Vietnam, he had moved back in, and although he had been working, on and off, at building an apartment over the garage, he was in no rush to get a place of his own. His parents' sturdy, one-story asbestos-sided house was the only home he had ever known. He had a lounge chair and an old TV and stereo in his room, and most days he got his meals cooked for him and his laundry folded. He had his old job back at Monsanto—though now he was operating machines that made synthetic hair to be shipped to China and fashioned into wigs—and was able to put aside some money. No one bothered him about his comings and goings, other than to tease him about which girl he was dating in a given week. He bought a used motorcycle and drove into the hilly country of Tennessee on his days off.

Ordinarily, the house was empty when he got in from work. His parents, who had given up farming in the '60s, both worked at Redstone Arsenal—his mother, Joyce, as a secretary at Missile Command, and his father, Bobby, on a NASA loading dock. This was not an ordinary day, though. Frank's sister Marilyn, who was a year older, had given birth to a baby boy, Mark, just six days earlier, and had decamped from her apartment in Athens to take advantage of her mother's offer of help. This meant that Marilyn's husband, Vergil McBay, who worked the swing shift at 3M, would be there, too, along with Marilyn and Vergil's older child, two-year-old Jason. It was like a family reunion—three generations of Orrs stuffed in one small house. Frank's chances of getting a good night's sleep—or, more accurately, a good day's sleep—were not promising.

He stepped inside. Things were quieter than he expected, which was illogical: Jason was on the living room floor, playing with his toys; Marilyn, in her nightgown, was cradling Mark, with Vergil beside her; Frank's mother was busy in the kitchen. The house smelled of baby—milk, lotion, the strangely appealing pungency of diapers.

Frank took in the stillness for a moment.

Then it struck him. It was the cats. Each morning when Frank came home from work a pack of cats—too many to count, a different number from one day to the next—swarmed around his feet. They were farm cats turned house cats, cats his mother couldn't resist taking in. They were there without fail when Frank opened the door. Often he had to pry them from his pant legs.

This morning, they were nowhere to be seen.

He pulled off his work boots. He glanced over at Vergil and Marilyn in the living room. They looked dead tired. Frank was tired, too. He went down the hall to his room and drew the shade on his window. He dropped his clothes on the floor and climbed into bed. The sheets were sticky from the damp air.

"I grew up in a family that always feared storms," the Civil Defense director recounted. One April night in the 1930s, before Spencer was born, high winds had blown the porches off his parents' house. "It scared them bad," he said. "When I was a boy, my daddy built what I believe may have been the first tornado shelter in this county. It was built of logs, sunk into the ground, with tin backing and a door on top to cover it. It was about eight by ten feet. We didn't know from 'tornado watch,' or any such thing. Hell, we didn't even have a radio back then. But if it started thundering and lightning in the afternoon, we were headed for the storm house. If we were at school when it started storming, Daddy would come by and take us from class and drag us into the shelter. Other kids would be laughing at us, but Daddy didn't care.

"Around 1950," Spencer went on, "Daddy decided to pull out the logs and build a concrete storm house. It cost two or three hundred dollars—man alive, that was a lot more money than we ever had. I believe he made payments on it. He built a little wooden bed for the babies and put a feather mattress on it. There were benches along the wall. And even if it was just raining hard, we went on in there, and we would set our asses down and be quiet. There wasn't any fun or games in there—it wasn't like today. We had kerosene lamps. I spent beaucoups of nights in there. I would climb out in the morning and go straight to school. Neighbors would come in there, too. The most we ever had in there at one time was thirty-six people, packed one on top of another." The last conversation Spencer had with his father, before he died of a heart attack in 1971, was to make a date to perform repairs on the storm shelter. "Daddy thought if you didn't have a storm house to protect your family, you weren't worth a thing," Spencer said. "To him, having a good storm house was like driving a Cadillac."

When Spencer took over as Civil Defense director, he "hit the ground running." Nationally, Civil Defense programs had originated during World War II as loosely organized efforts to detect the presence of enemy agents. After the war, Civil Defense shifted its attention to the Cold War perils of communism and nuclear attack, eventually extending its mission to man-made and natural disasters as well. "When I came on," Spencer commented, "it was all about weather and nuclear war." Spencer's sociability proved to be a great asset on the job. He supervised bomb drills in schools, and gave presentations to city and county agencies about planning for emergencies. "I drank coffee with some department head every morning," he said. He delivered lectures on tornado survival, stressing the need to get in a cellar, or, failing that, in a protected room or a ditch. He received some federal money to start a program called Skywarn, training a network of volunteers to spot dangerous weather. "The human eye," advised a 1971 handout from the program, "is still the only positive detector of tornadoes, and the eyes of SKYWARN volunteers across the Nation provide the first line of defense against these destructive storms."

Spencer's responsibilities also included maintaining the county's handful of fallout shelters, which were intended to protect against the effects of a nuclear blast. The shelters were supplied with metal barrels of water, packaged crackers and hard candies, a chemical toilet and toilet paper, and medical supplies such as aspirin, tongue depressors, bandages, and safety pins. Some contained radiation detectors as well. It was easy for the shelters to fall into neglect. "Kids got into them all the time and vandalized them for phenobarbital," Spencer remarked. He had no illusions about how effective the shelters would be in an actual emergency. "I hate to be plainspoken, but really and truly, the American people can be so gullible. If you got that close to radiation it would just burn you right up. You'd be just as well off hugging a light pole."

Spencer understood that the role of his two-person Civil Defense office in fending off disaster was more symbolic than real. As Wednesday morning went on, with a tornado watch in effect,

Spencer did what he could. He contacted schools, hospitals, nursing homes, the police, the sheriff, and spread the word. Most of those with whom he spoke seemed unconcerned. The weather out there looks nice, they would say. Spencer called his wife and told her he might be staying at work late waiting for updates from the Weather Service. He told her to take their children, ages two and five, drive to his mother's place in Clements, and head straight for the storm house. "Deep down, I really didn't know what to do," he acknowledged. "To be honest with you, there's really not a whole lot I can do for people when a tornado touches down. People have got to fend for themselves. If they don't get up and do something, they're pretty much sitting ducks."

By the time Annias had moved off M. Y. Dauthit's farm, Limestone was beginning to change. Agriculture was in decline. The proportion of county residents who farmed had dwindled from a majority before World War II, to a quarter by 1960, to a bare 10 percent in 1970. Annias began working construction in Huntsville. He dug ditches. He poured concrete and drilled wells. He picked up skills quickly, becoming proficient in carpentry, brick masonry, and operating an air tube and a jackhammer. "I might start out at the bottom," he would say, "but I don't stay there."

Annias also had a family to support. He had married Lillian, a childhood friend, in 1961. His first son, Ananias, Jr.—known to family members as "Rabbit"—was born a year later. (Annias's name, derived from a character in the Bible, had been misspelled on his birth certificate; in naming his son, he corrected the error.) Two other sons, Amos and Titus, followed by 1966.

In the mid-60s, Annias joined Local 366 of the Laborers' International Union, which supplied workers to the construction trades. The Local had integrated in 1964, and eager to increase its membership, had begun recruiting blacks. Annias was the first black to be asked to join the front office, as assistant manager, in 1969. At first he was reluctant to take the offer. He had been warned that some coworkers would not take well to having a black boss. "There were comments made that I'd be better off with a brick around my neck in the Tennessee River than working there," he said. One of the shop stewards was reputed to be a member of the Ku Klux Klan, and another supervisor was widely regarded to be racist. Annias mulled over the offer with his wife. The job paid far more than Annias could make as a laborer. It offered the possibility of a different kind of life. "We talked about the benefits," Annias said, "and we talked about the risks. We made sure that she and the boys would be taken care of if something happened to me. And I made the decision."

Annias was guided by his sense that every obstacle in his life had been purposeful. "I believe in predestiny," he said. He had always been deeply religious. At twenty-one, he recalled, "I was divinely called by God to preach. I felt the calling in my body. God was revealing the Word to me. I'd go off somewhere and preach to a group of folks and I'd feel the Holy Spirit." For most of the next decade, he attended night school classes at Bible colleges in Huntsville, and began preaching in local churches. He felt at home behind the pulpit. "I just wanted to be a servant. My message was simple: Everybody needs to be saved. You may have the greatest house, but it's temporary. Everything here is temporary. Someday you'll move out. But you've got a permanent home with Jesus."

When Annias got home from work early in the afternoon of April 3, he assumed he would be going fishing. It was his routine. It was strange, then, that he should have found himself delaying his outing. The air was heavy and it felt as though it might rain later on, but the weather wouldn't have bothered him. "I never was scared of a storm," he said. Still, for some unaccountable reason, he felt reluctant to leave home. It wasn't a matter of anything as specific as a foreboding. It wasn't even an anxious intuition. "I just stayed put. I can't explain it. I should have been gone." He did some chores, washing his truck, jotting down notes for his upcoming sermon. He spent the rest of his free afternoon waiting in the empty house for his family to join him. He was unused to being home alone.

Supercell

ornadoes do not come out of the blue. They are the progeny of thunderstorms, which strike the United States 100,000 times each year, but whose workings remained the subject of much speculation, and little hard science, throughout the first half of the twentieth century. It took a disaster to spur large-scale investigations aimed at getting a glimpse inside a thunderstorm.

On the afternoon of August 31, 1940, Senator Ernest Lundeen of Minnesota, a member of the Farmer-Labor Party, was on his way from Washington, D.C., to Minneapolis, where he planned to deliver a speech at an amusement park. Lundeen was a political maverick. In 1918, as a member of the House of Representatives, he had vehemently opposed the entrance of the United States into World War I. Then, after the war, he had argued bitterly against the formation of the League of Nations. His positions made him so unpopular that, in Ortonville, Minnesota, "he was ridden out of town in a locked refrigerator car . . . when he attempted to make an address on the League," as the *New York Times* recounted. On the eve of World War II, he continued to stand firm against American involvement in Europe, frequently railing against the prospect of the military draft.

Lundeen boarded a DC-3 operated by Pennsylvania Central Airlines, bound for Pittsburgh, where he would change planes. The flight took off from the capital at 3:18 PM, after a twenty-six minute delay due to severe thunderstorms and poor visibility. Twenty-two minutes later, the aircraft dove into an open field near the village of Lovettsville, Virginia, in the foothills of the Blue Ridge Mountains. As a dairy farmer living nearby observed, "Seems like this thing blasted out all at once. The pilot seemed to have given her the gun, and then—bango." Weather was the suspected culprit. "The wind was howling at a rate approaching gale force," the *Times* reported, "and the rain was pelting down through a fog that hid the nearby mountains and lightning bolts were seemingly finding a ground in the nearby woods." At first, witnesses believed the plane had exploded. All twenty-five passengers and crew members aboard were killed. Victims were strewn over a wide area.

Lundeen's death focused the attention of his congressional colleagues on the perils thunderstorms posed to aviation. The threat was hardly new. "Early airplane pilots quickly learned to respect thunderstorms," wrote meteorologists J. T. Lee and W. B. Beckwith. "Since the outward appearance of storms does not reliably indicate hazards within, most pioneering aviators who lived through hazardous weather experiences changed their flight procedure from storm penetration to storm evasion." By January 1945, as the end of World War II drew near, and the prospect of a burgeoning commercial airline industry emerged, Congress passed a bill authorizing the U.S. Weather Bureau, a branch of the Department of Agriculture, "to investigate fully and thoroughly the internal structure of thunderstorms." The U.S. Air Force contributed $19 million to fund the effort.

The Weather Bureau chose Horace Byers, a young meteorologist at the University of Chicago, to lead the project. Byers considered himself part of "the vanguard of the new generation" of meteorologists, who were engaged in exploring theories of the global circulation of upper-air masses, rather than focusing, as meteorologists traditionally had, on such practical matters as the impact of local weather conditions on crops. In 1940, Byers had prevailed on Chicago, "with its reputation for strong, innovative research, and convenient location in the path of storms," to venture into meteorology by opening a graduate program in the field, joining Cal Tech, New York University, and M.I.T., from which Byers had received his doctorate, as the only such programs in the country. Sewell Avery, chairman of the board of the Chicago-based U.S. Gypsum Corporation, which introduced Sheetrock to the construction industry, provided seed money for the endeavor.

The Thunderstorm Project, as it came to be known, was launched under Byers's direction in the summer of 1946. Byers's stated objective was "to study and probe the thunderstorm in much the same way that a zoologist studies a new organism." In the past, weather balloons, which provided the best means of measuring atmospheric conditions above the ground, had failed to provide reliable data from within the turbulent core of thunderstorms. Byers decided that to plumb a thunderstorm's depths required an all-out assault on the problem. He selected two large tracts of land for the frequency with which they hosted thunderstorms—one was near Orlando, Florida, which saw thunderstorms an average of eighty days each year, and the other was in southern Ohio, where thunderstorms struck about fifty days each year—and blanketed the areas with a variety of monitoring devices. Instruments on the ground would record temperature, wind speed and direction, air pressure, and humidity; radiosonde stations would release balloons to provide readings of conditions at a range of altitudes; and ground-based radar—still a top-secret technology, available only to the military—would track the movement of precipitation. These instruments, though, would be mere accessories to the project's most important means of detection: a fleet of Northrup P-61 airplanes, known as Black Widows, which had recently been decommissioned from reconnaissance duty in the Aleutians. As Roscoe Braham, a senior scientist on the project who would later join the meteorology faculty at the University of Chicago, wrote, the planes "were built to withstand strong maneuver loads." Such resilience would prove useful, Braham went on, since "[t]he planes themselves were the sensors of storm turbulence."

The success of the experiment would depend as much on human factors as on technology. When thunderstorms passed over the test areas, Army Air Force pilots were to take off from nearby bases and fly directly into the storm clouds. The planes would be stacked five deep, separated by 5,000 feet of altitude, at elevations between 5,000 and 25,000 feet. In order to take accurate readings of the movement of air inside storms, pilots were instructed to fly with a minimum of control once they reached their assigned altitudes. "The pilots had to turn off their instincts," Braham said. "Once they trimmed the plane for a straight, level flight, they would just turn it loose and fly through the storm and let the storm do what it wanted to do." Cameras were mounted behind the pilots' shoulders, recording images of their instrument panels, and also revealing, on the basis of the position of the pilots' arms and feet, the degree to which they had succeeded in flying handsfree. "The first flight or two, the pilots had difficulties," Braham remarked, "but very quickly, they came to tell us 'Hey, it works.'" It turned out that a plane going through turbulence would wobble all the time like a rowboat in the ocean, but would manage to waddle through. Of course, the pilots had to be very ready to take the wheel if the storm tossed the plane up at an angle they were unable to live with." When the pilots emerged from the other side of the thunderstorm, they were to turn around and fly back in. The pilots spent more than seventy hours inside thunderstorms, and Byers and Braham set about analyzing data from 1,362 "storm penetrations."

The project's results, published in 1949, revolutionized the understanding of thunderstorms. Instead of a chaotic and unpredictable outburst, the thunderstorm was described as dynamic and self-regulating, going about its business like a highly evolved, living creature. (Byers and Braham referred to its structure as a "cell.") The course of this creature's life was devoted to an elegant, efficient, and sometimes tumultuous effort to supply a measure of equilibrium to locally disturbed atmospheric conditions. The thunderstorm compelled incompatible elements—cold air above, warm below; dry air above, moist below—to blend, and in so doing to resolve the tension between them. Storms had the added benefits, frequently enough, of bringing rain to parched landscapes, and providing nutrients to soil. Were it not for the fragile existence of people and property below, the thunderstorm would have seemed to be a singularly admirable demonstration of nature's ability to impose order by force. After all, it did not take an expert to point out the cleansing, refreshing effects of a thunderstorm's passage, even if it was true that its process could, at times, cause misery and damage.

Warm air is the fuel of the thunderstorm, and the rapid upward motion of this air—convection—is the thunderstorm's engine. Convection has a number of sources: The sun's rays, heating the ground throughout the day, warm the air just above ground and induce it to rise, an action made visible in billowing cumulus clouds; or cold air, brought into contact at the surface with warmer air, lends the warm air an upward shove; or, on a much larger scale, the boundary along which a mass of cold air meets a warmer mass forms a frontier of convection that can stretch for hundreds of miles.

The thunderstorm gets underway innocently enough. As Byers and Braham wrote, "In its initial stage every thunderstorm is, of course, a cumulus cloud." Inside the cloud chamber of a brewing thunderstorm, though, warm air is surging upwards. Within the first few minutes of the thunderstorm's earliest stage, the cumulus cloud can grow to an altitude of 30,000 feet. Air pours in from the perimeters of the cloud, and its convection creates a sweeping "updraft," a streaking column of air moving vertically at up to 35 miles per hour.

"With the continued updraft during the cumulus stage," Byers's and Braham's report went on, "more and more vapor condenses, and the drops and ice crystals within the cloud become more numerous and increase in size." Rain is being prepared. As vapor turns to liquid, some of its stored-up heat is released. This discharge of heat slows down the cooling of the rising air, forcing the air to climb still further and faster. Thus the thunderstorm's energy is maintained by the heat it produces; in this way, the thunderstorm perpetuates itself.

The rising air reaches a height of forty or fifty or even sixty thousand feet, and is visible as the roiling crescents of cumulonimbus clouds, or thunderheads. The thunderstorm is now entering its "mature" stage. The speed of the updraft can approach seventy miles per hour. A mass of ice crystals and waterdrops collects atop the updraft until it can no longer support their weight, and they begin to fall. It rains. Often enough, it pours. If the updraft is a kind of elevator shaft for rising air within the thunderstorm, suddenly a separate elevator, of precipitation, starts tumbling down the shaft. Some of this downward current evaporates when it hits drier air within and beneath the cloud. Evaporation steals heat from the rain and vapor, and the cooled air shoots downward, spreading out in all directions when it hits the ground, and accounting for a thunderstorm's sudden gusts of cold wind.

"The downdraft," Byers and Braham noted, "develops at the expense of the updraft." (The "down" elevator impedes the movement of the "up" elevator beneath it.) The most severe effects of the thunderstorm—its heavy rains and strong winds—are the start of the storm's demise, as the downdraft snuffs out the updraft. When a simple thunderstorm is at its worst, it has already begun to end. After a half hour or so of strenuous activity, most thunderstorms enter their final throes, which Byers and Braham called the "dissipating" stage. "The downdraft weakens and finally dies out completely," they wrote. "The surface pressure, surface wind, and other elements then return to normal."

Over the course of its compact and well-organized life, the thunderstorm can provide a dazzling show for spectators. In abruptly shunting around the air that it draws into itself, the thunderstorm jars the electrical field within and around it. The ice crystals high in the storm take on a negative electrical charge; the rain lower in the storm is positively charged; and the impulse of electricity to restore its own equilibrium between oppositely charged fields produces flashes of lightning between upper and lower regions of the thundercloud. (Such "in-cloud" activity is thought to account for 80 percent of lightning displays.) The positively charged rain low in the storm drives similarly charged air on the ground to the peripheries of the storm, leading to the outbursts known as "positive flashes." Negatively charged air remains beneath the thunderstorm; its interaction with the air above is seen as streaks of cloud-to-ground lightning, whose veined forks are among a thunderstorm's most vivid effects. Lightning heats the air surrounding it to more than 43,000 degrees Fahrenheit in an instant; the heated air suddenly expands, and just as suddenly contracts again, and this exorbitant fluctuation is audible as thunder.

The apotheosis of thunderstorm evolution is a phenomenon called the "supercell," which is marked by enormous complexity, rarity (only one thunderstorm in a thousand belongs to this category) and, from a human point of view, savagery. If an ordinary thunderstorm can be likened to a fire, ultimately consumed by its own fury, a supercell is an inferno. It can remain active for hours, travel distances of hundreds of miles, and let loose punishing surface winds and grapefruit-sized hail. It can also set columns of air into terrifying spinning motion.

Supercells are bred by a particularly extreme mix of the same ingredients that produce ordinary thunderstorms—above all, sharp differences in temperature and moisture between upper- and lower-level air—and form in the presence of deep low pressure that serves to draw warm and cold air into collision. Typically the supercell also requires a layer of dry air to act as a cap, containing unstable air at the surface until it has the energy to rise propulsively. A supercell's most distinctive feature—its long-lived spinning updraft, called a "mesocyclone"—is ignited by speed shear, when wind at different altitudes moves at different speeds. (An example often invoked to illustrate the birth of spin: a pencil is held in the hand, and when air blows across it more quickly at the top than at the bottom, the pencil starts spinning.) Speed shear only serves to get air spinning horizontally. When spinning air makes contact with a thunderstorm's updraft, though, the thunderstorm can be radically altered. The storm's updraft, instead of standing firm as a vertical column, is given a diagonal shove. As a result, when moisture at the top of the tilted updraft begins falling, bearing currents of air with it in a down-draft, the downdraft falls away from the updraft, and fails to quash it. The thunderstorm is not pushed into its dissipating stage, but rather is allowed to stay alive longer.

The thunderstorm is still not a supercell, though, until a vital change takes place during the contact between the updraft and the horizontally spinning air: The rising currents in the updraft must lift the spinning air, pushing it into a vertical spin. The updraft would now be imbued with spin, itself becoming a swirling vortex, a mesocyclone. (In the northern hemisphere, a cyclone—the word is derived from the Greek word for wheel—rotates counterclock-wise; "meso," means medium-sized.)

The mesocyclone is the supercell's feeding tube, using the force generated by its spin to pump huge volumes of warm air into the storm. It can grow to six miles in diameter. As its spin tightens and accelerates, sculpted by winds moving from different directions, or directional shear, its updrafts can reach a speed of 150 miles per hour. Warm surface air is drawn upward with such force that it hits the top of the troposphere, between eight and ten miles above the earth, and, unable to climb further, spreads out horizontally in a sheet of frozen vapor called an "anvil" cloud. (Some air can even break into the stratosphere above, forming a dome, "the over-shooting top," above the anvil.) Dryer midlevel air, sucked into the supercell, causes rain to evaporate, and, in turn, chills the air; the rain-chilled air can be expelled from the storm in gusts of up to 75 miles per hour.

Downdrafts flare from both the storm's "front flank" and its "rear flank." At the leading edge of both flanks, on the boundary between the cold air being expelled and the warmer air in front, "gust fronts" emerge, lifting yet more warm air from the ground and shoveling it toward the supercell, where it is thrust upward, condenses—its rain falling in hooklike spirals around the meso-cyclone—and releases heat that, in turn, continues to power the storm. What all this activity means is that the supercell is a beast, and its dominant tenor is rage. Condensation held aloft by the force of the updraft, bouncing up and down in the supercooled up-per regions of the storm, accumulates ice until it weighs enough to plummet through the storm as hail.

In one of ten supercells, a further development—tornadogene-sis, or the birth of a tornado—occurs. The precise mechanics of tor-nado formation remain the stuff of conjecture. Some meteorologists believe that the rear flank downdraft, originating in the middle-to-lower reaches of the storm and making a furious descent, cuts into the mesocyclone on its way down, becoming wrapped around the mesocyclone's rotating updraft. (This can lend clouds around the mesocyclone a horseshoelike appearance.) When the rear flank downdraft hits the ground, its air fans out in all directions. Part of the flow from the downdraft spreads back toward the updraft, fur-ther intensifying the updraft's spin. Out of the extremity of this whirling column of air, a tornado begins to set forth. Fragments of cloud twist around it. At the tornado's center is a tiny core, perhaps fifty feet in diameter, of intense low pressure, like the constricted eye of a densely concentrated hurricane. Air circulates around this core with startling speed. Surrounding air is sucked into it, increasing its turbulence. The tornado trails along at the back of the supercell, spinning, slamming some of the objects in its path to the ground, lifting others in its vacuum. At first it resembles a swirling fog. Then, drawing in dirt and debris, it is painted with the earth, and becomes darkly visible.

"Steadily the cloud came on," wrote a Kansas farmer named Will Keller, describing the passage of such a storm on June 22, 1928. "At last the great shaggy end of the funnel hung directly overhead. Everything was as still as death. There was a strong, gassy odor, and it seemed as though I could not breathe. There was a screaming, hissing sound coming directly from the end of the funnel. I looked up, and to my astonishment I saw right into the heart of the tornado."

The archetypal American natural disaster: As much an emblem of the national imagination as a fact of the landscape. In a year like 1973, when more than 1,100 of them touched down from Osceola, Florida, to Sargent, North Dakota, the peculiar preference of tornadoes for the United States, site of three-quarters of the world's overland whirlwinds, could hardly be disputed.

Numbers do not tell the whole story, though. Indeed, the fear instilled by tornadoes, and the fascination with them, is beyond rational accounting; they are the weather-watcher's equivalent of charismatic megafauna. Their aura is not difficult to fathom. Descending suddenly, menacingly, and without reliable warning, the tornado serves as a near-primal expression of the mysterious and fraught relationship between individuals and the skies above them. Tornadoes are personal. Unlike hurricanes or earthquakes, which gather large communities in their grasp, the average tornado travels just six miles, measures under 150 yards in width, and lasts less than fifteen minutes. Even in the regions of greatest tornado activity— such as the so-called Tornado Alley, extending from Texas through Oklahoma and Kansas to the Dakotas, and home to 70 percent of American tornadoes—any particular piece of real estate is likely to host a tornado no more than once in 1,400 years, according to the formulations of statisticians. To be struck by a tornado, then, is to be cruelly singled out; even lightning kills more people in the United States than tornadoes. The visionary quality of a tornado sighting—part natural phenomenon, part spiritual emanation—is evident in a verse from the book of Ezekiel in the Old Testament: "And I looked, and behold, a whirlwind came out of the north, a great cloud, and a fire infolding itself, and a brightness about it, and out of the midst thereof as the color of amber, out of the midst of the fire."

Americans have documented their fears of tornadoes since the days of earliest European settlement. In July 1643, John Winthrop, governor of the Massachusetts Bay Colony, wrote, "There arose a sudden gust . . . so violent for half an hour, as it blew down multitudes of trees. It lifted up their meeting house at Newbury, the people being in it. It darkened the air with dust, yet through God's great mercy it did no hurt, but only killed one Indian with the fall of a tree." The tornado's ability to exact swift and precise punishment—leaving one man's house untouched while demolishing that of his neighbor—endows it with quasi-religious powers. So, too, do the uncanny physical effects that often accompany it: a greenish light in the sky, heralding its onset; an anticipatory hush settling over birds and animals, who seem to sense the imminent danger it poses; the deafening roar likened, often enough, to a moan, or a screech, or the din of swarming insects as it approaches; and, above all, its unmeasurably violent winds, which, until the 1950s, many scientists believed to travel at the speed of sound.

Above all, the mystique of the tornado rests with its transfiguring power. The root of the word itself, a corruption of the Latin "tornare" (to turn) not only describes the swirling motion of the storm, but indicates its ability to provoke change. The air turns; the terrain is altered; lives are thrown into disarray. Rev. Increase Mather, recounting a tornado that struck Cambridge, Massachusetts, in July 1680, wrote, "It passed along upon the ground, tearing all before it, bushes by the roots, yea the earth itself."

Though tornadoes have been sighted in every state, they remain a particular scourge of the heartland, predominating over the flatlands between Appalachia and the Rockies, where they are viewed as an indigenous menace. Indeed, as America's westward migration accelerated in the nineteenth century, and sightings of tornadoes became more frequent, the funnel came to symbolize the forbidding quality of open spaces. An article in *Popular Science Monthly* in 1883 suggested that the incidence of tornadoes was on the rise because of "radical changes" to the environment caused by the construction of railroads and the electrical discharges emitted by telegraph and telephone lines, and a writer in *North American Review* noted the "wide-spread impression that, with the deforesting and settlement of the West, tornado-visitations have increased." John P. Finley, a weather specialist in the U.S. Signal Corps, and the first government official to provide detailed studies of tornado damage, described the onset of an 1879 tornado strike in Marshall County, Kansas: "Many people actually believe that Judgment Day has come, and offer fervent prayers and loud appeals for preservation," he wrote. "But the hand of mercy stays not the dreadful carnage."

The deadliest American natural disaster to strike prior to the Civil War occurred when a tornado set down in the port city of Natchez, Mississippi, at midday on May 7, 1840. The *Natchez Weekly Courier and Journal* wrote of "a scene of desolation and ruin which sickens the heart and beggars description—all, all is swept away, and beneath the ruins still lay crushed the bodies of many strangers." The death toll was at least 317. In the luxuriant language that would come to mark disaster journalism, the *Mississippi Free Trader* remarked, "Our beautiful city is shattered as if it had been stormed by all the cannon of Austerlitz. Our delightful China trees are all torn up. We are peeled and desolate."

Tornadoes can come in batches, too, and the first notable American tornado contagion struck on February 19, 1884, when sixty of them barraged eight states, from Virginia to Kentucky, killing 800 and taking down 15,000 homes. The breadth of the disaster was not matched again until March 18, 1925, when the "Tri-State Tornado" crossed from Missouri into Illinois and Indiana, carving a continuous 219-mile-long track in the ground, and killing 695 people. "The death-dealing funnel," writes weather historian David Ludlum, "was imbedded in a dark, amorphous mass of whirling clouds and assorted debris that prevented a sighting of the approaching calamity."

As a side effect of their inscrutable nature, tornadoes are nearly always accompanied by what Snowden Flora, a onetime senior meteorologist with the U.S. Weather Bureau, referred to in his 1954 volume *Tornadoes of the United States* as "freaks of the storm." These are rural myths of a sort, and though they can include cautionary tales—babies wrenched from their mothers' arms and blown a half-mile, schoolchildren mutilated beyond recognition, families divided between survivors and victims—most tell of miraculous survival, or offer adamant testimony to a tornado's otherworldly powers. Certain motifs recur. Tornadoes drive lengths of straw into walls, pluck feathers from chickens, send cows and horses aloft, and lift rail cars from their tracks and set them down facing the opposite direction. No traditional account of a tornado is complete without an episode like one Flora mentions, telling of "a jar of pickles that was carried twenty-five miles and then lowered, unbroken, into a ditch." In such visions, the tornado proceeds by its own capricious logic.

It can seem almost impious to admit one further aspect of a tornado's fascination: its beauty, which is inseparable from the terror it provokes. Nature produces no sight more ravishing than that of the tornado slipping, spritelike, from a mountainous cloud to the ground. As the observer looks on, the tornado builds itself, leaping out of invisibility and then returning to it. Its most salient feature, its funnel, can take many forms: a narrow tail of white smoke, or a sharply defined geometric cone, like an inverted pyramid, or a wedge, or a tube that seems to stretch from the sky to the center of the earth, or the so-called finger of God. The tornado is a sculptural marvel, simultaneously solid and sheer, compact and monstrously enlarged. It seems to inhale the earth. Then, suddenly, it disappears.

Tornado hysteria reached its peak during the spring of 1953. At 4:45 PM on May 11, a mechanic named Ira Braden was installing automatic doors at the Amicable Life Building in downtown Waco, Texas. The weather turned gloomy, but Braden did not take shelter. "The hypnotic terror of witnessing this unbelievable scene kept me glued to the rain," he would recount in the *Saturday Evening Post*. He went on:

> From the sidewalk where I clung desperately to my steel rail to avoid being sucked into the vortex, I saw the tornado's incredible forty-five-second thrust through the business heart of the city. I saw the fronts and the walls of buildings explode outward. . . . I saw roofs pop up like corks from champagne bottles and burst apart. . . . I saw automobiles—some unoccupied, others bearing passengers—crushed like bugs and buried out of sight. . . . I saw one car, an old model, leap upward and disappear into the air as if by magic.
>
> I saw blocks of stone and timbers blown horizontally through the atmosphere at unbelievable speed, and razor-sharp chunks of glass and steel flew toward me as though shot from rifles.

The tornado killed 114 people in the city of 90,000. Across the street from Braden, a six-story furniture store collapsed, burying dozens of people in rubble and killing at least thirty. Elsewhere, fifteen teenagers died in a pool hall, and five more people were crushed while fleeing in cars. Twenty square blocks of the downtown were reduced to ruin.

The Waco tornado caused a sensation, in part, because tornadoes were popularly believed to be a blight exclusive to the countryside. Indeed, over the next four weeks, tornadoes returned to the hinterlands, dozens of them, striking meagerly populated areas from South Carolina to Michigan. In early June, a tornado "which appeared to have 'five fingers'," touched down in eastern Nebraska, killing the entire Mads Madsden family—ten members spanning three generations—while they enjoyed Sunday dinner. A photo in *Life* magazine showing the family's underground storm cellar bore the caption "Unused Refuge."

Then, on successive days, tornadoes offered further evidence that they do not distinguish between city and country. On the evening of June 8, "Six savage twisters . . . raked sections of a 350-mile belt above and below Detroit," according to the *New York Times*. Worst off was Flint, General Motors's center of production. As *Time* reported, "It was 8:30 o'clock when the big one hit suburban Flint. Cars and trucks bounced like baseballs through the ruined fields. Homes were flattened; factories, schools and shops were ripped apart board by board, block by block." One hundred and thirteen were killed.

The next day the 200,000 residents of Worcester, Massachusetts, few of whom recognized a tornado threat to New England, were visited just before sunset by what was described in the *Times* as a "huge cone of black smoke." "Homes exploded to kindling and automobiles were whisked about like cardboard toys. . . . When the machines finally came to a halt, they were as flat as if crushed by a giant press." Ninety people died. Four thousand buildings were destroyed or badly damaged, and airborne debris made its way to Boston, forty-five miles distant.

What was going on? President Eisenhower examined the wreckage of Flint and Worcester a few days later from the comfort of his airplane, but the spring's rash of tornadoes, causing 420 deaths and at least $200 million in damage, prompted a brief political furor. Ray Madden, a congressman from Indiana, was among those who suggested that the tornadoes might be a Cold War byproduct. Madden pointed out that the onslaught had arrived close on the heels of the detonation of eleven atomic weapons over the Nevada desert. "The public is entitled to know if there is any connection between the A-bomb explosions and the tornadoes which have followed," he said in a radio interview. "Thousands of tons of this radioactive material drift across the nation. We know that this material pollutes the air we breathe and the water we drink. Does it also generate abnormal atmospheric conditions?"

Officials from the Atomic Energy Commission dismissed the suggestion, though their reasoning offered little comfort to those who feared tornadoes. As a spokesman pointed out, "A major atomic explosion is a tiny force compared with the energy unleashed by a natural storm."

Limestone:
Law and Death

I n 1974, nobody in Limestone made the mistake of calling the county's best-known resident, M. W. Evans, by his given name, Martin. He was "Buddy" to friends and family, "Mister Buddy" to less familiar acquaintances, and "Sheriff" to the rest. At age 45, he had already logged seventeen years as an undertaker, eight years as county coroner, and three terms as sheriff. (Some of the service was concurrent.) There was little doing in Limestone that escaped Buddy's notice, and few hideouts in the county's 607 square miles of alternately marshy, wooded, and ruggedly hilly territory that he had not visited on one occasion or another. "If I didn't know someone in Limestone County," Buddy would say, "then they didn't live in Limestone County. I didn't need a street address to find a person. I knew who lived just past that old oak tree on the right hand side of the road, and who lived down in the creek bottom through those woods, and so forth. I knew every pig paddy."

He had taken over as sheriff in 1963, inheriting a staff of three deputies and two jailers from a predecessor whose approach to investigating crime, particularly those of which the victims were black, was described as casual. At the time, the department had no secretary and no radio contact with its two aging cruisers. State law required the sheriff to take lodgings at the county jail, and, with some trepidation, Buddy had moved his wife, Bobbie, and two boys, Johnny and Jerry, into a spartan apartment adjacent to both the drunk tank and what he called the "insane tank." "We would hear those drunks hollering all night long," Buddy recalled. "But they were always careful to use polite language around the boys." Bobbie did the grocery shopping and cooking for the prisoners, who usually numbered around a hundred, and whose ranks could be swollen by inmates that Buddy accepted from other counties, for a charge. The sheriff's department was often in straits. Until late 1970, it had been structured like a small business, one in which Buddy, rather than earning a salary, was paid a $10 fee by the county for each arrest he made, in addition to a daily stipend of sixty cents for each prisoner in his custody.

Balding, puggish, and physically unimposing, Buddy came to preside over Limestone like a one-man force. "People voted the sheriff in, so they expected to be looked after," he remarked. Constituents would not hesitate to call about missing pets or malfunctioning household appliances, and Buddy learned to keep his uniform beside his bed when he slept. "There was no such thing to me as 'off-duty,'" he said. He was Limestone's personal embodiment of the law, its guardian. He sported a seven-pointed star on his chest, a Colt revolver on his belt, and, when protocol required, a Stetson atop his brow.

There may have been numerous signs that Limestone's steady small-town way of life was slowly disappearing—its farmers auctioning off their land and livestock, its youth looking for more thrills and better opportunities elsewhere—but few such indications of change were to be found in the local newspaper, the *Athens News Courier*. On April 3, 1974, alongside coverage of the freakish April Fool's Day storm (the front page headline screamed, "Twister

Damage Extensive"), the morning paper performed its typical survey of what passed for news in Limestone. It reported on the mayor's proclamation of an upcoming blood drive as "Save-A-Life Day" and ran a half-page portrait of the plaid-bedecked members of the Owens Junior High School Beta Club. The Lifestyle column provided reassurance that traditional family roles remained respectable in Limestone, noting, for instance, that on Wooley Springs Road a meeting of the Oak Grove Homemakers' Club had lately been convened, with Mrs. Campbell's demonstration, "Let's Clean House," as the highlight. The paper offered reminders, too, that in Limestone neighbors still looked after each other, and listed those who had paid a call at the house of Mr. and Mrs. Frank Williams the previous Sunday. "Mr. Williams is recuperating at home from back surgery," the item explained. "He remains bedfast most of the time even though the body cast has been removed." On the next page, a row of photographs were dedicated to local children celebrating their birthdays, and an advice columnist described how to cope with the trials of swayback and gout.

Limestone's veneer of sedate Christian propriety could, however, wear thin quickly when one occupied the sheriff's point of view. Buddy Evans was the most efficient and prolific crime-fighting sheriff Limestone had ever seen. In 1973, his office set a record for arrests, with 4,578—an average of one for every nine residents—including a murder, eight cases of assault with intent to murder, a rape, two arsons, armed robberies, drawing a deadly weapon, and kidnapping. Luckily, violent crime was still relatively rare, but Buddy took seriously the more basic challenge of patrolling the unflattering excesses of day-to-day life in the county. Crimes attributable to alcohol—in particular, violations of the county's prohibition law, and related charges for drunk driving, public drunkenness, disturbing the peace, abusive language, and escape after arrest—accounted for a third of Buddy's total activity. He had a close-up view of the petty anguishes that afflicted his neighbors, and racked up arrests for forgeries, passing bad checks, carrying concealed weapons, fist fighting, contributing to the delinquency of a minor, causing malicious injury to property, using the telephone for harassment, running away from home, fishing without a license, cattle thieving, failing to dim lights, failing to stop at a blinking light, and countless other lapses of character, judgment, intelligence, and luck. No infraction was too minor to pursue, whether it was a case of a multiple "pignapping" at Wilbur Marbutt's farm—the missing "were described as two blacks, one black and white streaked, two white, and one a dingy gray"—or the apprehension, in January 1974, of forty warm cases of canned Shlitz beer.

As Buddy could attest, Limestone had always had a well-concealed dark side. Although he, like others in the county, was reluctant to admit it, much of what was darkest and most violent involved the county's legacy of race relations. Limestone's first census, conducted in 1820, counted a population of 6,922 whites, 2,919 slaves, and thirty "freed coloreds." As cotton growing thrived—aided by such new technologies as the spinning jenny, the self-acting loom, and, above all, the cotton gin—the county's racial balance tilted rapidly. By 1830, the white population had risen only modestly, to 8,077, while the number of slaves had more than doubled, to 6,689. On the eve of the Civil War, when a solid majority of Limestone's residents were slaves, landowners suddenly woke up to the potential for disaster. "It seems that the negroes have concluded that Lincoln is going to free them all," noted one leading citizen, Daniel R. Hundley, in his 1861 diary. Rumors of planned slave rebellions abounded, and "county vigilance committees" were formed to contain the perceived threat by any means deemed necessary. As Hundley, a member of one such committee, recorded, "Our task to-day was to examine the slaves of Mrs. Rice, many of whom had to be severely whipped and some will be hung."

During the Civil War, terror and lawlessness were, in turn, directed against the few whites—mostly women and children—who remained in Limestone.

In May 1862, days after Confederate troops had ambushed Union soldiers occupying Athens, Union forces avenged the attack with such wantonness that James Garfield, the future president, termed their actions "the most shameful outrages on the country here that the history of this war has seen." In Limestone, the episode came to be referred to, with sullen pride, as "the Sack of Athens." It started when Union colonel John Basil Turchin, after retaking the town, stood in Courthouse Square and directed his troops to go on a rampage. Businesses were ransacked, houses and churches set ablaze, and women raped. The pillage soon spread to the countryside. Turchin ordered his men to respond to rebel attacks by punishing civilians and burning their farms. So complete was the destruction that a Confederate general, John Bell Hood, passing through the area more than two years later, described "once prosperous and happy homes, long since reduced to heaps of ashes." Bell went on, "Only the birds seemed unconscious of the ruin and desolation which reigned supreme."

The cycle of violence continued after the defeat of the South, when whites, disenfranchised and aggrieved over the collapse of their social order, conspired to reclaim power. Late in 1865, a half-dozen veterans of the Confederate army gathered in Pulaski, Tennessee, thirty miles north of Limestone, in the office of a local judge. The meeting, as Susan Lawrence Davis, a native of Athens, wrote in 1924, was one of those extraordinary occasions on which

the depredations of nature reflected the morale of those in attendance. "It was Christmas Eve and their town was saddened not
only by the wreckage of Civil War," Davis recounted, "but by the
visitation of a cyclone which had killed and injured many of its in-
habitants and destroyed many homes."

"Boys," proposed one of those assembled, "let's start something
to break this monotony, and to cheer up our mothers and the girls.
Let's start a club of some kind."

Thus, in Davis's mythologizing account, the Ku Klux Klan was
born. "They established regular headquarters at the home of Dr.
Benjamin Carter which had been recently wrecked by the cyclone,"
Davis wrote. "Around the ruins of this home were the storm-torn
trunks of trees which had once been a splendid grove . . . [I]t was
most suitable for the purpose of the Ku Klux Klan as it had the appearance of being haunted."

Davis's father, Lawrence Ripley Davis, learning of the secret society, opened the organization's second chapter, or clavern, in
Athens. Athens would become the Klan's Alabama headquarters
during Reconstruction, and it was there, too, that the Klan would
be transformed from a social club into a militia, as its members undertook a campaign of intimidation designed to "tell all the negroes that they must give up the idea of social equality in the
south." Davis reminisced about seeing her father in "his regalia"
for the first time, as a young girl: "I watched my father out of the
gateway on this bright moonlight night and saw many hundreds
of the Ku Klux Klan in their white robes, filing over the hill to join
him, and follow the signaling bell towards Athens."

Buddy settled into office as the counterculture of the '60s began
making a middle-class hobby of illegal drug use around the country. In this respect, as in others, Limestone seemed, for a time, to

belong to a different era altogether. Indeed, Buddy's major initiative as sheriff was his relentless fight against moonshining. "Moonshine was a lot cheaper than the bonded stuff," he explained, "and a lot of guys just liked it better. It would really knock you out." There were hundreds of improvised stills hidden around the county, mostly in the sparsely populated woods near the Tennessee River, and Buddy knew of several locals who had died from lead poisoning caused by whiskey brewed in the pipes of rusted radiators. Limestone had also seen bouts of violence, including murders, in "shot houses," abandoned sharecropper's shacks that were used as transient speakeasies. Buddy had an additional incentive to crack down on moonshine: The state rewarded the sheriff with $50 for every moonshiner arrested, $25 for a confiscated still, and fifty cents for every gallon of whiskey retrieved.

"It was hard to catch moonshiners," Buddy remarked. "You'd look for a tiny path on the side of the road, and then you had to follow it way into the woods, wading through creeks and what have you. Then you'd have to lie down in the mud and snow and ice and keep watch. People told me I was crazy to do it, but back when I became sheriff—man, I was full of piss and vinegar." Once, in December 1970, Buddy staked out a farm in West Limestone for sixty hours in the bitter cold before moving in to break up a 400-gallon butane-powered still. Captured stills were destroyed with axes or dynamite.

When routine surveillance failed to produce arrests, Buddy went undercover. At one point he disguised himself as a woman. Cloaked in a wig and dress, and covered by a long housecoat, he set out to buy moonshine from suspected bootleggers. The ruse, however improbable, worked. In 1973 he tried a new costume. "The Sheriff, one of the best known men around . . . got himself a fairly long, hippie-type wig," according to a local news report. He donned sunglasses and ragged clothes, "substituted his familiar pipe for a cigarette," and spent two weeks venturing across the county in the costume. On one fruitful day, he arrested fifty-seven moonshiners.

It was only a matter of time, though, before trends from the outside world began to reach Limestone. At the end of 1973, Buddy pointed to "an alarming growth" in drug cases; he made close to 250 drug-related arrests that year, three times as many as the previous year. (In 1968, by contrast, only two arrests had been made on drug charges.) He suspected that marijuana and heroin had infiltrated county schools, and blamed the introduction of drugs squarely on a new breed of students who had arrived in the county to attend Athens College, a small Methodist school that, having hit on hard times, began recruiting out-of-state applicants. "In 1967 Athens College took in a bunch of New Jersey draft dodgers," Buddy said. "They plastered the county with drugs."

Buddy's counterpart in Limestone's shadow landscape of law and death was a man named Ralph Padgett—a bank manager by day, and, when circumstances required, acting Limestone County coroner. The position had become available in 1972 when the sitting coroner was killed in a car accident on his way to an embalming school. (Buddy had given up being coroner a decade earlier, when he was elected sheriff.) Ralph had taken some chemistry courses in college, and regarded himself as more qualified to be coroner than most. "Of course, you could pump gas and still be coroner," he observed. He saw the job as community service. It carried a biweekly stipend of $36, plus a fuel allowance of ten cents a mile.

In his first twenty months on the job, Ralph presided over 167 cases, enough to dispel any illusions he may have held on the subject of the dignity of life. Many deaths were the outcome of terrible caprice—a child accidentally strangled, or a man burned to a crisp by a lightning strike, or a horseback rider thrown from his mount, or a farmer caught in a corn picker and torn to bits. Ralph was still frequently moved, or appalled, by the wretchedness he encountered, particularly when young people were involved, whether it was the teenage rodeo queen whom he had pronounced dead of injuries from a car wreck, or the local baseball star who had been killed in a motorcycle accident. "That boy's Daddy was down in the sand trying to dig up pieces of brain," Ralph recalled. Soon after taking office, he investigated the dreadful case of a fourteen-year-old girl who was killed in the front yard of her house, accidentally shot in the neck when her brother and a friend were hunting snakes.

Drownings, too, were routine occurrences in Limestone. In early spring, when water temperatures rose, the gases in a submerged body would expand and long unaccounted-for corpses would break the surface of local waterways. Ralph had once identified a victim who had been missing for 110 days. "We found him up in a slough," he said. "Turtles were eating on the guy's back." It was not unusual to find bodies in such compromised states. One man was out hunting near Tanner when he was struck by a 111-car freight train of the L&N Railroad, bound for Nashville. According to Ralph's measurements, the man was dragged nearly 137 feet. "I had to go pick up the body parts right away before dogs got to them. The abuse a body can be put through is amazing."

Ralph had already investigated enough suicides to have formed strict opinions on the subject. "Carbon monoxide poisoning is the best way to go," he commented. He had seen hangings and drug overdoses and no shortage of self-inflicted gunshot wounds. He visited the suicide scenes of elderly people who were sick and feared they were burdening their families, and those of the young and lovelorn. "I had a guy who wore a thick pair of glasses and put a .22 right up against the lenses and shot himself. I had to go get the wife—she was in a motel room with a fifteen-year-old boy. It was a nice rifle. Later on I bought it from her."

Every so often, Ralph got involved in the intrigue of a murder, and would cross paths with Buddy, with whom he enjoyed an easy rapport. In August 1973, he was called to the house of 38-year-old Rosetta Anderson. She had been dead about a week. "She was all wrapped in blankets that were tied with wire," Ralph said. "Her body fluids—we call it 'pizza juice'—were running out of her. I cut those wires and maggots were crawling everywhere. My God, we couldn't keep her skin on. We did the autopsy right there in the house, on the dining table. We had a sheriff's deputy with us, holding a spotlight so we could see, and he puked in his gas mask." Ralph found a knife wound in the woman's chest. Her scalp was coming off—"the brain was like blackberry cobbler"—but Ralph managed to trace the opening made by a gunshot to her head. The woman's husband was arrested and charged with murder. In standard fashion, Ralph's report identified the woman as "c/f," or "colored female."

In the first months of 1974, Ralph's caseload had been unremarkable. Two duck hunters who had gone missing a few weeks earlier turned up in the Tennessee River. A motorist suffered "complete brain ejection" in a crash. A six-month-old baby fell from a sofa and stopped breathing. A pair of men died near the rural village of Belle Mina when their kerosene lamp exploded. A forty-year-old man shot himself on Elk River Mills Road. When infant Melissa Kay Walker was found dead, Ralph dispensed with official detachment in his report. "This is one of those unfortunate crib deaths," he wrote. "Melissa was due to have her six-week checkup tomorrow."

By April 3, Buddy had spent eleven years wearing the sheriff's uniform. He had well-deserved confidence in his ability to control any form of chaos that might encroach on his territory. In a month, he would be running in a primary election to determine the Democratic party nominee for sheriff, and it seemed certain that his tireless efforts on behalf of Limestone County would be rewarded. Just in case, he was spending more than $3,000 on his campaign. "A vote for Buddy is a vote for continued honest efficient capable courteous experienced law enforcement," one of his ads read. His competition for the nomination was not particularly strong. Clyde Ennis, whom Buddy had unseated in 1962, was running for office again. Ennis had written a poem, called "The Sheriff's Job," for his campaign:

Now this Sheriff's job is a curious one,
Like the housewife's work it's never done.
Calls come by night and come by day,
They may be near or miles away.
Do hurry up, says the caller,
You're badly needed in Possum Holler.
Pa's on a rampage; he's got a gun,
Been looking for Maw since half past one.

Buddy did not pretend to have Ennis's homespun charm, but the people of Limestone knew that he never failed to respond to a call, and that danger and discomfort did not put him off. There were, however, some matters that were beyond his jurisdiction. Once he had seen a tornado up close. It was late in the afternoon of March 11, 1963. He had just taken over as sheriff, and was returning to Athens from the community of Copeland, in northeast Limestone. He was carrying a prisoner named Billy Ray Knox, whom he had just picked up, on the basis of a fingerprint, for robbing a grocery store. Knox rode in the back of the cruiser, in a secure cage. "We were crossing a bridge over a creek on Nick Davis Road, and all at once a black cloud came toward me. I didn't know what it was." Buddy laughed. "That's how dumb I was about tornadoes. The car just started bouncing. I stalled out on the bridge. I was afraid it was going to take me into the creek." When the cloud passed, Buddy looked to his right. "A minute before there'd been a barn standing there. Now it was gone."

A man ran up to Buddy's car and told him there were people lying injured in a field. Buddy's prisoner was beside himself with fear. "I didn't have time to go look for those people and also take a prisoner to jail," Buddy said. "But I figured that if I left the guy sitting there alone in the cruiser he'd run."

Buddy whispered a few words to his prisoner, then trudged into the field to look for wounded. None of the injuries was serious. When Buddy returned to the car, he was pleased to find that the prisoner had not budged. "I had told him, 'Okay, I'll let you sit in place. But here's the thing. If you try to run, I'm going to shoot you.'" Buddy enjoyed retelling the story. "Oh, I wouldn't have shot him, really. Still, it was a good thing to say." He added, "That's how I knew what a tornado looked like."

Mr. Tornado

On August 8, 1953, a young Japanese physicist named Tatsuya Fujita boarded a Pan American propellor-driven plane at Tokyo's Haneda International Airport, bound for San Francisco. Although he could not have known it at the time, he was about to embark on a lifelong, single-minded pursuit of the violent mysteries of tornadoes. He held a one-way ticket to the United States, which had cost him $650, the equivalent of thirteen months of his salary at the Kyushu Institute of Technology. He left behind a wife and an infant son.

Fujita was a slight man who dressed primly, wore round metal-frame glasses, and observed his surroundings scrupulously. He had been abroad only once before, in 1940, on a geological field trip as a student, when he took a ferry across the Sea of Japan to visit an iron mine in Korea. "In comparison with the flying range of migrating birds," he would later write, employing his bent for novel analogies, often drawn from nature, "the traveling distance in my childhood years was extremely short, only less than 50 km (30 miles) from my birthplace. Consequently, my vision of the world was no more than that of a small frog in a deep well."

As the plane took off, Fujita was both wide-eyed and workman-like. "I spoke to myself that I was now flying for the first time in my life. Without wasting the expensive flight time, I began sketching the vertical cross section of clouds along the flight path."

Thus occupied, Fujita landed in San Francisco twenty-seven hours later. He was carrying all of $22, the maximum amount he could take from Japan under postwar currency regulations. A three-day train trip to Chicago, his final destination, still lay ahead of him. He stocked up on fig bars and bottles of Coca-Cola and departed from Oakland. The view from the train window was evidently less absorbing to him than the aerial vista had been. "After a long sleep, I took a fig bar breakfast when the train was passing over the dike in the Great Salt Lake, followed by a fig bar lunch after departing Green River, Wyoming . . . After drinking Coca-Cola, I fell asleep until the train stopped at Cedar Rapids, Iowa, early next morning."

Fujita was born in October 1920, in the town of Sone, population 1,000, on the upper tip of Kyushu, Japan's southernmost island. He referred to Kyushu as "my wonder island." As a child, he would venture across nearby rice fields to the edge of an inland sea and wait for the tide to withdraw, exposing a broad sandbar in which he would hunt for clams. The sand would heat up rapidly under the afternoon sun, and Fujita would scamper barefoot to a tiny island across the tidal flat, then rush back before the tides shifted and cut the island off from the mainland. "The return trip was very tricky," he noted. The fluctuations of natural forces fascinated him. Kyushu "was adorned with two active volcanoes . . . I visited these volcanoes during eruptions, observing the angry face of our living planet." His father, a grammar school teacher, would remind him "that nothing in this world will remain unchanged. 'Look up at the full moon in the sky,' he said, 'it will have to turn into the new moon.'"

The family lived in a small compound surrounding a carefully laid-out garden, which featured pink and white magnolia trees, a black pine, orange, persimmon, and fig trees, and a hundred-year-old tree called a muku, the trunk of which was covered with mushrooms known as "chairs of monkeys." Fujita had a younger brother and sister, and the entire family celebrated birthdays on New Year's Day, "when everybody became one year older simultaneously." As he remarked, "My childhood life was by no means rationalistic."

It quickly became clear that Fujita's mind was given both to strenuous exertions of reason and to flights of idiosyncrasy. As a teenager, he was taken on a class trip to view a tunnel that a Buddhist monk had bored through a cliff, toiling for thirty years with a hammer and chisel. Asked by a teacher to comment on the monk's efforts, Fujita submitted an essay expressing dismay. " 'If I were asked to dig a tunnel, I would first invent a digging machine,'" he wrote. His insight was not welcomed. "Unfortunately, I did not receive a passing grade after all, because I failed to appreciate the monk's spiritual achievement." Nonetheless, Fujita was notably dogged. He fabricated a handmade telescope to track the location of sunspots and neglected schoolwork to build himself a slide rule. Evidently, he preferred to devise his own tools rather than use those provided by others. " 'You spent over ten days to generate the logarithms which you will be learning in less than ten minutes in your regular class next month,'" his math teacher told him on seeing the slide rule. The teacher, Fujita wrote, "did not tell me if I wasted my time or not."

He entered the Meiji College of Technology in 1939. As an assistant to a geology professor, he was given the task of drawing bird's-eye views of the calderas of four volcanoes based on topographical maps. "After working on [t]his project for several months, my eyes began seeing contour maps as if they were three-dimensional mountains." Indeed, the bird's-eye view—hovering above the landscape, observing the intricate workings of physical forces, maintaining a studied distance from the untidiness of human behavior—would come to be Fujita's favored perspective. He was intrigued by maps, and showed an extraordinary aptitude for precise visualization and for draftsmanship.

Immediately after graduating in 1943, Fujita joined Meiji's physics faculty, at a monthly salary of $17.64. War would soon interrupt his academic work. In July 1944, after American forces massed in the Pacific, Fujita was recruited by the Japanese navy to develop a means of detecting incoming aircraft by use of searchlight beams. The project required that he factor into his calculations the effect on the beams of both the earth's curvature and its atmospheric conditions. Fujita, who would come to avoid commentary on his military experience, noted only, "At this time I became very interested in the meteorological aspect of the global atmosphere."

As it was, Japanese meteorologists, working with far less sophisticated instruments than their counterparts in the West, had already been responsible for some significant discoveries. A Japanese researcher, Wasaburo Ooishi, had determined, on the basis of experiments conducted from the peak of Mount Fuji in the 1920s, the existence of strong upper-level winds that flowed east across the Pacific. He published his research in the utopian international language of Esperanto, ensuring that it went almost entirely unnoticed. These winds, which would eventually become known as the jet stream, were exploited by the Japanese in a campaign to send bomb-laden, pilotless balloons to the United States. The Japanese launched nine thousand such balloons, made of paper derived from mulberry bushes; 300 landed in the United States; a single one proved lethal, killing a woman and five children who were picnicking in Oregon on May 5, 1945.

* * *

F5

It would take years for Fujita to make an explicit connection between the effects of aerial bombardment and those of tornadoes. In the meantime, he gained firsthand experience of airborne destruction as American forces, persuaded that persistent cloud cover over Japan's coastline made pinpoint attacks impossible, began blanketing Japanese cities with incendiary bombs. The campaign was launched on Tokyo on March 10, 1945. More than three hundred B-29 bombers set off from bases in the Mariana Islands, each carrying some 1,400 bombs. The planes flew over the city at low altitude, under cover of night. On impact, the bombs released a flammable petroleum compound. Fire swept through the city, consuming so much oxygen that many victims suffocated. Some 200,000 Japanese—mostly women and children, since all available men had been conscripted to military service—are thought to have died, and sixteen square miles of the city were incinerated. "I happened to be in Tokyo in March 1945 when several waves of B-29s firebombed the city, burning down 230,000 houses overnight," Fujita noted, with seeming casualness. He offered little elaboration, except to say that he and a friend "heard a bang from a close distance, after which we noticed that distant houses were on fire. Early next morning we walked around the neighborhood and found unexploded cylinders of incendiary bombs stuck deep in the ground."

It would not be possible to know exactly what Fujita saw while wandering around Tokyo, or whether he took in scenes of carnage similar to those noted by a witness named Fusako Susaki, who observed, "Stacked-up corpses were being hauled away on lorries. Everywhere there was the stench of the dead and of smoke. I saw the places on the pavement where people had been roasted to death."

The firebombing campaign culminated, of course, in the atomic blasts in Hiroshima and Nagasaki. "In September 1945," Fujita recounted, "several weeks after the Nagasaki bombing, President Heihachi Kamura of our college sent a group of our faculty and volunteer students on a ground-truth mission to Nagasaki and then to Hiroshima." Fujita was a member of the group. Once again, he would render his impressions of what he encountered with unusual, almost steely, reserve and obliqueness. "I visited both Nagasaki and Hiroshima, noticing that the train fares to these two cities were identical. In fact, the railroad distances to Nagasaki and Hiroshima from Tobata, the city of our college, are 216.0 km (134.2 mi) and 219.7 km (136.5 mi), respectively. Our college is therefore located halfway between Nagasaki and Hiroshima."

"Because damage areas were still radioactive, I told my students, 'Do not sit on or touch anything in the bomb area.' In spite of our precaution, some suffered diarrhea, nausea, and headache."

Fujita described the bombed cities as though they were scientific curiosities, like archaeological sites. In Nagasaki, he happened upon a collection of shattered bamboo flowerpots that had decorated a cemetery, and that were scorched with odd, crescent-shaped burns. Studying the pattern of burns, he was able to calculate the height, location, and dimensions of the blast. It was the beginning of Fujita's long dedication to a novel, and sometimes grisly, brand of investigative work. "I hopped around from one cemetery to another on the hillsides north, east, and south of ground zero," he wrote. "A number of burned bodies were still lying on the hillside." He proposed that the bomb had detonated some 1,500 feet above the city, and not on contact with the ground, as other researchers assumed. Further, he suggested that the airflow from the blast had apparently fanned outward on contact with the ground, creating what he would refer to as a starburst pattern of damage.

* * *

F5

"My daily life under the postwar inflation was miserable." The misery, Fujita determined, was most effectively rendered in quantitative terms. "The rate of inflation, as measured by the price of rice, rose 260% (1945–46), 220% (1946–47), and 210% (1947)." Fujita returned to his home island of Kyushu, seeking to enhance the poverty-level wages of his physics position, and applied for a grant to be retrained as a meteorologist. "I thought that 'weather science' was an excellent topic to choose, because it could be studied rather cheaply with pencil and paper." He began collecting raw atmospheric data, from which he would produce detailed maps of surface wind flow, and added color to his maps using a silk-screen process. In August 1947, he set about studying air currents from the top of nearby Seburiyama Mountain, at whose 3,500-foot peak there was an old weather observation station. It was bare-bones science. He and a friend "took a bus from Fukuoka to Wakiyama village at the foot of the mountain. We backpacked at the bus terminal and climbed the steep slope while watching fast-growing towering cumuli." Before long, they found themselves caught in a thunderstorm, during which Fujita managed to record temperature, wind, and air pressure measurements. "We were very lucky to have had an opportunity to be in the heart of a severe thunderstorm at the mountaintop." He went on to produce a detailed analysis of the storm, arguing that it was marked by a sharp downward current of air. He presented his findings, which defied current Japanese models of airflow during thunderstorms, to a group of meteorologists in 1949. "As anticipated, I received no comment on my downdraft concept."

After he delivered his paper, though, a member of the local weather service approached Fujita and told him of reading a similar report, by University of Chicago meteorologist Horace Byers, that had been found in a trash basket at a U.S. Air Force installation. Fujita grew fixated on contacting Byers, although initiating such a correspondence proved difficult. "I tried to use a[n English-language] typewriter belonging to my Physics Department, but it had been broken down for some time," he recalled. But he would not be deterred:

> On January 25, 1950 I bought [an excellent used] typewriter for 20,000 yen ($55.56), paying 10,000 yen in cash and borrowing the rest, interest-free. . . . The cost of the typewriter was 2.7 times my take-home monthly pay. Nevertheless, I was very pleased to own a typewriter which turned out to be the most expensive item I had ever purchased to that point in my life.
>
> Although I do not remember how Tatsuko [his wife] and I survived for several months thereafter, I was busy translating my papers into English and typing with a single finger.

Finally, in August 1950, Fujita wrote to Byers, enclosing samples of his research. Encouraged by Byers's reply, which commended him on "very careful analysis," Fujita decided to send Byers his skeptically received study of the mountaintop thunderstorm. This time, the response that came back was remarkable. Byers applauded Fujita's ingenuity, writing, "in view of the fact that you were not familiar with the work of the U.S. Thunderstorm Project on this subject your conclusions are highly valuable and really represent an independent discovery of some of the factors derived from our work. In particular you deserve credit for noting the importance of the thunderstorm downdraft." Working with rudimentary resources, Fujita had arrived at conclusions similar to those produced by the high-tech, military-financed efforts of the Thunderstorm Project.

Byers invited Fujita to the University of Chicago for a two-year research stint. On August 13, 1953, he was greeted at Chicago's North Western Railroad Station by Byers's secretary, who "found me walking down the station platform, carrying an aluminum suitcase with a handpainted white cross for identification." Fujita was taken to a dormitory room in the university's International House, and treated himself to a dinner costing $1.50.

"In my childhood days in Japan," Fujita remembered, "we were told that four fearful things are, in the order of fear, Zishin, Kaminari, Kaji, Oyaji (Earthquake, Lightning, Fire, and Father), because Japan is the land of earthquakes which occur without warning." He went on, "An equivalent fear in the Midwest could be Tornado, Lightning, Fire, and Crime."

Arriving in the United States at a time of intense interest in tornadoes—the trio of deadly storms in Waco, Flint, and Worcester had struck a few months earlier—Fujita soon realized he had come to the right place to tackle this most elusive meteorological phenomenon. "The Gross National Product (GNP) of U.S. tornadoes in recent years," he would observe, employing another of his favored metaphors, "is 750 per year, while the estimated Gross International Product (GIP) of global tornadoes is 1,000 per year." To illustrate his point, Fujita would produce a map of the world showing international tornado distribution, with the United States appearing as a blackened smear. His interest, though, went beyond the abstractions of mapping. "I wished I could fly over a damage area to determine wind effects."

He spent his first few years in Chicago researching minute airflow patterns within storms, and posited the existence, within certain severe thunderstorms, of a concentrated area of rotation, which he believed was associated with the formation of tornadoes. Further, by exhaustively analyzing radar images that had, by chance, detected a tornado in 1953, he suggested that the strange hooklike shadow that appeared on the screen represented the flow of precipitation around the storm's spinning air currents, and that such a "hook echo" could be considered a signature of tornadic activity. Byers invited Fujita to join Chicago's meteorology faculty permanently, and in 1955 he flew to Japan to retrieve his wife and son, returning to Chicago the following year.

Then, in the early evening of June 20, 1957, the city of Fargo, North Dakota, was struck by an immense tornado. Its cone resembled a gyrating tower of soot. As the tornado moved toward the edge of town, it was spotted by eastbound motorists on U.S. Highway 10, who alerted the Fargo police department. Warnings soon spread. The warnings had two effects. First, residents had time to scramble for shelter, and although the storm pounded 1,300 homes, only ten lives were lost, including six within one family. The second effect was that numerous locals grabbed their cameras and rushed to document the remarkable specter that appeared in their skies. At that point, the Fargo storm became the most widely photographed tornado in history.

When Fujita learned of the existence of the photographs, he enlisted the help of one of Fargo's local TV weathermen, who implored viewers to lend their keepsakes to science. Fujita collected 150 snapshots and five super-eight films. He spent the next two years on a rigorous photogrammetric analysis of the storm, converting the evidence from the photos into maps of the tornado's structure and airflow. It was forensic meteorology of a new order. On visits to Fargo, Fujita followed the tornado's path on the ground, choosing fifty-three locations from which pictures had been taken to determine the angles at which the tornado had been viewed and the distance of the photographer from the storm. He corrected for variations in the lenses of the different cameras, and for the effects of camera movement. He rephotographed the prints in order to establish uniform scale and perspective, and triangulated measurements taken from multiple positions in order to construct a three-dimensional model of the storm. When he finished, he had pieced together, frame by frame, a short and comprehensive disaster film that told the story of the onset and development of a tornado.

He established, first, that the "swirling cloud" that had been reported by motorists was not, itself, a tornado, but a rotating thunderstorm—a supercell—from which five separate tornadoes would descend. (Fujita used the term "tornado family" for such a group, which was spawned by a single "parent cloud.") Further exercising his penchant for coining phrases, he dubbed the ominous, low-hanging block of cloud at the base of the Fargo thunderstorm a "wall cloud," which formed when humid air on the ground was swept into the storm's updraft. Above the wall cloud, Fujita identified a spinning ring of air, which he called a "collar cloud," and which connected the wall cloud to the thunderstorm above. From the front end of the wall cloud came a long, sinuous projection, a "tail cloud," where rain-cooled air was being pulled back into the storm. When all of these features were in place, a tornado began descending from the rear of the thunderstorm. Fujita put together a sequence of fourteen photos showing the tornado dropping, increasing its diameter, consuming the slot of clear space between the wall cloud and the ground, then "turning into a huge cone surrounded by a thick debris cloud." The entire process took less than thirty seconds. He divided the tornado's life cycle into four phases: the dropping stage; the rounded bottom stage; the shrinking stage, and, as the tornado retreated, the rope stage.

Fujita's study was published by the U.S. Weather Bureau in 1960, "costing only forty-five cents per copy," he noted. "I was told that most of the 3,000 copies printed were purchased by the Fargo-area residents."

After Fargo, Fujita became a celebrity in the field of severe storm research. He began attracting large grants from the U.S. military, NASA, and, in time, the Nuclear Regulatory Commission, which was trying to assess the risk that tornadoes posed to the rapidly expanding nuclear energy industry. His ability to bring money into the University of Chicago would not only become a point of pride, but would ensure him a large measure of autonomy in his research, and freedom from teaching. He took over an entire floor of the building in which Chicago's geosciences department was housed, and had at his disposal a personal secretary, a draftsman, a technician, two photographers, and a staff of graduate student researchers. He developed a talent, too, for wooing visitors from funding agencies, and made up for his broken English—which some of his colleagues suspected he exaggerated to charming effect—by showing off his range of visual aids, including maps, diagrams, an extensive collection of weather-related photos, satellite film loops, and, eventually, a tornado machine that used fans and dry ice to simulate a funnel cloud. He would frequently host parties in his offices, and tended to work from seven in the morning until ten at night, returning to his house, two blocks away, only to sleep and take meals. (Years later his son, Kazuya, would remark, "His staff knew him better than his family.") His drive and his perfectionism impressed his colleagues, though it occasionally frustrated his crew. "It's all wrong!" he was known to shout at staffers. "Do it over! Time is money!" In 1968, Fujita, having built his sinecure in Chicago, became an American citizen and added the middle name Theodore, preferring to be called Ted. The same year,

F5

he and his wife, Tatsuko, divorced. She returned to Japan, and soon after he married a Japanese woman named Suzuki.

Fujita was never without a project, and after Fargo, he became increasingly determined to get closer to the heart of a tornado's mechanics. Instead of relying exclusively on photographs provided by witnesses, he began chartering small planes to fly over tornado-damaged areas himself. He grew into the habit of rushing from his office to Meig's Field, a single-runway airstrip on an island off Chicago's downtown lakefront, after hearing reports of destructive storms. Spreading a topographic map in his lap and holding a camera with a telephoto lens in his hands, he would guide his pilot to follow visible paths of damage at an altitude of 10,000 feet, then return for a closer look at 2,000 feet. What might have appeared to other observers as randomly strewn wreckage was, to Fujita, the fingerprint of the vanished storm. He began to decipher and categorize a tornado's seemingly random destructive behavior, getting to know a tornado's habits the way detectives learn the habits of a thief.

Fujita scanned the damage left behind by the so-called Palm Sunday outbreak of April 11, 1965, in which fifty-one tornadoes struck Iowa, Wisconsin, Illinois, Michigan, Indiana, and Ohio, killing 253 people. He came to recognize that the vast majority of tornadoes were decidedly minor, plowing down crops, perhaps knocking over a barn or two. These did not excite him. He focused his attention, instead, on a small and particularly vicious subset of tornadoes, those that accounted for the bulk of the destruction of life and property.

In 1970, after studying the wreckage left behind by a huge tornado in Lubbock, Texas, he drew an elegant diagram of overlapping spirals—ten separate high-powered vortices that he believed to have been operating within the tornado, each producing its own swirl of suction. He pinpointed which "suction vortex" was responsible for which of the storm's twenty-eight deaths, labeling each of the vortices with a blunt caption. "Woman died after being swept out of house and wrapped in sheet metal," read one. "Boy sucked out of car stopped at traffic light, killed by flying debris." "Girl died crouching under house."

Fujita collected such details of disaster like a connoisseur, and argued that death by tornado could be a highly systematic event. Knowing that tornadoes defied measurement during their brief, unpredictable lifespans, he devised a scale that he maintained could effectively rate their violence and estimate their wind speed on the basis of the ruin they left behind. Damage, he contended, told the story of a tornado. Although critics pointed out the flaws of his approach—noting that the variety of construction techniques and materials made it impossible to apply a uniform standard, since the same tornado could, for instance, leave one building standing and another, similar one, wrecked—Fujita was undeterred. After all, no previous scientist had gained as much intimacy with tornadoes as he had. Indeed, the popular press had come to refer to him as Mr. Tornado, much to his delight. In 1971, he issued a paper introducing "The Fujita Scale Classification of Tornado Wind Intensity," promoting a new system to organize the study of all tornadoes.

According to Fujita's scale, close to four in ten tornadoes should be rated as "very weak," or F-0. (The F stood for Fujita.) To be sure, these tornadoes produced brisk winds, blowing up to 72 miles per hour, but they were nonetheless capable of little more than bending street signs, knocking branches from trees, or loosening a few bricks from an old chimney. Another third of tornadoes, Fujita argued, qualified as F1, with winds up to 112 miles per hour. These "weak" tornadoes could overturn trailers, peel shingles off roofs, uproot the occasional tree, and blow moving cars off the road.

Tornadoes grew "strong" at F2. Winds of up to 157 miles per

hour would unroof houses, wreck mobile homes, and topple railroad boxcars. Such tornadoes accounted for less than one in five of those encountered in the United States.

An F3, or "severe" tornado was, then, an uncommon event. Only one in twenty tornadoes reached this level of severity, which was marked by the capacity to lift cars off the ground and roll them "some distance," or upend most trees in a forest, or leave "some rural buildings completely demolished or flattened." The winds in an F3 tornado, as Fujita calculated, could exceed 200 miles per hour.

It was not surprising that, on such a scale, an F4 tornado—1 percent of all tornadoes—should be classified as "devastating." Among the remnants of such devastation, produced by winds of up to 260 miles per hour, were "well-constructed frame houses leveled, leaving piles of debris; structures with weak foundation lifted, torn, and blown off some distance; trees debarked by small flying debris."

Rarest of all, though—an event occuring only a handful of times each decade, a one-in-a-thousand tornado—was an F5. F5 winds, Fujita contended, blew at between 261 and 318 miles per hour. Even a well-built house, under such circumstances, would be "lifted clear off its foundation and carried a considerable distance to disintegrate." Steel-reinforced structures would take a hard hit, too, and an F5 would launch "automobile-sized missiles" for a hundred yards or more. In an F5, Fujita noted, "Incredible phenomena can occur." Indeed, the F5 was labeled an "Incredible Tornado."

Fujita's charisma, and his standing in his field, was such that by 1973 he persuaded the National Weather Service (the new name assigned to the U.S. Weather Bureau in 1967) to adopt the scale as its standard tool for analyzing tornadoes, much as the Richter scale was the accepted standard for seismography. Fujita then set his staff to the task of going through all documented records of tornadoes—

government agencies had been maintaining such data since 1916—and attaching an F-scale rating to each of thousands of tornadoes. In this way, Fujita's name would be appended to nearly every American tornado in the twentieth century.

He remained eager, though, not simply to demonstrate that the F-scale was useful as a retrospective tool, which might help to determine patterns of tornado risk, but also to see that his scale gained currency with the public, providing a new vocabulary for the discussion of tornadoes. For such a breakthrough to occur, Fujita needed an event that would, through its wide-ranging effects, reawaken awareness of tornadoes, and lend him a platform on which to display the powers of his scale. He needed an outbreak.

It was with mounting excitement, then, that he watched the atmospheric elements on April 3, 1974, fall into place over the center of the country. As the edge of a supercell thunderstorm clipped Chicago, temperatures dropped, skies darkened, and hail fell. Before long, reports of regional damage started reaching Fujita in his offices. In the words of one of his staffers, "He went wild."

Limestone:
Wednesday Afternoon

Brown's Ferry Landing, a once-bustling depot along a calm pocket of the Tennessee River, was the only place in Limestone whose name had even come close to entering American folklore. The renown of Brown's Ferry had less to do with its function—though without it, generations of Limestone's residents would have found themselves stranded at the riverbank, cut off from the rest of Alabama—than with the success of a homegrown musical duo called the Delmore Brothers. Alton and Rabon Delmore were sons of a tenant farmer from Elkmont, north of Athens. Alton played six-string guitar, and Rabon strummed the ukulele-like four-string tenor guitar. The brothers' high-pitched, gospel-tinged harmonies captured the pleasures and woes of rural life and brought them to the attention of audiences at the Grand Ole Opry during the Depression. An early photo of the pair showed them performing in overalls and straw hats, with checkered bandannas tied around their necks, and sitting on milk crates. Among their most popular songs was "Brown's Ferry Blues." "Hard luck poppa standing in the rain," they sang. "If the world was corn he couldn't buy grain. Lord, lord, got those Brown's Ferry blues." In the late '60s, after both brothers had died young—Rabon of lung cancer, Alton of heart failure—there was a revival of interest in their music.

Bob Dylan cited their influence on him. Jerry Garcia of the Grateful Dead performed "Brown's Ferry Blues" in concert.

By that time, Brown's Ferry, like much else in Limestone, was getting ready to undergo steep changes. In 1966, the Tennessee Valley Authority—the entity responsible, in the '30s, for damming the river and inundating 50,000 acres of Limestone's farms and forests—began construction on Brown's Ferry Nuclear Plant, a $700 million undertaking designed to be the world's largest producer of nuclear energy. On March 22, 1974, the first of the plant's two generators was finally activated, with a projected annual output of a thousand megawatts of electricity. The installation was a futuristic sight. Its conical exhaust stack soared above the river's edge, casting shadows on a giant crate of cooling towers. The steel reinforced concrete walls of the reactor, which contained 764 bundles of uranium fuel rods, were as much as eight feet thick. The plant had created more than 3,000 jobs, making it by far Limestone's largest employer, and each morning a long line of vehicles headed to the site along a formerly sleepy country road.

All those workers needed places to live. Limestone had lots of empty space and little new housing. An enterprising farmer named Buddy Lawson, a longtime resident of the newly renamed Nuclear Plant Road, took the opportunity to develop some acreage he owned along Highway 31 into a trailer park. The land, it turned out, yielded a more reliable stream of income from renters than from crops. By 1974, Lawson's Trailer Park consisted of ninety-five neatly landscaped lots, all of them occupied. Rent was $25 a month. The community was quiet, safe, friendly, and family-oriented. Cattle still grazed along the edge of the property.

Paula Marbut, whose husband, Russell, supervised a crew of insulators at the nuclear plant, moved to Lawson's in December 1973.

F5

She had charge of six children, ranging in age from nine to twenty, plus a two-year-old grandson, and she had not yet gotten used to living in a mobile home. The storm on April 1, during which she and her children had hunkered down while the roof clattered and the walls seemed ready to splinter apart, had given her a case of bad nerves. "I was fearful," she said. "We had one of those roofs that kind of bounced up and down. There would be a wavery sound going back and forth overhead. It got you torn up. I didn't feel safe."

On the morning of Wednesday, April 3, Paula's husband set off for a business trip to Atlanta. It was payday for his two dozen men, and before he left he directed Paula to remain at Lawson's until his workers came by to pick up their checks later that afternoon.

It was another windy morning. Paula tried not to let it trouble her. She was on her own, and she would have to make do. But as the day continued—getting pale, hazy, damp as midsummer—the winds kept blustering. There were steady high winds, then periods of lull, then sudden gusts that seemed capable of blithely tossing her and her trailer aside. Lawson's lay exposed to the wind, surrounded by open farmland. Little plumes of dust would suddenly rise from the fields. As midday passed, and the day got still hotter, the wind offered no relief. Paula grew restless. The hum of traffic from the highway was a familiar backdrop. Otherwise, the trailer park was dead quiet. She wanted to leave. She glanced at the clock on the wall. It was two. The wind rose up, and the clock rattled on its hook.

A school bus paused along the highway to drop off Paula's children. They ran into the trailer, threw down their notebooks, grabbed a snack, ran outside to play.

By 4:00 PM, her husband's men began to arrive from the nuclear plant to collect their checks. There was no small talk. They came and went. Ragged clouds streamed through the sky. Paula watched the stack of paychecks dwindle. She waited for the last man to arrive.

Don Lauderdale lived in a grand antebellum-style manor known throughout Limestone as the Old Orr House—his nearest neighbors included Frank Orr, whose father had been raised in the house. Don should not have been in Limestone on Wednesday afternoon. He was booked on a flight that morning to Erie, Pennsylvania, where he had been offered a job in the jet engine division of General Electric. At 37, Don was a veteran of Huntsville's aerospace industry. He had spent the past decade working at GE in the Apollo space program, as a production planner for electrical equipment in the Saturn V rocket booster. He loved his job. It was high status and well paying. In north Alabama, any association with the space program was glamorous. On a few occasions, Don had even met with Werhner von Braun, the former Nazi rocket scientist who was the first director of the Marshall Space Flight Center. "And me, I was just a peon," Don recalled, not a little starstruck. "A poor old country boy who came up out of the cotton fields."

He had, indeed, been born on a small farm south of Athens, the youngest of nine children in a house lacking electricity, indoor plumbing, and most any other touch of comfort. But his life had gotten harder than that. One winter morning in 1941, when he was four years old, Don was awakened by cries urging him to flee his bed. A kerosene heater had exploded. The house was in flames. Don was carried to safety, but as he stood in his night clothes on the frozen ground, he saw his father, who was unaware that the rest of the family had made it out, run back into the fire. His father was killed. After that, the family was swiftly reduced to poverty and forced off their farm. For years they lived in a succession of temporary lodgings. Don managed to graduate from Tanner High, where he was a standout on the football team, but had to pass up the offer of a college football scholarship in order to support his mother. Nonetheless, he nursed high ambitions for himself, and despite his lack of a college degree he had worked tirelessly to overcome his disadvantages and to build his career.

On April 3, though, he was at an impasse. The Apollo space exploration mission had been discontinued, and GE was shutting down its local operation. Just the previous day, Don had driven to his office in Huntsville to attend his exit interview. In a way, he was lucky: He was one of a few dozen employees who had been asked to relocate to Erie. But it was not an easy decision. Don was firmly rooted in Limestone. His widowed mother was still alive, and he and his wife had an eight-year-old son, a married 18-year-old daughter, a three-month-old grandson, and a large collection of friends and relatives. He had also recently completed an expensive and elaborate restoration of his house. Neither his wife nor he wanted to move away. After leaving his exit interview, he drove straight to Decatur to inquire about the job outlook at a GE refrigeration plant that was under construction. The meeting was not promising.

He headed back to Athens demoralized. He tried to resign himself to leaving Alabama. Everything was in place. He had a ticket to Erie the next day. He would get himself settled at work, find a place to live, then return for his family.

On his way home, though, something unexpected occurred. "I'm a Christian," he explained. "I was riding in the car and talking to the Lord. I said, 'Lord, you're gonna have to help me. I'm in trouble. I need guidance.' And then—I can show you the exact spot on Highway 31 where it happened—I got a clear signal. The signal told me not to get on that airplane Wednesday morning. The signal was not an audible thing, not a voice. It was something moving in my spirit. It said, 'Don, don't go. It's not the time to go.'"

Mark Levine

* * *

On Wednesday afternoon, Walter McGlocklin, Jr., was getting ready to celebrate his second birthday—or, more accurately, given his vague understanding of the meaning of the event, to have his birthday celebrated for him. His family—three older sisters, a teenage cousin, and parents Ruth, 31, and Walter, Sr., 30—lived in a modest, low-slung brick house on a seventy-acre farm on Ingram Road, a few miles west of Lawson's Trailer Park, and a mile above the Tennessee River. The mood there was particularly festive as the birthday party approached. Little Walter had overcome long odds just in reaching this milestone. As an infant, he was frequently weak and feverish. He would easily grow short of breath, panting, as his father observed, "like a dog pants when he wants water." After many rounds of doctor's visits, his parents were told Little Walter had "a hole in his heart," meaning that the wall between ventricles was breached, allowing oxygen-depleted blood to leak through his circulatory system. Doctors suspected he was in the early stages of heart failure. High-risk surgery was scheduled, to be performed in Birmingham before his first birthday. His doctors worried, though, that he was too sick to survive the operation. Admitted to the hospital, Little Walter developed double pneumonia while awaiting surgery. His parents watched him linger. They were told he was dying.

Little Walter, though, proved unaccountably resilient. He not only recovered from his pneumonia, but surprised his doctors by continuing to regain strength and vigor, until it seemed that even his heart defect might be healing on its own accord. By his second birthday, he was robust, if a bit thin, and, according to his father, "just as normal as could be." Playful and good-natured, he was doted on by his parents and three sisters. In Wednesday's *News Courier*, the horoscope noted, "Born today, you are possessed of insatiable curiosity. Travel will take a great deal of your time—if not

106

actually, then by means of books, films, slides, and so on." To his father, the significance of the date could be put more succinctly: "It was a miracle he was still with us."

As evening approached, the party preparations began in earnest. Little Walter's mother had two cakes in the oven, and stood above a mixing bowl making frosting. His sisters—Grace, 7, Sandra, 5, and Nancy, 3—eagerly helped to decorate the house with streamers. A small stack of gifts, neatly wrapped, lay on a shelf, out of reach but within sight. The children were anxious for the party to start. That would happen, they knew, when their father came home.

Having determined to miss his flight to Erie, Don Lauderdale woke up unemployed on Wednesday. It was a peculiar feeling. He left home in the morning to play a round of golf. He was not much of a golfer, though, and the morning was blustery, so he gave up after nine holes. He ate lunch with his wife. On a weekday afternoon, that, too, was peculiar. After lunch, Don wandered across a few hundred yards of unplanted fields to Frank's house, hoping to get a look at the new baby there. (Frank's sister, Marilyn, was married to Don's nephew, Vergil McBay.) No one seemed to be stirring at the Orrs', so Don drifted over to the adjacent lot, where Marilyn and Vergil were building a house of their own. The house was nearly done. Bricklayers were at work. Don had worked construction for a while as a young man, and offered to lend a hand to the crew. It was hot, but Don was not too old, or too proud, for hard work. He removed his shirt. In no time at all, the finer points of laying bricks came back to him.

After a few hours, he returned home. He wife wanted to do some shopping before going to Wednesday evening prayer meeting, so she rushed him into the shower, and they left around five. They stopped at Rose's Department Store, where Don waited on the sidewalk while his wife went inside and picked through fabrics. He struck up a conversation with another similarly stranded man. The man mentioned that he was from Pulaski, thirty miles north. "There's some bad trouble moving in," the man observed. Don didn't know what he meant. "Storms," he said. "I'll be glad if my wife would hurry up so I can get out of here."

The man from Pulaski moved on. Don was in a fine mood. He reflected that after many years of long hours at the office, it was a nice change to have spent a weekday afternoon at home, and even to have done some manual labor. His wife finished shopping. The couple headed downtown to First Baptist Church of Athens, of which they were loyal members.

Around 4:30 PM, a school bus let off fifteen-year-old Jerry Beckham at the McGlocklin house. Jerry, a ninth grader at Tanner High, had spent weekends with his Uncle Walter's family since he was a child. He kept a horse in their pasture and helped with farm work. When Jerry's parents separated and his mother moved to Florida, the McGlocklins took him in despite the fact that their home, which Walter had built, was already crowded. (Their three girls shared a room, two of them in the same bed.) "Uncle Walter and Aunt Ruth treated me like their own son," Jerry said. He was grateful for the stability of the family's life. The McGlocklins always sat down to dinner together; Ruth spent the better part of her day in the kitchen, and excelled in preparing what her husband called "country food." (Her peach cobbler was particularly coveted.) On Saturday nights, the family stayed home, playing cards or checkers. Everyone went to bed early and most of the year they rose in darkness. Jerry, waking at 5:00 AM to help Walter feed and milk his cows, would find Ruth already at work in the kitchen. Often Sandra, the redheaded, tomboyish five-year-old, would trail her father to the barn.

F5

Arriving home on Wednesday, Jerry didn't stay in the house long. He put down his school books, changed clothes, and went back outside to work in the fields until it was time for dinner and Little Walter's birthday party. He climbed atop the John Deere tractor and set about preparing a plot of land for planting cotton. "We call it 'turning it up,'" he explained. "We use a turning plow, which turns the ground over, and then after you do that you take what we call a disc—it looks like a bunch of pie plates standing up all tied together, picture that—and you go over the ground with that and it breaks up the big clods and makes the ground smooth. Once you get it disced up, you're ready to plant your seeds."

By 5:00 PM, Walter was getting ready to leave his shift at the Athens Electric Department, where he was a lineman. He called Ruth from work to let her know he would be on his way shortly. Ruth worried that she wouldn't have enough ice cream for all the children at the party—another nephew, Steve, was also coming over—and asked Walter to stop at the grocery on the way home. Walter was glad to oblige. He was in good cheer. He adored his three daughters, but having a boy—someone with whom he could share his love for "fooling with soil," and to whom he might one day pass on his farm, as he had passed on his name—was a different kind of feeling. Then, too, as Walter admitted, "I always wanted a boy to play ball with."

Walter's own father had abandoned him and his eight siblings when he was young, and Walter worked fiercely to be responsible to his own family. He tended to the farm on mornings, evenings, and weekends. His day job at the Electric Department afforded a good, steady wage, with plentiful opportunities for overtime, and two weeks of paid vacation each year, which Walter had scheduled, four of the past seven years, to coincide with the birth of his children. The lineman's job could be dangerous; two of Walter's coworkers had been electrocuted not long before. "I respect electricity," Walter said. "It's invisible and it doesn't make any noise, but if you don't watch what you're doing it won't give you a second chance." Walter, whose dense Alabama twang could make it difficult for strangers to follow his speech, was what people in Limestone referred to, euphemistically, as being "not very well educated." Nonetheless, he had a reputation for honesty, generosity, and decency, and was altogether without guile. Some of his black neighbors were wary of him, because his brother, Bill, was active in the Ku Klux Klan, but Walter insisted he didn't share his brother's sentiments. "I'm no racist. I surely never wanted anything to do with the Klan, and I'd warn anyone that thought of bothering me at my house, Klansman or otherwise, that I'm ready to defend my family."

Walter turned from Ingram Road onto his drive, a quarter-mile-long strip of rough gravel that ran beside a creek and was shaded by cottonwoods, willows, and oaks. He crossed the creek on a narrow concrete bridge that he had built himself, then continued toward his house. He could see Jerry on the tractor, far out in the fields. Walter's land sat in one of the more idyllic spots in the county. When the crops were in, and the rust-colored soil, sloping gently toward the Tennessee River, was flecked with green and yellow grasses, and the thick row of hardwoods at the edge of the property was in full leaf, Walter could be nearly overcome with gratitude for his good fortune. It was true that the recently installed TVA transmission towers, coming from the nuclear plant eight miles west, and crossing Walter's farm, were an eyesore. But as a power company man, he could not help but be impressed by the massive high-voltage lines. He had heard that the towers themselves, which rose 120 feet above ground, could withstand winds of more than 200 miles an hour.

When he stepped through the door at 5:20 PM, Walter was

greeted with bad news. Ruth had just taken a call from his supervisor at the Electric Department. High winds had blown through a northern section of Athens, knocking down some utility poles. Walter was being ordered back to work.

It wasn't in Walter's nature to complain, but he insisted it wasn't his turn to go out on emergency calls: He had finished his on-call rotation the previous day. Moreover, as he told his supervisor, he had a special reason to remain at home.

He was told he had no choice in the matter. He assured Ruth he would be back soon. She suggested he might pick up more soda for the kids on his way home. He nodded. Then, full of disappointment, he turned and left.

Frank Orr's sister, Marilyn McBay, had a brief moment to herself on Wednesday afternoon. Most of her family was sleeping—her two children, Vergil, and Frank. She should have been sleeping, too. Naturally, she had been up through the nights since Mark's birth a week earlier, and she had not yet recovered from the delivery. But she relished the momentary quiet. Barefoot, in her nightgown, she stepped from her parents' house onto their back porch and lowered herself to a lawn chair. She could see men working on the house next door. She was anxious to move in. She couldn't imagine living anywhere but Limestone. She had gone to grade school in the last two-room schoolhouse in the county, and though she was only twenty-four, she had a fond sense of the old ways of life. Mostly she was attached to her family. When Frank was in Vietnam, she would ship him tomatoes and a jar of mayonnaise so he could make tomato sandwiches, his favorite. It must have seemed silly, she thought, sending such things halfway around the world, but she knew it made a difference to him. They had been close growing up, though Marilyn—tall, skinny, and a good student—did not have Frank's wild streak. She met Vergil when she was sixteen. No doubt it was ironic that his uncle Don lived in the Old Orr House, which had been sold off, much to the dismay of Marilyn's father, in a dispute with extended family. But no one held it against Vergil. Now that they were married, it was almost like having the house back in the family.

Marilyn could not get comfortable on the porch. The heat was hard to bear, and the gusting wind kept blowing her nightgown around her waist. She watched the sky. It seemed to be the strangest color—greenish-yellow, as though she were looking at it through tinted glasses. Everything was quiet in the wind. She was so tired. She heard her baby cry and went back inside.

A half-mile away, across busy Highway 72, which ran east to Huntsville, Annias Green's children were coming home from school. Rabbit, the oldest, just shy of twelve, was in sixth grade at Tanner Elementary. He was a bookworm and an A student, which had helped to ease some of the awkwardness when he was bused to a newly integrated school in East Limestone at the beginning of third grade. (Before that, he had gone to all-black Dogwood Flat, where his teachers still remembered his parents.) "When you're making good grades, the teachers treat you nicely, whether you're black or white," Rabbit noted. His best friend was his brother, Amos, a year younger. Amos was an avid basketball fan, and had developed a particular interest in the fortunes of the New York Knicks, who had won the championship the previous year, and who had just entered the first round of this season's playoffs. Titus, their baby brother, was in second grade. Unlike Rabbit, who was sometimes teased for being a "Mama's boy," Titus would often follow his father wherever he went. Of course, between the demands of his job and his ministry, Annias was not home nearly as much as Titus, or the other boys, would have liked. The task of looking after them fell primarily to their mother, and she was involved in every aspect of their lives—feeding them, shopping for them, taking them to visit friends and relatives, overseeing their homework. Lillian was a busy woman. While her children were at school, she worked as a custodian at Athens College, where, despite the past five years of integration, the majority of blacks on campus were employed as grounds people and food service workers.

When Lillian returned from work Wednesday afternoon, she wasn't surprised to find that her children had gotten home before her. She was, however, startled when she saw Annias in the living room. On his fishing day, it was not uncommon for Annias to be out past the boys' bedtime. She asked him if he were feeling sick. He assured her that nothing was wrong, he had simply decided to stay home. "Well, okay," she laughed, "but I just know something unusual is bound to happen. You're not supposed to be here!"

The Athens Broadcasting Company, owned and operated by the family of Robert Dunnavant, ran both of Limestone County's most-listened-to radio stations, WJMW-AM and WJOF-FM. The Dunnavants were Limestone's version of media royalty. Robert Dunnavant hailed from Pettusville, population fifty-seven, in the heavily wooded and ravine-carved northern end of the county. According to *The Heritage of Limestone County*, a compilation of local history, "From the time Bob heard the Grand Ole Opry for the first time on a community-owned battery-powered radio, purchased by members of the Pettusville Community, he was hooked." In the '40s, Dunnavant passed up the opportunity to buy a Model A Ford and instead invested with his father, Homer, a farmer and barber, in the equipment needed to start his own radio station.

In 1974, while Dunnavant oversaw the FM station, his 24-year-old son Bill was in charge of WJMW-AM. Bill, a Boy Scout troop leader who had volunteered for Barry Goldwater's presidential campaign as a thirteen-year-old, was steeped in the family business. He had helped out at the station since childhood in a variety of capacities: errand boy, file clerk, advertising salesman, advertising copy writer, announcer, news reporter, and his most important role in recent years, sportscaster. Bill loved sports but had been too small to play on school teams, and reveled in providing crisp play-by-play commentary for high school football and Athens College basketball games. He had become one of the most familiar voices in Limestone.

Bill did other live reporting, too. Among the innovations that his father had brought to radio in Limestone was the area's only remote broadcasting unit—a 1971 Ford Econoline van outfitted with a mobile transmitter and a fifty-foot length of microphone cord and dubbed the "King Country Rover." Late in the afternoon of April 3, 1974, after hearing reports that tornadoes had hit an area about fifty miles south of Limestone, Bill got ready to set forth in the van to investigate the local weather conditions. He didn't expect much action. The skies were limpid and fair, and a nice breeze was blowing. It seemed that people were always making a lot of needless drama about storms. Still, before leaving, Bill decided to insert a tape into a new Norelco cassette recording device that was hooked into the station's AM feed. It was a good opportunity to test the gadget. It would let Bill hear how he sounded to listeners.

Five o'clock at Lawson's Trailer Park. Paula Marbut had had enough. She told herself, "I'm getting out of here." Two of her sons were due at Little League baseball practice. She rushed to round up the six children who were home, including her grandson, crowded them into her old Riviera, and left behind only Cocoa, the family's chocolate poodle. She pulled onto Highway 31, turned south, and crossed the river toward Decatur. The water below was choppy. She continued into town and stopped at Delano Park. Her sons ran from the parking lot to join their teammates on the baseball diamond. One of Paula's daughters, 20-year-old Vanessa, opted to stay in the car, out of the heat and wind, with her two-year-old. The other children wandered off to play. Paula headed for a bench in the park and listened to the shouts of the ballplayers, the smacking sound of balls being hit, of balls hitting the webbing of a fielder's glove. It was now close to 6:00 PM. The sky was darkening some, and was the color and texture of aluminum foil.

Suddenly Paula lifted her head to see Vanessa running toward her, baby in arms. She was shouting. She had been listening to the radio in the car. When she reached Paula she was out of breath. "They came on and said there were tornadoes heading in our direction," she said. "*Killer* tornadoes."

That was all Paula needed to hear. She scrambled onto the ball field, summoned a coach, and repeated what Vanessa had told her. The coach looked to the sky. He told Paula not to worry. He turned his attention back to the practice.

Paula ran toward her sons and pulled them off the field. She didn't care if she was making a scene. All she could think to do was to get away. She drove, circling back and forth on Decatur's main street. Stores were closed, the library was closed, and the only person Paula knew in Decatur, the boyfriend of one of her daughters, wasn't yet home. She kept driving. Her children demanded to know what was happening. She pulled up to Krystal's and bought a bag full of hamburgers, fries, and Cokes. The food kept everyone quiet for a while. She continued driving. Finally she turned into a parking lot by a motorcycle dealership, within sight of the banks of the river. It was beginning to rain. Her boys jumped out of the car and roughhoused beneath the awning of the dealership. Soon there was lightning, and, for a moment, pinpricks of hail. Paula summoned her children back to the car. The family sat together silently, watching, even as the rain stopped and the skies seemed to clear.

Something, a figure, came out of the clearing to the west. At first, Paula took it for a ribbon of smoke drifting across the sky, perhaps fumes being vented from Monsanto, stretching out in the wind. It unfurled toward the ground, swaying this way and that, languidly, like a kite with a streaming tail that some child had released into the sky. It seemed to be taking its time, dallying along the edge of the river, undecided about whether to leave the shore and venture across. Then it began to move on, and as it approached the smokestack of another factory, slabs of masonry began to drop to the ground. It appeared to Paula that the cloud had inhaled some of the stack's emissions. It was infused with streaks of pink and green. The colors allowed Paula to follow the cloud's motion as it turned north, a sheer pastel wedge of sky, fluttering. It moved across the river. Water leapt up, as though from a fountain. It was a vision. It moved away from Paula, making for Limestone. It terrified her. The thought of her dog, Cocoa, alone in the trailer, filled her with dread.

At around 6:30 PM, Mike Davis, the studio announcer at WJMW-AM, broke into the evening's broadcast of easy listening music. "We just had a report from the Civil Defense office that a tornado was moving across the Tennessee River," he said, calmly. "Of course, it could have come up and bounced back up. We don't know for sure that it's hit anywhere in that area. But one was spotted."

He went on, "Bill Dunnavant is currently fixing to hit the road to go and find out the extent or if any tornado at all has hit in that area." Until further word came in, Mike had a cautionary suggestion for listeners: "You folks please be rushing—or not rushing, but getting on to, a place of shelter."

"Spring is officially here," said a chipper voice. "And that means summer is just around the corner—at Rose's Department Store! And summer means swimming!" Plastic pools were available for $6.96. A five-foot Whip Slide was on sale for $14.88.

Before the ad ended, Mike returned to the air. Now the softness was gone from his voice. He sounded official. "At twenty-two minutes before seven o'clock," he said, "here's Spencer Black of Civil Defense."

Spencer seemed startled to find himself on the radio. "My job— we just—this thing is spotted and it's coming up the Tennessee River and possibly now will cross somewhere around the Tennessee River bridge, so it evidently is moving up the south end of what we'd call our county."

Station owner Robert Dunnavant joined the conversation. "It's going up?" he asked. "It's still in the river?"

Spencer could not answer. "They say it evidently must be in the river area now, in the river bed," he said. "Now it's not confirmed yet that it has touched down anyplace."

"They don't know whether it has touched down?"

"Right," said Spencer.

Outbreak

It started at ten past one in the afternoon. A farmer spotted a tornado crossing a bare field near Morris, Illinois, twenty miles beyond Chicago's southwest suburbs. The tornado stayed on the ground for a minute, displacing dirt for a half mile before vanishing. It hurt no one. It was an F-0: the mildest of prefatory spasms.

Earlier that morning, a satellite photo had captured the image of a broken line of thunderstorms extending on a diagonal from north Texas into Illinois. From space, the line appeared as a sinuous, frayed tissue of cloud. It formed ahead of the cold northern Pacific air that was pouring across the country as warm air on the ground was drawn upward. The line generated a few small tornadoes, and it pushed northeast through the day, headed toward Appalachia and beyond, following the path of the jet stream.

Tropical air originating over the Gulf of Mexico had continued to spill overland, as though the door of a vast steam room had been opened. By 2:00 PM, the humidity was oppressive. Something had to give. Indeed, with notable suddenness, the layer of warm, dry air that had moved in from the desert southwest and that was holding back the humidity at the surface began to form cracks. The constrained unstable air sought out the fissures, pushed through, and shattered the cap, soaring upward. The upshooting air then ran into air from the cold Pacific mass, and was rapidly organized into two additional lines of thunderstorms. These lines—one stretched from the center of Tennessee into southern Indiana, the other linked St. Louis and Chicago—stacked up behind the first, and dwarfed it in intensity. It was a highly unusual situation. A single line of thunderstorms can afflict a large region with severe weather. Three such lines, arrayed in elegant formation, like a display of knives, were the recipe for a spectacular and repetitive pummeling. One supercell thunderstorm after another began battering the country.

The heart of the drama—it would be long-lived, it would have many acts—began at 2:03 PM. A tornado landed north of Chattanooga, Tennessee, within sight of the Great Smoky Mountains, and churned the ground for thirteen miles. (At the same moment, tornadoes also alighted in Illinois and Indiana.) Along the way, a woman came to rest amid the tatters of her trailer home. Hers was the day's first death by tornado.

Soon after, a tornado set down in far southern Indiana, near the settlement of Carefree, and rambled sixty-two miles through Depauw and beyond. It swelled until it was a mile-wide cylinder. Near Tell City, a school bus driver and his wife were on their way to make a pickup when, seeing the mass of it approaching, they pulled over and made for a ditch. Their abandoned vehicle chased them down, rolling fifty feet and crushing them.

The tornado kept moving. In the tiny German-Catholic colony of Hamburg, a pregnant woman was thrown into a tree and killed. By 3:00 PM a separate tornado hit the nearby town of Kennard, destroying an elementary school into whose basement dozens of children had been hurriedly hustled. The children survived, but a baby born to a woman whose labor was induced by her injuries did not.

F5

Twenty minutes later, in quaint Madison, Indiana, on a bend of the Ohio River, Steve Wilson, a police department patrolman, stopped his squad car at the water's edge and watched a tornado cruise past. "It crossed the Ohio, touched the Kentucky shore, then turned back," he said. "When it hit the river, water went straight up in the air. The whole river went up. There was water as high as . . . smokestacks." The tornado's effects on land were not less dramatic, though they were less benign. Buildings collapsed. Cars rolled over. Eleven people died.

Then, at 3:30 PM, a tornado descended on the lush, rolling tobacco lands of northwestern Kentucky, announcing its arrival by blowing a school bus full of children off the road—none was harmed—and storming toward bluegrass country. After twenty-five minutes, a disc jockey at the only radio station in the hamlet of Brandenburg eyed the oncoming funnel through his window. "We're going off the air and taking cover," he shouted to listeners. Brandenburg was a town of 1,600; its two largest neighborhoods lay atop bluffs overlooking the Ohio River, and its one-block commercial district ran down a steep gully to an old steamboat landing. "It was a Mark Twain town," commented one native. It had been destroyed once before, when the Ohio flooded in 1937. This time, the tornado made quick work of it. An insurance agent named James English rode out the storm in the basement of his office. "When I looked around, across the hill, there weren't any buildings left," he remarked. The downtown was flattened, and homes on the hilltop high above were in ruins, too. Thirty-one residents—one in fifty—were killed, and 300—nearly one in five—injured.

Just before 4:00 PM, Dick Gilbert lifted off from a small airfield on the outskirts of Louisville, Kentucky, in a two-seat canary yellow Bell helicopter. Gilbert, 49, the "traffic tracker" for Louisville's most popular radio station, WHAS, climbed to an altitude of 500 feet and looked to the west. The skies, he observed, had "a definite chartreuse tint." At 4:08, he delivered his first dispatch to commuters. "Well, we do have a pretty wild and rugged weather picture on our hands here," he announced, describing "wet pavements all the way, lightning and gusty winds, and sprinkles and bursts and gusts of rain here and there." He headed toward the southwestern edge of the city to begin his tour of the main traffic arteries, saw a thunderhead looming in front of him, and turned around. "The weather looked a bit suspicious out there," he told listeners, "so you folks out there will have to be on your own for a little bit."

Gilbert had been raised in Louisville, but had returned to the city only three years earlier after a long absence. In 1942, as a seventeen-year-old, he had enlisted in the Army Air Corps, flying thirty-one missions as a bombardier before being shot down over Germany and taken prisoner. After the war, he trained as an Air Force helicopter pilot and was sent to the Pacific. There, among other assignments, he was a member of the Air-Sea Rescue crew during the detonation of the first hydrogen bomb, over Enewetok atoll in the Marshall Islands, in November 1952. "As I approached the site," he recalled, "it was apparent that the atoll no longer existed." He returned stateside to become one of the nation's first helicopter traffic reporters, first in Chicago and then in New York. He found his way back to Louisville after his wife was killed in a car accident in 1969, leaving him alone with a nine-year-old daughter, Candy. "I live at 500 feet," he would say. "I'm at home there. Cars are toys. People are little foreshortened creatures running around."

Now, after offering his first glimpse of the afternoon's rush hour, Gilbert zipped back toward the center of Louisville at seventy miles per hour. He had a daily ritual of buzzing his house in order to greet his daughter on her return from school. At around 4:20, he dipped down unusually low. Candy, running outdoors, could see he was upset. He repeatedly pointed his finger toward the ground. He was shouting, too, in an exaggerated manner. Candy could read his lips. She rushed back into the house and headed for the basement, where she crouched anxiously, listening to a transistor radio tuned to her father's broadcast.

"I don't actually physically see any tornado activity at the moment," Gilbert announced in his next report, "but it does look highly suspicious down there."

At 4:37, his suspicions were confirmed before his eyes. "Well, it's a spectacular sight," he calmly announced. "The low clouds, very black, low clouds. . . . And it is swirling around, and it looks like smoke underneath it. There is no tight, definitive tornado as such—it's still turning at a—." He broke off. "Yes! There's one now, starting. Yes, dipping down from the bottom of the cloud."

Gilbert then tagged alongside the tornado as it began an eleven-mile stampede through Louisville, its winds approaching 260 miles per hour. It casually unroofed Freedom Hall, where the Kentucky Colonels of the American Basketball Association were scheduled to host a first-round playoff game that evening, and it grew wider as it crossed Calvary Cemetery, on its way to densely populated residential neighborhoods. On shop-lined Bardstown Road, a Grateful Dead album was playing through the speakers at Karma Records when the windows blew out, spraying glass on customers. (According to the *Louisville Courier-Journal and Times,* "about $800 worth of 'smoking papers,' used to roll marijuana cigarettes, blew away.") In Cherokee Park—the city's prized swath of greenery, designed by Frederick Law Olmsted in the 1890s— 20,000 hardwood trees came down. "The park was left a hideous skeleton of its former self," said one report, "3,000 tons of debris scattered on its floor." As the storm headed out of town, passing through the affluent Indian Hills and Rolling Fields neighborhoods, three people were killed, another three died of heart attacks, and more than 200 were injured. The low casualty toll, in the city of 360,000, was attributed, above all, to Gilbert's broadcast, which spread the warning of danger and led residents to take shelter. As far as anyone knew, Gilbert was the first person to escort a tornado through the air.

"The city to me is like a model railroad layout down there," Gilbert would say. "When the tornado hit, it was like someone had wiped his hand through it." As he flew over the neighborhood where he had been raised, he observed, "My old homestead here— Pennsylvania Avenue—is . . . just about wiped out. . . . This area is no longer an effective community."

Gilbert reflected, "A tornado is mindless. That's the scariest thing about it. When someone is shooting anti-aircraft guns at you—there's a reason for that. But a tornado . . ."

Deaths mounted. Strangers, going about their days in far-flung places, came to be united by misfortune—felled by one or another of what was already shaping up to be a barrage of tornadoes. In central Illinois, near Decatur, an elderly man died in his trailer near the county fairgrounds. In southwestern Kentucky, the village of Temperance lost one of its residents, another died in Three Forks, and a third was killed at Rocky Springs. Two more lives were taken along the "Miracle Mile" strip mall in Elizabethtown, Kentucky. At Sylvan Lake, Indiana, "a man was killed in his island home, and a mother and child died in their trailer." Further, "a couple were drowned as their mobile home was thrown into Turkey Lake." Near Juno, Georgia, a woman and two children were fatally buried in their house. (Relatives next door were spared.) Not far east, in Sugar Valley, "neighbors found the home of the Goble family demolished and nine-year-old Randall Goble running in circles in the backyard, screaming hysterically," according to *Time*. "He was alive only because the tornado's winds had picked him up and carried him 200 yards before flinging him to the ground."

The same tornado killed 50,000 chickens.

In Monticello, Indiana, midway between Chicago and Indianapolis, Karen Stott, seventeen, was among five teenage girls traveling in a minibus, returning home to Fort Wayne from a Mormon youth conference in Nauvoo, Illinois. As the drive wore on, Karen dozed off. Then, suddenly, while the vehicle was on a bridge crossing the Tippecanoe River, she opened her eyes. "The weather was calm but black outside," she said. It didn't stay calm for long. "The wind just took complete control of the bus. It rolled us over and over and off the bridge." The bus plunged fifty feet to the river. "We landed nose down in the water, and I guess that's how I was able to get out." She pulled herself through a shattered window and clung for a moment to the edge of the sinking vehicle. Two of her friends reached for her from the water. They surfaced briefly, then were carried off by currents. Karen tried, without success, to swim to one of the bridge's pilings. "I was fighting the water very hard," she said. "There was a point when I felt I was going to die and was ready to die, but something clicked in my mind and I knew I wouldn't." She rolled onto her back and floated. She was swept into the branches of a fallen tree and pulled herself to shore. Her four friends and their driver did not join her there. "I love each and every one of them very much," Karen said. "Someday, I'll be with them again."

In Xenia, Ohio, population 25,000, a twenty-nine-year-old Choctaw Indian named Thomas Youngen was sitting in the window of his rented room on West Street, pointing the microphone of his tape recorder to the street below. It was 4:45 PM. Youngen, an unemployed physician's assistant who had recently moved to Xenia from New York City, was preparing an audio letter to send to a friend. "It was an 'irony' tape," he said. He lived on a heavily trafficked street, near railroad tracks and not far from an old foundry, and wanted to share with his friend some less-than-tranquil sounds of small-town life. "There was thunder that afternoon, so I thought I'd record that," he said. "I was sitting there and the thunder, rain and wind all stopped." He looked up and saw a tornado taking shape. Two rags of sooty cloud were spiraling to the ground, and as they lowered they twisted around each other. "I could see that cloud coming across a graveyard—that's apropos—coming straight for me," Youngen recounted. As the tornado neared, "I could see solid things in it but was too shocked to identify them." He tried to duck behind a stove but was carried through a doorway. His ceiling collapsed. "I thought, 'Oh hell, I'm dead.'"

Over the next eight minutes, as the tornado shredded Xenia with winds of more than 300 miles per hour, the town emerged from obscurity to become the public face of the day's national disaster.

It fit the role well. In more ways than one, it was a typical American small town in 1974, the kind of place many Americans had grown up in and left behind. Its population was aging. It could attract few large employers (it had been bypassed by a nearby interstate highway) and those older industries that remained—the foundry, a rope factory, a furniture manufacturer—were not flourishing. It boasted some handsome turn-of-the-century architecture, but many older homes were in disrepair, and downtown storefronts were beginning to empty, victims of competition from nearby shopping malls. Xenia—the name derived from the Greek term for hospitality—was on a well-established declining course when the wind came through to speed things along.

The tornado entered town at a subdivision called Windsor Park, whose modest two- and three-bedroom Levittown-style houses had been erected on slab foundations. Joyce Behnken, twenty-two, eight months pregnant, was home alone. Her mother called to warn her about the oncoming storm, and Behnken covered herself with pillows and a mattress. She was killed nonetheless. Down the street, seven-year-old Brian Blakely had been watching *The Flintstones*. He was thrown a hundred yards to his death. Michael Ehret, 16, was minding his sisters at home. He led them to a hallway, assuring them, "It's only a little wind." He and a sister were crushed by their house's collapsing roof. Prabhakar Dixit, a fourteen-year-old immigrant, "was killed immediately, when tornado-propelled debris hit him in the head." Virginia Walls, 32, pushed her three children into the bathtub and lay on top of them. She saved them, but not herself.

The tornado crossed a highway, entering the four-year-old Arrowhead subdivision, whose treeless streets had names like Wigwam, Buckskin, and Peacepipe. Will Armstrong, seven, was playing in his backyard. His mother, Gloria, went out to retrieve him. Neither made it back. The neighborhood lay in such shambles that surviving residents wandered the streets as if lost. Arrowhead Elementary was destroyed, one of five Xenia schools, including Xenia High School and Xenia Junior High, that were rendered unsalvageable. At least the schools had been empty. Had daylight saving time not been extended in 1974—Congress, mindful of the energy crisis, had mandated moving the clocks forward on January 2, rather than on the first Sunday in April—Xenia would have been struck at 3:45 PM, while after-school activities were in full swing. As it was, only a few dozen students remained in the auditorium of Xenia High, rehearsing a production of "The Boyfriend," and all had run to the school's front door to watch the approach of the storm. It was lucky they hadn't remained on stage. Three school buses landed there after being hurled through a wall.

The tornado continued on through the center of town. At the A&W root beer stand, a young couple was smothered with their infant child, the assistant manager was mortally wounded by a hurtling stainless steel countertop, and an attractive twenty-two-year-old carhop, about to be married, lay beneath a freezer stocked with hamburger.

Xenia was broken in half. Fifteen hundred buildings were seriously damaged or destroyed. Thirty-four people died and 1,150 were injured. As the tornado left town, it moved to Wilberforce, three miles east, where a pair of black universities were located, and killed a postal clerk, a student, a janitor, and the director of the credit union. Lee Esprit, a professor at one of the colleges, took refuge in a hallway. When the tornado passed, he saw students wandering dazed across the campus. "It looked worse than a war scene from Vietnam," he said.

As for Thomas Youngen, the man with a tape recorder and a sense of irony: He did not die. He was merely shaken up. When he brushed himself off, though, he realized that his tape had continued to roll all the while, leaving him in possession of an unusual document. He had captured the sound of a monstrous tornado. Like most extravagances of nature, tornadoes tend to thwart attempts at physical description. Their sound is most often compared to mechanical sources, like freight trains or jet engines. But such approximations can't quite convey the tornado's capacity to strip people of safety, and, on occasion, to turn their homes into graves. According to a description of Youngen's recording in Xenia's *Daily Gazette*, "You can hear nails popping out of his apartment."

Even the national pastime was drawn into the fray. At 5:28 PM, a massive tornado set down near Rising Sun, Indiana, crossed and recrossed the Ohio River, and stomped through the western outskirts of Cincinnati. There was some question about whether the destructive fallout from the storm might affect Opening Day of the 1974 Major League Baseball season, which was set for the following afternoon in Cincinnati's Riverfront Stadium. The game had attracted great fanfare and was slated to be televised nationwide, with Vice President Gerald Ford on hand to throw out the first pitch. The hometown Reds—the vaunted "Big Red Machine," whose stars included Pete Rose, Joe Morgan, and Johnny Bench—were not the reason that the game was so anticipated. Instead, all eyes were focused on the lowly visitors, the Atlanta Braves. The Braves' slugger Hank Aaron—"Hammerin' Hank," "Bad Henry"—was one swing away from matching the most glorified record in American sports, Babe Ruth's career total of 714 home runs, which had stood since 1935.

Throughout the previous season, Aaron had been besieged by attention in his pursuit of the mark. He had appeared on the cover of *Time* and *Newsweek*, and his visits to opponents' ballparks attracted thousands of additional spectators. He received more mail, some 930,000 letters, than any other private citizen in the country in 1973. Not all were from well-wishers, though. "Dear Mr. Nigger," began one, "I hope you don't break the Babe's record. How do I tell my kids that a nigger did it?" Another, opening with the greeting "Dear Jungle Bunny," went on, "You may beat Ruth's record but there will always be only one Babe. You will be just another Black fuck down from the trees." The Braves were the only Major League franchise located in the former Confederacy; Aaron had long been the object of racial taunts there, and had an embattled relationship with Braves fans. Remarking on the paltry attendance at Atlanta's ballpark, he said, "Here I am with all these records behind me and the big one in front of me and no one really cares. If I were a white man going for the record, the place would have fifteen to twenty thousand every night."

In addition to name-calling and neglect, Aaron endured countless death threats. "Retire or die!" warned one correspondent, who listed Atlanta's schedule for June and July, promising, "You will die in one of those games. I'll shoot you in one of them. Will I sneak a rifle into the upper deck or a .45 in the bleacher? I don't know yet." The Braves provided Aaron with two bodyguards, one of whom would sit in the stands with a weapon concealed in a binoculars case. Aaron advised teammates to keep their distance from him in the dugout; between innings he often retreated to the solitude beneath the stadium to smoke a cigarette. He registered in hotels under an assumed name—Diefendorfer—and rarely ventured into public, spending his free days watching soap operas on television. Despite the pressure, he hit forty home runs in 1973, ending the season just one shy of Ruth's mark.

Aaron then spent the off-season capitalizing on his fame. He signed a million-dollar contract to promote Magnavox televisions. Although he had long been regarded as aloof and introspective, he appeared on the *Flip Wilson Show*, donned an apron alongside Dinah Shore for a cooking demonstration on *Dinah's Place*, and was the guest of honor at *Dean Martin's Celebrity Roast*. In mid-February, he returned to his native Mobile, Alabama, which had proclaimed "Henry the Great Day." All the while, the threat of racial violence dogged him. At one point he was notified by the FBI that agents had disrupted a plot to kidnap his daughter, Gaile, a student at Fisk University in Nashville. Then, on April 2, 1974, after the final exhibition game of the preseason, in Birmingham, Aaron was leaving his hotel for dinner with teammate Paul Casanova when a pair of police officers stopped the players and warned them that Aaron's life would be in danger if he left the premises. According to Casanova, Aaron responded, "I'm sick and tired of this," and brushed past the officers. "I'm going to tie the record in the first game."

F5

Aaron traveled with his team to Cincinnati early the next morning. It was April 3. His flight landed in a thunderstorm. He checked into a suite in the Netherland Hilton, then went to the stadium and learned that practice had been rained out. He was anxious to get the season underway. He was irked, too, that the Reds' management had rebuffed his request to begin the game by marking the sixth anniversary of the slaying of Martin Luther King, Jr., with a moment of silence. With the afternoon stretching in front of him, Aaron set out to the airport to pick up his father and brother, who were coming in for the historic game.

As he made his way, he said, "I saw funnel clouds in the distance."

Distance was crucial. From far off, the tornado was a braid of cloud and dust, silhouetted against the dimming day. Up close, though, it was more like a runaway train that had leapt its tracks. At Cincinnati's Longview State Hospital, it knocked a wall onto a thirty-year-old patient, killing him. Another young man perished beneath a fallen tree. An eighty-year-old driver "stepped from his car, apparently uninjured, then dropped dead while talking to bystanders," the *Cincinnati Enquirer* reported. He had had a heart attack.

In suburban Sayler Park, where Pete Rose, the National League's Most Valuable Player for 1973, had grown up and continued to reside, winds badly damaged half of the neighborhood's 1,100 homes. The elementary school Rose attended as a child was destroyed. His wife, Karolyn, told a reporter, "The tornado passed right over our house. I've never seen one before and I hope I never see one again." Not far away, Rose's neighbor and teammate, pitcher Jack Billingham, who was scheduled to take the mound in the opener, spent the night on a mattress in his basement with his children, fearing more tornadoes.

The tornado, Aaron commented, "made me forget all about Babe

Ruth and Jack Billingham for a while." He told reporters, "It was really something," adding, "It didn't worry me, though."

At 6:30 PM, a series of unsettling but harmless "earth tremors," measuring 4.5 on the Richter scale, shook Indiana. Meanwhile, tornadoes covered an ever-expanding geographical range. At 7:30, five people died in Moodyville, Tennessee. Fifteen minutes later, a couple in Hillsdale, Michigan, were killed when a tree smashed their mobile home. Towards 8:00 PM, a tornado took seven lives in central Tennessee before throwing a tractor-trailer into a house. An hour later, a motorist was killed near the Civil War battlefield at Shiloh. Around that time, fifteen tornadoes were on the ground simultaneously in Kentucky and Tennessee. Some tornadoes had multiple funnels. Some simply appeared as vagrant clouds that had meandered to earth. As night fell, the ambiguous advantage of being able to see a tornado's approach was eliminated. Tornadoes came from nowhere and passed on. At 10:15 PM, one crisscrossed the Hiwassee River, on the border between Georgia and North Carolina, killing three people.

One tornado even dropped into Canada—albeit, in Windsor, Ontario, within sight of its unruly sister city, Detroit. The tornado struck the Windsor Curling Club, where four dozen members were engaged in a tournament. Curling, a sport whose roots were in Scotland, but which had found its most ardent following in Canada, was a low-key, civilized affair. On each team, one member slid a weight, called a "rock," across ice, aiming at a target area. A second team member scurried alongside the rock, trying to steer its course by sweeping the ice ahead of it with a broom. Among the curlers that night were accountants, dentists, and engineers. At 8:10 PM eastern standard time, eight of them were killed when the building's west wall gave way. A priest was called to the rink to ad-

minister last rites. Among the dead was Windsor's building com-
missioner.

April 3 turned into April 4. Past midnight, infant twins died in
a tornado in Sunrise, Tennessee. At 3:15 AM a teenager was killed
in Saltville, Virginia. Finally, at 3:30 AM, the death toll halted after
a three-year-old girl was thrown to her death in Meadow Bridge,
West Virginia.

It would be time to catch one's breath. But the broad survey of
mayhem, misfortune, miraculous escapes and extravagant phenomena takes on a different dimension when seen up close. All disaster is local. A storm is on its way to Limestone County, Alabama.

PART TWO

F elica is in the passenger's seat. It is all happening very quickly— whatever it is, an accident, perhaps, an accidental turn toward something new and unforeseen—and very slowly. The accident has nothing to do with her or Donnie, though it is happening to them, though it barely enlists their participation, though it has taken hold of them, though it is devoid of meaning, though it unfolds like fate. It happens.

Donnie has finally spoken up—has ordered Felica out of the car—but his words seem to have come from elsewhere.

Felica tugs the door's handle. It doesn't want to yield. She presses against the door with a shoulder. Nothing. She is trapped. Then, as though detonated, the door bursts open and is ripped from its hinges. It might as well have been holding back all the air in the countryside, which now rushes in, flooding in. The air carries with it a sound, dense and opaque, of the fractured landscape and all its dislodged matter—stones peeled from creek beds, grasses peeled from soil, soil from fields, roofs from rafters. The sound is a scraping and a groaning and a whistling and a broad, indifferent howl. Felica's voice would join it, if only she could gather herself to speak.

She can't. She is busy being thrown back against her seat. A pressure bears down on her, like a body, bearing down.

She is being pelted by a rain of stones. Sandlike bits, more glass than

137

stone, prick her skin, and are accompanied by a spray of gravel, and by larger, smoother, egg-sized rocks, polished by wind and water. She raises her arms to her face in a reflex of self-defense; but this leaves her chest exposed; so she bows her head and crosses her arms over her torso; but this leaves her head unshielded once more.

Donnie, too, is taking a beating. Perhaps it occurs to him, in the moment of awareness remaining to him, that poor delicate Felica, positioned between him and the wind, is unwittingly shielding him from worse abuse.

He is hardly getting off easy, though.

A rock careens toward the car. Among the spray of flying objects, this one is on a singular course. It finds the gap in the car where Felica's door used to be, and sails past her. The arc of its flight is synchronized with the motion of Donnie's head, which jerks forward in the bouncing vehicle. The rock strikes the back of his skull. It leaves a shallow dent. He jolts sideways. His face slams into the Mustang's steering wheel.

Felica is now, in a sense, alone, although Donnie remains beside her in the driver's seat, limp, unconscious.

The moment wears on. It seems to Felica that nothing is likely to stop it. It is like the dream in which she is chased, and runs from her pursuer with all she can muster, but barely moves. She remains dimly aware of the hurling of stones, and beyond the stones, of the sky's beautiful upheaval, its filaments of light, and of the sour smell of minerals rinsed from soil.

In the midst of such a moment it is even possible, perhaps preferable, to withdraw from the car to a vantage point in the sky. Seen from above, the red car on the side of the road seizes and bucks in place. Its body is being mashed like wet clay beneath a heavy footstep. Its hood flips up. Its innards are jarred free and tossed. The windshield shatters, glass dousing the occupants, who have ceased their attempts at struggle. The car seems to lift from the ground—a few inches, nothing more—and to hover, in a brief and prolonged instant of hesitation. Then the grip of the wind tightens beneath the passenger side, and the car is flicked over, and dropped on its roof. The thud of the roof on the road is blended with the shallower thud of Felica's skull on the roof's interior. The car continues its reel. Seen from above, Felica can be said to have switched places with Donnie, and now reclines to his left, though upside down. A moment later she is righted. She counts—one—and the wind continues its play, flipping the car again, and once again her skull smacks against the roof— two—and while she is being whirled back into place Donnie disappears, pulled through the hole where the windshield was as though on a string, and spun into the darkness; and the backseat, too, has somehow been unfastened from its bearings and wrested from the car, and only Felica remains in place, her head knocking against the roof once more— three—and from within the car the distinction between up and down has become a curious irrelevance. It is as though the tumbling could go on and on, if only Felica could count higher than three—that magic num- ber—which she cannot, for she is getting very drowsy, until finally, with- out knowing precisely how, she makes her way out of the car.

She wakes to darkness. She is sprawled in a ditch. Mud is packed on her face like a mask. She scrapes openings for her eyes but remains in dark- ness. The air is still and cool. It is not raining. Felica does not know whether she has been in the ditch for a moment, or an hour, or a day. She recognizes nothing of her surroundings. A thick belt of wires is wound around her legs. She squirms free and rises, off-balance, to her feet. She is freighted with mud. It requires an enormous effort to climb from the ditch. Much slipping. Much grabbing for a handhold, only to lose her grip and come away clutching a fist of mud. Nearby, a steaming form pokes from the soil, like the hull of a beached ship. It is the cracked shell of the Mustang. Donnie is not in it.

Finally Felica makes it to solid ground. Her shoes are gone. She asks herself if she is in pain and decides she is not, though she seems to be wafting alongside her body, like a spirit, and is perplexed by the movement of her limbs. Nonetheless she straggles along the side of the road for a bit, then stops and turns back. There is nothing to help her see through the night, no landmarks by which she might guide herself. "Donnie," she calls. "Donnie Powers!" She repeats the call over and over. Maybe she is crying. She can't tell. All she knows is that she needs to find Donnie, and that he is nowhere. She calls his name across the dark fields, up and down the road. For the first time, she is scared. She wanders back and forth, stranded, her dress torn, her voice like an animal's cry.

Suddenly she spots a pair of lights, pinpricks in the distance, approaching her. She walks to the middle of the road and raises her arms. The car brakes in front of her. Its driver rolls down his window and stares. Felica speaks haltingly. She has difficulty explaining her circumstances. It all makes little sense to her. She tells the driver her name. What else is there to say? She was in a car with Donnie Powers. Now she can't find him.

The driver gestures for her to get in. She is reluctant to leave without Donnie, but too shaken to resist. She is taken to a darkened house. The people inside the house are wielding flashlights and rushing from one room to the next in a panic. She recognizes a few of them—girls—as classmates of Donnie. She can't for the life of her remember their names. They are crowing about getting to the basement. Felica doesn't move. Someone spreads a blanket on the living room floor and tells her to get on the blanket and wait.

Wait for what?

Then it is quiet again, and again Felica is alone. She lies on the floor, looking out the window. The sky flares with lightning. Felica watches with a child's rapt attention. The lightning is not, she observes, string-like, unspooling from the sky to the earth, but rather an all-over light-

ning that pops, like a flashbulb, spreading its glow from one side of the night to the other, and then being washed from sight. It is a glaring momentary brightness, a version of daylight. If Donnie were anywhere in it, she would find him.

She must have drifted off. A man crosses the room and picks her up in his arms. She comes to with a start. His name, he tells her, is Mr. Glass. He carries her from the house and lays her down in the backseat of a car. Then the car glides off into the darkness. Felica stares up at the rain-spattered back windshield, which has been scrawled with greasy shoe polish. It takes her a while to flip the backwards lettering around in her head: "For Sale."

When the car stops, Felica is surrounded by faces. They are gawking at her. Their mouths are moving. She is hoisted onto a gurney. She turns to look for Mr. Glass, but he is gone. She is wheeled through double doors. The crowd parts to make way for her. Voices call to her and hands fumble over her and she observes the commotion as if from a distance. Out of the blur of faces, one—ashen, sorrowful—comes into focus. It is Donnie's father. He is saying her name as though it is a question. "Oh, I'm fine," she tells him, and indeed she feels far more concerned about him than about herself. "Where's Donnie?" he cries.

She is transferred to a wheelchair and pushed into a cramped hallway. The floor is wet and stained. Mud-covered bodies are slumped against walls and in doorways. Other people push past, calling out names, bending down to examine faces. Felica wonders what has happened to these people, these casualties, and why she has been brought here among them.

Soon she is taken behind a curtain and laid on an examination table. Dr. Waddell—her family's doctor, who knows all there is to know about Felica—is waiting for her. He looks her up and down and shows her his familiar kind smile. No longer does anyone ask Felica what happened. The doctor seems to be spending a long time touching her leg. After a while it occurs to her that he is tugging at it with something like a pair of pliers. You let me know if this hurts, he says, and though until now she had not considered the possibility of pain, suddenly she is gasping. It is as though he is twisting the bones out of her foot.

There are shouts in the distance. A voice comes over a loudspeaker. Dr. Waddell leaves and then returns. Another one is coming at us, he whispers.

Felica is lifted back into the wheelchair and taken to a small corridor. People are fleeing, some of them carrying others in their arms, some of them in such a hurry to move the wounded that they drag them across the floor. As she is being pushed through the mayhem she sees a wheelchair coming toward her, framed by the bleached walls. It carries Donnie. "Oh my Lord," *Felica says. As they near each other she stretches her hand out to him and touches his arm. She can hardly believe it. She left him behind but he found his way back. His eyes are open. He looks straight at her.* "Donnie," *she says, soothingly,* "everything is going to be okay."

He glances back at her. His expression is tranquil. "Who are you?" *he says. He is wheeled away.*

The corridor is lined with bodies laid feet to head, and Felica is set down among them. Who are you, *she thinks. There is no telling.* Who were you a moment ago? Who will you be tomorrow? *She must have conjured Donnie. He could not have gotten here on his own. He is missing. He is in the mud. She has to find him.*

She turns her head. A young man lies nearby, his face streaked with thick blood. There is no telling whether he is dead or alive. The hall is full of such people. The only sign that there is life around Felica are the sounds of labored breathing and moans.

A nurse kneels by her and begins cutting her dress from her body with a pair of shears. The mud has begun to dry, and as the dress is removed

F5

it is as though Felica's skin is being stripped away. Deep snakelike burns encircle her legs.

She is hauled away once more. Now she gazes up at a bright lamp. A tray of medical instruments is open beside her. Dr. Waddell looks down at her brow. He is wearing a mask. She sees the outline of his lips moving behind it. She can't make out what he is saying.

A nurse steps up behind Felica, and grabs a handful of her hair. "We can't wash out all that stuff," *she tells Felica.* "We're going to have to cut it off."

"No!" *Felica's voice rises.* "You're not cutting my hair!"

She goes blank.

The Crossroads

A t 6:43 PM, while Bill Dunnavant sat behind the wheel of WJMW's King Country Rover, roaming across Limestone County in search of a tornado, Mike Davis, the station's announcer, was providing listeners with an extemporaneous update on the situation at hand. "You've had plenty of warning now," he reminded them. "You folks go ahead and be taking your places of shelter. If you can't get to a place of shelter, in a storm cellar or something similar to that"—he paused to clear his throat—"get in your hallway of your home, and put something over you, maybe your couch or something of this type nature, to keep things from hitting you, in the hallway of your home, and open your windows to the east, open the windows to the east, and that way might, um, keep the house from exploding."

The station resumed its broadcast of music. A singer named Johnny Rodriguez began to croon, "I've lived my life in vain. / Every dream has only brought me pain. / All my life I've always been so blue. / Born to lose, and now I'm only losing you."

A moment later, Spencer Black's voice could be heard breaking through the song. "Mike?" he said. "I can't hear you." There were background sounds of great commotion at Civil Defense, the squawk of a two-way radio, a melee of raised voices, calls for every-

145

one to quiet down. Dozens of frightened people had begun pouring into Spencer's office as soon as word of tornadoes had gotten out. Spencer had given up trying to control the crowd. An elderly man lay on a cot beside a sick child. Others sat on the floor. Some asked to be taken upstairs, to the shelter of the county jail. "They getting ahead of their self over here at the National Weather Service," Spencer cautioned Mike and the radio audience, "but this, the hook, is down within the river around the Brown's Ferry area now."

The phone line cut out. There was a moment of awkward silence on the airwaves.

"Okay," Mike said, hesitantly. "This is the real thing. We're getting a tornado. It's—the hook—is reported down. When we say hook we're talking about the tornado. Heading northeast, forty miles an hour."

Around the same time, Buddy Evans, who had been winding down his day visiting a friend in Athens, lured by the promise of a steak dinner, was summoned to the phone. It was a jailer, calling from the sheriff's department, and speaking so rapidly that Buddy had to urge him to slow down and repeat himself. "Anytime something bad happened," Buddy would remark, "those jailers went all to pieces." Buddy was finally able to gather that a deputy had reported seeing a tornado enter the river near the nuclear plant. Buddy sighed deeply, eyed the meat on the grill, and got into his patrol car.

He was in no hurry as he threaded his way down the county. There was still plenty of watery light in the sky, and a pale gleam in the west marked the progress of the setting sun. The day's heat had not abated, and though the wind had picked up—gusts of it were causing the cruiser to fishtail now and then—the sky was clear and unthreatening. False alarms were a daily part of Buddy's routine, as was the need to strike a posture of diligence in responding. He proceeded slowly down Highway 31, using the loudspeaker mounted on the roof of his car to warn anyone who could hear him that it was prudent to find a hiding place. It felt a little foolish, but it was all he could do. He approached Tanner Crossroads, the only interchange of any significance between Athens and Decatur, where the Huntsville-Brownsferry Road crossed the highway. A pair of competing all-purpose shops—Craig's Grocery on the southwest corner and Laughmiller's on the northeast—faced off across the intersection, each boasting its own dedicated clientele, some of whom spent afternoons sitting out front holding court.

As he passed the crossroads, Buddy saw a group of people standing in front of Laughmiller's gas pumps, staring at the tinted sky to the southwest. He barked a warning at them over his loudspeaker. They smiled at him and waved.

It was a few minutes before 7 PM. Frank Orr sat in the den of his parents' house, biding time until supper. The black-and-white television was tuned to Channel 19, and *Truth or Consequences* was in its last moments. No one was paying much attention to the show. Marilyn was playing with Jason, her toddler; the baby was asleep. Her husband, Vergil, had woken not long before, showered, and now lay on the sofa, dozing, trying to squeeze in some rest before leaving for his 10 PM shift. It was quiet time: the end of Jason's day, the approach of the mens' workday, a pause in Marilyn's ongoing infant care.

Suddenly everyone looked up, at once, toward the television. Programming was being interrupted by a bulletin. A grainy image of weatherman H. D. Bagley appeared on the screen. Bagley, a fatherly figure who favored loud suits and signed off his broadcast each Friday by reminding viewers, "Have a good weekend and wherever you go, go to church on Sunday," had been north Alabama's first television meteorologist, and remained its most popular. The tone he adopted now was unusually grim. He gestured to the display of an old radar monitor—a murky gray screen, speckled with blips of light—and said that a tornado had been sighted near Moulton, the 2,470-person seat of Lawrence County, fifty miles southwest of Athens.

Frank thought nothing of the report. As far as he knew, tornadoes didn't travel that kind of distance. Besides, the Tennessee River formed an impassable barrier between Lawrence and Limestone counties. Marilyn remarked that the blurred radar screen to which Bagley pointed looked like something one would see in an old war movie set on a submarine. Indeed, the weatherman's somber alert seemed to be little more than an accessory to the evening's televised entertainment. Soon a light rain began to fall, and the TV reception became irregular. The set was shut off.

Buddy continued south. Night was coming. The sky had grown darker quickly. A spark of lightning ignited to the west. Wind rushed through the open windows of his cruiser. To his right, dust stirred in the fields, then was tamped down by a sudden stream of rain. In an instant the road was washed from sight. Then, just as quickly, the rain stopped. The view cleared. Buddy slowed down. A change was happening before him. Whether the change was coming from the ground and shooting skywards, or starting in the sky and diving to earth, was not yet clear.

Then he knew. Of course, it looked nothing like the wispy snakelike funnels of children's movies. It was, instead, a dark cylindrical tower, extending from a flat-topped black cloud to the ground. It approached him on the diagonal. The sky was a blank on which it appeared stainlike, blotting the pristine landscape. Indeed, the more he stared at it, the more it seemed nearly architectural in its solidity, and anchored in the ground. Then the illusion began to give way, and Buddy could tell that the mass was spinning. Loose matter drifted in its currents. Just a moment earlier the tornado had seemed distant and discrete; now it consumed the sky. If he continued driving, he would get pulled into it.

At Annias Green's house, it was dinnertime. That meant that the television was not on, and that the radio—which would not have been tuned to WJMW, in any case, since country music was not Annias's preference—was switched off, too. Nor were he and his family within earshot of the sheriff's loudspeaker. Any suggestion of danger, whether imminent or remote, would have caught Annias off-guard. As he took his seat at the dining table, all he knew was that it seemed to have started raining—he could hear the rain beating on the windows—and to him, rain was no news at all.

As usual, the meal was preceded by prayer. Annias was glad he had stayed home rather than going off fishing. He didn't get enough chances to relax at home with his family. Perhaps the phone would be quiet tonight, too, and he would not be called to attend to a parishioner in need.

Next door, Joe Isom, Annias's landlord, was following H. D. Bagley's report with interest. Ever curious about the weather—Joe farmed 240 acres, and his peach orchard was easily menaced by hail or frost or drought—he went to a south-facing window, looked down a long gully, and scanned the dusky skies. He squinted. There was nothing unusual to be seen. A bit of rain had passed through, but that was it. His rows of young peach trees stood upright and undisturbed in the shadowed light. Joe was about to write off Bagley's warning as a hoax when something caught his eye. Far off—a good six or seven miles away, in the direction of Tanner—he saw a smoky trail drifting in the sky, as though someone were burning straw. The smoke was dangling from a storm cloud, and churning. Joe turned back to his wife and teenage son to report his sighting. He teased his wife by saying that if the tornado came close, they would have to dart from the house and duck into a ditch and then, he joked, it would be every man for himself. Joe could tell, though, that it wouldn't come to that. The storm was traveling well to the east, and would skirt the house by a mile or two. Nonetheless, he decided it would be prudent to leave home and check on his parents, who lived nearby. It did not occur to him to stop by Annias's house on his way out. Even though they were neighbors, such a visit would have been out of the ordinary. Joe did not believe in barging in on his tenants.

The grander a house, the more it can feel haunted by the absence of its occupants. At 7:00 PM, Don Lauderdale and his wife, Sheila, were at church, among friends, in the midst of prayer. The only thing moving through the rooms of their house was the wind.

There may not have been another man in Limestone County who was as house-proud as Don. In 1963, his father-in-law, who ran a local car dealership, had bought the Old Orr House from a man named Harry Orr, a disreputable uncle of Frank's who maintained two households, each with a wife and children, unbeknownst to each other, in separate counties. Don and Sheila moved in on the day of John F. Kennedy's funeral. The house was quietly opulent. Four slender columns, in the neoclassical mode, extended from the ground to the overhanging gable roof, which shaded a long front porch adorned with antique rocking chairs. A companion porch ran along the back of the house, each end outfitted with a custom-built porch swing. When Don's son, Don, Jr., was a baby, Don would soothe him to sleep with the motion of those swings.

The house contained some 4,000 square feet of living space on two floors, and, like all well-loved homes, had become a den of memories. Quilts made by Don's mother were hung throughout, and most of the furniture had been passed on by relatives. Under a ten-foot ceiling, a formal dining room held an antique oak table and sideboard and an heirloom poplar cupboard. A large round still life of fruit hung on one wall. The living room contained a Shaker-style cherry desk, a drop-leaf cherry table, and a long coffee table with delicately carved spindles. On the mantle was a hand-blown decanter, crystalline blue with gold trim, and six matching glasses. Across the hall was the children's game room. A pool table sat in the center, and a miniature race car track was spread across the floor. Against one wall stood an upright piano that held sentimental value for Sheila. She had bought it as an eleven-year-old with the proceeds she received, $125, from the sale of a cow she had raised.

Each room on the second floor was organized around a decorative motif, and a ledger inside each doorway described the room's furnishings. Don and Sheila's eighteen-year-old daughter, Shwan—a name invented to blend those of her parents—had grown up in the Blue Room. In addition to its blue carpeting, the room retained its four-poster bed, whose white cotton canopy with lacy blue trim Sheila had sewn, along with the matching curtains and bedspread. Shwan's large doll collection was still on display.

Don, Jr.'s haven was the Red Room, whose details were chosen to evoke the University of Alabama's Crimson Tide football team: Carpeting, drapery, and linen were all in team colors. There was a drum set in one corner, and a toy chest, built by a favorite uncle, filled with Matchbox cars, a G.I. Joe doll and accessories, and what Sheila called "boy stuff."

The Green Room was reserved for guests. It contained a set of antique furniture, all painted olive green, and featuring pineapple-shaped ornaments. "The pineapple represents hospitality," Sheila would note.

The master bedroom, the Sea Foam Green Room, was similarly stocked with well-kept antiques, except for the addition of a new king-sized bed, which lent the room a touch of contemporary luxury.

Don had remembered to leave a single light on before going out for the evening.

By now, the announcement of warnings had reached enough residents of Limestone to throw the county into a tornado frenzy. Spencer Black was getting besieged by reports of unverifiable funnel sightings all over the county—at the nuclear plant; throughout Athens; in the daintily preserved antebellum village of Mooresville, in southernmost Limestone; and, on the opposite end of the county, in Ardmore, on the Tennessee border. Repeated distress calls came into Civil Defense from the small community in western Limestone where Spencer's mother lived, and where his wife and children were sheltering. He didn't know what to think. He was trapped in his office with a mob. The air was getting stale; the bathroom was already unusable. He called the radio station again and used the airwaves to appeal to residents "not even to worry about listening about what's going on . . . until this whole thing is over with. The whole thing," he reiterated, sounding as though he might be lapsing into panic, "I mean the whole county, not just one particular section. . . .

F5

Cause the conditions and everything is just perfect. And they dropping out everywhere."

Buddy braked. As he jumped from his car his feet were cut out from
under him. He clawed his way into a rut along the side of the road.
He thought he heard a huge truck racing toward him, out of control, and he braced himself, but peering up he saw there was nothing on the road. It was the sound of the storm.

He lay facedown in a full-bodied embrace of the ditch. He
grabbed fistfuls of shrubs and struggled to maintain his grip. His back
and legs stung. He wondered if he was being buried. He glanced up
from the rut and saw his cruiser tottering above him. It dawned on
him that he could suffer the indignity of getting crushed by his own
squad car.

Then the brunt of the wind came. It seized him by his uniform
and plucked him up.

He lost hold of the ground. He rolled, he tumbled, he was
dragged down the ditch. He might as well have been plunging down
a steep hill. There was no telling where bottom was.

Then it was done. It was as quick as a car wreck, as quick as getting shot. He didn't bother taking stock of his condition. He could
feel his arms and legs. He knew he was still in one piece. He rose
and brushed off his uniform. The tornado strode away from him,
leaving blue skies in its wake. For a moment he could not find his
car. Then, squinting down the road, he saw it parked where he had
left it, two hundred yards away.

Walter McGlocklin had finished resetting the errant utility poles on
Elm Street, on the north end of Athens, and returned to the Electric
Department. He was more than ready to get home to his son's birth-

day party. His supervisor, though, needed him to remain on the job, and told him that a bad storm was on its way. Shortly before 7:00 PM, Walter called his wife to apologize that he would be delayed a bit longer. He asked her how the weather was down at home. Her reply: "It's a real pretty night."

Ten minutes later, a call came into the Electric Department reporting that power had been knocked out at Lawson's Trailer Park. Walter and his partner, Maxie Loggins, were told to take a repair truck and investigate the damage. They headed south on Highway 31. Walter was glad to be given the assignment. Lawson's was less than two miles northeast of his house. When he was done, he would be able to drop in on his family.

At 7:10, Spencer had his secretary, Martha Moore, contact the radio station once more. She announced over the air, "We have reports that the tornado has just leveled Lawson's Trailer Park."

WJMW opened its lines to callers from the community, who gave vent to expressions of collective fear and amazement. A man breathlessly announced that he had picked up pieces of ice "larger than a half dollar" at a place called Jones' Crossroads. A woman, her voice trembling, claimed to have seen a funnel cloud trampling through the west side of Athens. Another caller described two tornadoes veering in opposite directions north of town.

Between calls, a song played on and off. "Double exposure," went the refrain, "I've lost my composure."

At 7:17, announcer Mike Davis remarked, "These things are touching down in every direction under the—under the—clouds. They're just hitting a little bit everywhere."

Bloodied, his rain-soaked uniform caked with dirt and mud, Buddy continued down the road. The storm seemed to have spilled its contents onto the pavement, like a reckless dump truck. There were remnants of construction—an impressive range of cuts of lumber, and gnarled sheaths of aluminum siding, and sodden batts of insulation, and masses of wiring, and cast iron and copper and clay piping; and there were remnants of domesticity—stove tops, unhinged refrigerator doors, bedsteads, cookware, shredded quilts, the mangled frames of family portraits and dressing mirrors; and there were remnants of nature, foremost among them the limbs of trees, as well as limbless uprooted boles, and even a few hardwood canopies that had been plucked, like giant florets, from their bases. And there were, too, occasional remnants of biological life, guts, mostly—presumably, and hopefully, those of cows or pigs.

Buddy painstakingly maneuvered around the debris. Somehow, he found himself in the midst of a traffic jam.

Within minutes of the tornado's passage, the road had attracted a throng of vehicles, picking their way haphazardly along, clogging the route, and carting their freight of onlookers. There is a kind of unbalanced person, Buddy reflected, who has a scent for distress—fires, traffic accidents, drunken brawls, crime scenes—and who always manages to get to the scene ahead of officials.

He halted at the entrance to Lawson's. Power lines blocked the way; as far as he knew, the wires were still live. He smelled gas, too. He began shouting over the loudspeaker for those on the road to stay back, and for those in the trailer park to remain where they were until help arrived. The spectators around him seemed oddly buoyant, and eager to test their capacity for heroism. Buddy tried to restrain them. He could hear cries coming from Lawson's, and through the dwindling daylight he could see a handful of people tripping over mounds of rubble. A few of the trailers were untouched. Flags fluttered from poles extended above their doorways, and potted geraniums sat in windowsills and on doorsteps. Surrounding these trailers were charred gaps from which homes had been taken whole.

Buddy did not trust that his jailers back at the sheriff's department would be competent enough to handle the job of dispatching personnel during the crisis. His fourteen-year-old son Jerry, though, was an expert on the radio. Buddy radioed Jerry and told him to round up help for Lawson's. He wanted everything Limestone and surrounding counties could muster—law enforcement, ambulances, fire trucks, and members of a volunteer rescue squad. He wanted workers from the gas and electric company. He added, too, that Jerry should get hold of the coroner. He surveyed the wreckage further, then told Jerry to place a call to the family's church, First Baptist of Athens. Buddy knew there would be a large gathering there for evening services. Have the pastor round up as many able-bodied men as he can, he instructed. Have them come to Lawson's to look for survivors.

After seeing H. D. Bagley's televised warnings, Frank, though doubtful, had remained curious about the storm reports. He turned on the radio, and, amid all sorts of wild rumors, heard an official statement that Lawson's Trailer Park had been struck by a tornado. That made him prick up his ears. He drove past Lawson's daily on his way to work; he knew of a few men at Monsanto who lived there. He wondered what the wreckage would look like.

Marilyn, too, was taken aback by the report, though it seemed like a sad bit of news from a faraway place. "A tornado," she thought, "is just some little spout running along the ground. Worst it does is take a roof off." She had too much on her hands to welcome any added drama. She was determined to believe that the TV and radio were, as always, exaggerating.

Frank stepped out to the porch to take a look at the sky. Rain had ended, and some grains of hail glimmered on the lawn. He caught sight of what he took to be the storm that had struck Lawson's. It was a few miles to the east now, passing them by, headed for Tennessee. It didn't look like much from this distance. It was becoming a pleasant evening.

On the radio, Marilyn heard someone from the sheriff's office saying that Buddy Evans was ordering Highway 31 shut to traffic. Okay, she thought. That means Vergil has a good excuse to stay home from work.

The King Country Rover arrived at Lawson's at 7:23 PM. In his past experience of making live reports, Bill Dunnavant had raced to the scene of car wrecks and gotten glimpses of dead bodies. "But nothing like this," he said. "It wasn't so much maimed bodies—it was too hard to see if there was any of that—just unbelievable destruction." He couldn't tell if there were casualties, but he imagined there had to be. "There was a cotton field next to the trailer court, and I could see them digging people out of it. It looked like people had been buried alive. I kept hearing mothers yelling for their babies."

His first words to the radio audience were emphatic: "It is unreal what it has done here!"

Over by Ingram Road, Walter McGlocklin's fourteen-year-old nephew, Jerry, watched the dusky skies turn overcast. It was time to call it a day. He drove the tractor in from the field he was plowing and went to the barn to milk the cows. He could see it raining a bit to the east. He had no way of knowing that the rain fell alongside a tornado that had narrowly missed his uncle's farm, and had, instead, gone on to hit Lawson's.

Around 7:10 PM, Jerry's aunt, Ruth, had shown up at the barn, accompanied by her girls, and toting Little Walter. She told Jerry that Walter would be home before long. She said, too, that it looked as though it was about to storm, and that it would be a good idea to hurry back to the house. Indeed, as she was talking, rain began thrumming on the barn roof.

It was a hundred yards to the house. Jerry, Ruth, and the children stood by the barn door waiting for the rain to let up. The barn was dank and smelled of hay and wet cowhide. The cows, agitated, shuffled and stomped and pressed against their stalls.

They waited another ten minutes for the storm to slacken. The barn creaked, and rain and wind plied their way through chinks in the planking. Ruth told Jerry she would rather get soaked and be in her house than remain in the barn. She pressed Little Walter close against her, and Jerry picked up Nancy, the youngest girl. Sandra and Grace stood beside them. All together, they made a run for the house.

Rain filled their eyes. They were drenched in an instant.

Ruth and Jerry entered the house, peeled off shoes, shook the rain from their hair, and began helping the children out of their wet clothes. Walter's twelve-year-old nephew, Steve, who had come by for the birthday party, was in a corner of the living room, standing in front of the television. It was hard to tune in a clear picture. Jerry could hear a voice through the static, though. The voice was repeating the words "tornado warning."

Towards 7:30, WJMW took a call from the southern end of the county. "We have seen the funnel cloud," the caller said. Mike Davis was confused. A tornado had passed through that area less than a half hour earlier. "I think now we're kind of a little funnel happy," Mike commented. "We're seeing them now when we might not be."

* * *

F 5

Buddy's badge was not enough to allow him to control the flow of people moving to and from the trailer park. It had started pouring once again. Cars were parked on the highway and in the median; other vehicles tried to find clear passage by driving into fields and got mired; injured people lay on the sides of the road. Ambulance lights cast watery streaks on the road and on the shambles of the trailer park. Some of the people who had emerged from Lawson's were telling the sheriff that against all odds there seemed to be few, or even no, fatalities. Most everyone, they said, was gone at church when the tornado hit.

Buddy turned his sights across the highway. On the western horizon, the last band of daylight was narrowing beneath storm clouds and nightfall. He peered into a vivid nest of lightning. Against the darkening sky, he began to trace the outline of a darker shape. It was rocking gently from side to side. It was enormous— a mile across, Buddy thought—and it couldn't have been more than three or four miles away. At first, he could not fathom what he was seeing. Such visions do not occur twice in a lifetime, let alone twice in an evening. Yet it was unmistakable. And it was on its way. "That's when you think the world is coming to an end," he mused.

Don Lauderdale approached Tanner Crossroads on his way to Lawson's Trailer Park, riding in one of two vans that had set out from First Baptist Church of Athens, in response to the sheriff's call, filled with volunteers.

Don watched a swirl of colors in the distance. It was, he thought, a particularly vibrant sunset. Then, as he watched, the colors turned black. The van swerved around debris and came to a sudden stop. It seemed to be hurling itself straight into a massive wall. "Turn back!" Don shouted. The van veered onto the median and changed direction. There was a church on the side of the highway—First Baptist of Tanner—and Don shouted for the driver to stop so he could provide warning to those inside. As he ran from the van toward the church he heard howling behind him. He turned his head and saw a car flipping past, end over end. People in the church were standing by the windows watching the storm approach. Don called for them to get under the pews. He saw a man he knew, a circuit court judge, who was one-armed and had an artificial leg, and he threw the man to the ground, pushing him under a pew. Then Don dropped to his belly and covered his head with his arms. "Lord, if this is it, I'm ready," he said.

Bill Dunnavant had parked the King Country Rover in the median of Highway 31, across from Lawson's, and now stood beside the van staring down the hour's second tornado. A black cloud surged from the evening sky. Bill counted four or five funnels twisting within the cloud. His brother Bob, Jr., a reporter for the *Huntsville Times*, who had been dispatched to Lawson's by his editor to gather impressions of the damage, now appeared beside him. Together they watched the tornado climb from the direction of the Tennessee River, cross the embankment of the Louisville and Nashville Railroad tracks, and bear down on them across a vast open field.

Behind them, Buddy was scrambling back and forth on the road, urging the clutch of rescuers, survivors, and those he called "sightseers" to take cover. Not everyone shared his sense of alarm. Some stood transfixed, as though watching a movie of a tornado. Others climbed into their vehicles and headed north, directly into the storm's path, whether to get a closer glimpse of the rare phenomenon, or to make a misguided attempt to outrun it, was unclear.

As Buddy struggled to prevent mayhem, a van from the Electric Department approached the trailer park and slowed down. Buddy watched Walter McGlocklin get out of the truck and examine the electrical lines, seemingly oblivious to those sprinting past him in the downpour. Cars blared their horns and spun their wheels on debris. Walter spotted the sheriff and trotted over to him. "The power is dead," he told Buddy. "No need to worry about getting electrocuted."

"You all get out of here!" Buddy shouted. Walter was bewildered. Then he saw a man pointing to the west, in the direction of his house. "Yonder comes another one," the man called.

Walter's nephew Jerry stared past the television, through the living room window. The sky was bright with lightning. What Jerry saw was strange and wondrous. Clouds were riding across open fields to the west, moving just like clouds do across the sky. As the clouds passed a steel TVA tower, it snapped out of the ground, and began rolling across the field. A moment later, a second tower was toppled. To Jerry, the scene resembled something out of a cartoon, with the 120-foot-high girders skipping like tumbleweeds.

The house went dark.

Jerry kept gazing into the night. He was eye level with the lightning. The clouds were glowing red. Rain continued to lash the house. The red clouds began to swirl. Jerry could now see two distinct shapes, conical, side by side. They were darting toward the house. Ruth appeared beside him at the window. "What do we do?" she said.

"Let's get down on the floor," he said.

Ruth gathered her children to her on the dark living room floor, crouching beneath the masonry column of the chimney. Steve and Jerry lay down too.

The wind was bellowing. The children began crying. The wind came closer. The children shrieked.

Then there was silence. The rain stopped. The sound of wind ceased. The house was still and the darkness total. Jerry remembered something he had once read in a book: a directive that windows be raised during a tornado. He rose to his knees on the floor and began to reach for the window. As he moved forward, the noise of the storm returned in a violent rush. The children cried out for their mother. "Everybody start praying," Ruth said. Jerry put his hand on the window and tried to raise it. Then he was thrown back and slammed against the floor.

The tornado neared Lawson's like a huge wave about to break on those who had been abandoned on shore. Driverless cars began to slide across the highway. Pieces of scrap whistled past. By now, most of those remaining at Lawson's recognized what they were facing. Men lunged for the drainage ditch in the grassy median of Highway 31. At least three dozen lay there.

Bill Dunnavant leaned against the King Country Rover, microphone in hand, until the van was quaking so hard that he was thrown to the ground. His brother grabbed him and pulled him toward the ditch. Bill looked over his shoulder and saw the storm collapsing on him. He issued a final comment to the radio audience. "I gotta go," he said. "I'm hitting the ditch." His transmission ended.

Walter watched in horror as the tornado streaked across the railroad tracks toward Lawson's. He and Maxie Loggins ran back to their truck. Maxie gunned the engine and put the truck into gear before Walter made it into the cab. Walter grabbed the door. The wind was pulling him off the truck. He held onto the door and managed to haul himself in. The truck was laden with electrical wires and coils of insulating sleeves and tools. It had a hard time gaining speed. It listed from side to side in the wind, and seemed closer to tipping over than to moving forward. Finally it began to creep south, shuddering as it went. It passed Ingram Road, which led to Walter's house, and kept going. Walter heard a piercing sound. "It was like being in an old house in wintertime during a wind, when you hear the house whistling bad, ringing almost— well, this cloud was ringing loud as can be." The sight of it was even more striking. "There was a red cloud and a white cloud behind it. You could see the bottom twisting."

One of the last to make it to lower ground at Lawson's was Fred Lackey, pastor of First Baptist Church of Athens. Known as Brother Fred to his parishioners, he had arrived at Lawson's ten minutes earlier to offer help, accompanied by a van full of church elders. (His van had left the church just ahead of the one carrying Don Lauderdale.) Brother Fred had ignored the downed power lines and headed straight for the damaged trailers, stepping through the ruins in his suit and dress shoes, calling for survivors. Then, suddenly, he had looked up and seen Buddy Evans motioning toward the horizon.

"It was coming," he said. "There was lightning on both sides of it. Everything was lit up. The cloud itself was all the way on the ground. I kept staring at it. It looked like a dragon's tail, and it was really moving, from left to right."

He sprinted to the ditch. Chest down in mud and weeds, he continued to fix his gaze on the tornado. He saw a pair of farmhouses, dwarfed by the black cloud, suddenly disintegrate into meager puffs of dirt. "It was sucking up everything in its path," he remarked.

Brother Fred had attended countless people on their deathbeds. Now it occurred to him that he was the one about to die. He was surprised to find himself recalling an obscure article he had read some twenty years earlier in a dog-eared copy of *Reader's Digest*. The article had recounted the experience of a group of people who were caught in a tornado and saved themselves by locking arms. Brother Fred shouted at the men in the median to get hold of each other. They did, lying there in a long, unkempt, vulnerable chain. Brother Fred looked to his side and saw the sheriff rushing over to join them. "He was the last in the ditch," the pastor said. The noise of the storm rose like an incalculable swarm of bees. Brother Fred raised his voice. "Fellows," he announced, "if any of you are not right with God, you'd better get right now. This is it." Cries of prayer were shouted into the storm.

The wind passed over the ditch. Men grabbed at each other, at the grass, at clumps of dirt. Faces were driven into the mud. Bill Dunnavant felt a body smothering his, and realized it was his older brother offering himself as a buffer. Gusts of water washed across the ditch. Men were scraped along the ground. To Brother Fred, it seemed to go on for hours. He felt as though the oxygen were being sucked from the air, and thought he was suffocating. He looked up and was stunned to see a white car hurtling through the air overhead. He saw the wind take Buddy Evans and blow him down the highway, fifty, sixty yards. The sheriff clawed at grass as he was dragged along.

Bill Dunnavant rose to his feet dazed, disheveled, and with a mixture of fear and adrenaline-driven exhilaration. He grabbed his microphone. "We all locked arms trying to keep from being blown away," he told listeners. "It did come."

He turned to a man standing beside him and put the microphone to the man's face. The man spoke breathlessly. "It's the most terrifying thing I've ever seen in my life, I tell you."

"Where'd you ride that one out?" Bill asked.

F5

The man chortled. "I was in a ditch across the road from you, hugging the ground."

Bill's brother Bob would later provide a description of the scene at Lawson's for readers of the *Huntsville Times*, writing, "I laid in a shallow highway ditch and watched what we thought was sure death pass by Wednesday night near Tanner. There were about 30 of us . . . all competing with the grass for a connection to the dirt." He continued, "It was like something out of the Old Testament, a pillar of clouds, black, majestic and ominous, moving across the farmlands of southern Limestone County."

Now, Bill stood and watched in awe as the tornado moved on toward Athens. Over the radio, he was heard to exclaim, disjointedly, "It looks like we have one going just south of us—we can see through the—uh, just north of us—in the clouds here, the lightning lightens up the sky. Yes—it is a funnel cloud! It is a funnel cloud! Just north of us, just about four miles north of us, close to the Athens city limits, and it is headed in a northeasterly direction. It is not down but it is a funnel cloud."

Barely recovered from his own brush with death, Bill took a moment of radio time to worry about those who were soon to be chased down by the same wild winds. "All I could say is, if you've seen one, you've probably seen one of the worst-looking, most frightening experiences you've ever seen. And I can understand what some of those people are going through now, in these tornadoes."

Home

It was 7:35. As a precaution, Frank Orr and his extended family were now gathered in a hallway in a center of the house. Frank's sister Marilyn thought they were overreacting, and was irritated. Nonetheless, she had grabbed six-day-old Mark from the cradle in which he had been sleeping, and held him against her. "This is ridiculous," she thought. "I just woke my baby to come sit in a hallway." Frank brought a portable radio into the hallway, and the family listened to its broadcast with intense interest. They heard live descriptions of the chaos at Lawson's, and they sat tensely as Bill Dunnavant tracked the approach of the second tornado in his dramatic sportscaster's delivery, and they started when he cried that he was running for his life. A few minutes later, when Bill returned to the air, the family was collectively relieved, though Bill was now warning that the action was on its way toward Athens.

Frank thought about it. If, as the radio suggested, the second tornado was reprising the path of its predecessor, it stood to reason that it, too, would pass far east of them. All the same, it was worth taking a look. He returned to the back porch with his father and Vergil. The men gazed across farmland and down the hollows of stream beds, following the slope of the land toward Tanner and Lawson's.

The cloud cover had once more thickened on the horizon. Lightning was flashing. Night was here, Frank remarked, but you could still sit out on the porch and read a newspaper by the glow of the sky, or see a man walking toward you across the field just as surely as if it were midday.

Walter and Maxie Loggins had succeeded in fleeing south to Calhoun Community College just as the second tornado was arriving at Lawson's. The storm passed quickly, and the men turned back toward Tanner. Before reaching the trailer park, though, Walter prevailed on Maxie to turn west at Ingram Road. He needed to make sure everything was in order at home. It would only take a minute.

A mile from his house, at the L&N rail crossing, Walter and Maxie found the road blocked by fallen pine trees. They got out of the truck and strained to clear a path. The trees would not be budged. Within a few minutes a caravan of search-and-rescuers backed up behind them. Walter spotted Buddy Evans, and figured that if the sheriff had made it, being directly in the tornado's sights, the storm might not have been as bad as it looked. Buddy was trying to organize the men to drag the trees to the roadside, but it became clear that without a chainsaw or a tractor, the task would not get done. Everyone was still abuzz with excitement about what they had been through. Bill Dunnavant pulled up in the King Country Rover. "A car was completely carried across this field," he told listeners. "Where it came from we don't know. One traveler on 31 said he saw it go, or completely be carried, over the highway." He climbed up the railroad embankment and sized up the surrounding damage. "It looks like we have another house here demolished," he said. "Let's see—yes, it's a house completely torn down here." He made an on-air plea for a wrecker to come join them and clear the road.

Walter could not wait. He and Maxie backed up to Highway 31, and began to detour to his house on narrow backroads. With electricity gone, the beams of the truck provided the only source of light. Walter was glad to find the roads empty of debris, as though the tornado had confined its worst damage to the highway, leaving the interior of the countryside intact.

As the truck slowed to turn north at Lucas Ferry Road, Walter was met by the sight of a group of people slogging through a field, waving flashlights against the darkness. It took him a moment to realize that the old house that had stood on the corner had been gouged from the earth. He gasped and moved on. A bit further up the road, the truck's headlights picked out the site of a small church. As far as Walter could tell, the only thing left of the church was its pulpit.

He and Maxie finally turned back onto Ingram Road and drove toward his house from the west. Maxie slammed the brakes. More electrical lines lay across the road. Walter retrieved a set of nine-inch cutters from the back of the truck, donned rubber gloves that extended to his elbows, and sliced cleanly through the bundle of wires. He looked off into a field. Something—an odd shape, not quite discernible through the night—caught his attention about thirty yards off the road. He strode into the field and found an overturned car. Five of his neighbors were sitting on the ground beside the vehicle. They had been tossed from the road. It didn't make sense to Walter. This was a big car, and these were big people—two of the men weighed at least 300 pounds each. Still, no one was badly hurt. Indeed, they were all in remarkably good humor.

By the time Annias Green and his family had finished dinner, the rain had picked up again. The storm was now difficult to ignore. Wind streamed through the planks of the floor and the window frames. Doors slammed shut on their own. Thunder raised a thud on the roof. The boys sat quietly in front of the television, entranced by the storm and more afraid, perhaps, than they would let on to each other. Lillian, cleaning up in the kitchen, saw washes of lightning on the walls. She called to her boys to turn off the television, lest lightning enter the house through the rooftop antenna.

There was a sudden spattering sound, as though handfuls of sand were being flung at the house. Annias called the children to come join him at the window, quickly. Together they watched an icy spray of hail blanket the ground. The boys had only seen snow a few times; hail-fall was magical.

The lights in the house blinked, went off, came back on for a moment, then went down for good. Lillian joined Annias and the children in the darkened living room. The family sat side by side on the sofa; Titus, the youngest, was in his father's lap. Everyone followed Annias's lead, and refused to show fear. In Annias's mind, there was, after all, nothing to be afraid of. It was just weather. The family sat quietly, watching the streams of light cast by the storm. There was nothing to do but hold tight. Soon enough, no doubt, power would be restored.

While the men were outside, Marilyn and her mother continued listening to the radio. "We're in an emergency," reiterated WJMW's Mike Davis. "These things can snuff you out in a matter of seconds." The two women stared at each other. "Folks," Mike continued, "if you are taking this thing lightly, let me tell you something. In all my life I have never seen nothing like this. I'm setting here behind this microphone, my teeth chattering, scared half to death. This is an emergency. This is a disaster. You folks take cover! We warn you!"

Marilyn's anxiety was beginning to overcome her skepticism about the warnings. There was no question of retreating to the cellar of her parents' house—it was a dank, unfinished dugout, with dirt walls and a low ceiling, and a perpetual pool of water on the floor. It was not a place to take small children. Marilyn suspected that her parents, left to their own devices, would have headed up the road to a neighbor's storm cellar, but having the grandchildren at home ruled out that option. Dressing both children, carrying them to the car through the driving rain—it all seemed like a great deal of trouble, especially since these warnings always turned out to be a lot of noise about nothing.

Bill Dunnavant came back on the radio. "Goodness gracious alive!" he said. "Would you look at these trees! It is unreal." The report was making Marilyn feel sick. "Buddy Evans is stopping and checking out for possible injuries," Bill went on. "We are headed towards where supposedly five people are entrapped and they're going to use a wrecker to pull them out."

Frank ran into the hallway and halted. Marilyn stared up at him. He seemed to be searching for the right words.

"It's out there," he said.

Marilyn did not say a word. Frank continued. "It's like a huge hill turned upside down—with the peak facing down. It's solid black," he added, "except for lightning—a solid chunk, going as high as you can see."

He guessed it was a mile away, coming towards Isom's Orchards across the road.

Frank's father, too, returned to the house from the porch. He was pale and spoke in a whisper. "What are we going to do?" he asked.

The sight of her father's face terrified Marilyn. She realized: He thinks we are going to die.

As he neared his house, Walter recognized every landmark in the terrain, every dip and bend in the road. This was home. Somehow, though, the scrim of familiarity seemed indelibly, if mysteriously, changed. A tractor lay upended in a ditch. The disfiguring TVA power lines were not to be seen. The last small hill before Walter's house stood strikingly bare.

If the storm had gotten bad, Walter told himself, his wife would have called on her parents, who lived just down the road, and the extended family would have sought safety together. Perhaps they were all in Athens now, crowded together in the car. Perhaps Ruth had taken the kids to the drive-in to buy them a treat.

He and Maxie reached the long driveway to his house. Evidently the rescuers had still not cleared the road from the other direction, for Walter and Maxie were alone. They made their way slowly. Their truck was as wide as the dirt track it hobbled along. Some of the trees that lined their path were bowed, but nothing more than torn branches impeded their progress.

They came out of the corridor of trees onto the broad front yard. Walter saw that his car—a hulking Dodge Rambler wagon—was gone. Okay, he thought. Ruth has driven the family away.

He dismounted the truck and took in the scene. Rivulets of water ran in broken lines on the ground. Dust motes floated in the white columns of the truck's lights. There was no wind, no rain. The air was cool and heavy. All vegetation—weeds, grass, flowers, shrubs, trees—had been cleared away. The ground was pitted, as though it had been scraped clean by a backhoe.

It was difficult for Walter to believe he had returned to the right place. He could not square the ruins he was looking at with the home he had left only a few hours earlier. Home: he had built it from nothing, laid its bricks, poured concrete for its porch, dug a well out back for its water, cleared its lot of tree stumps and rocks, put up a barn and outbuildings, installed swings for his children, turned the ground in the adjoining fields. Now, none of it was recognizable. The fields lay stripped of topsoil. And his family was nowhere to be seen.

He stepped into the emptiness. He kicked the ground and discovered the edge of the foundation on which his house had risen. Here and there stood oblong mounds of brick and stone, like strange cairns. Remarkably few traces of the house remained. The floor was gone, and the roof, and the walls and the appliances and the furniture.

Walter turned away from it. He would attend to property matters later. For now he needed to get back to his truck, locate his family, look after them. He saw headlights in the distance. Rescuers must have cleared the railroad embankment. They were coming toward him. He stood frozen.

Then, from off to one side, Walter heard a weak cry—like a bird's, broken, high-pitched, feeble. The cry repeated, and repeated again. Walter walked toward it. Maxie walked toward Walter. The cry repeated. It was coming from a pile of rubble.

Some things happen too quickly for the mind to process. Some things are too embedded in pain to be remembered.

You are at home. It is a normal enough night. You are a cautious person, but home is where your guard is down.

An intruder bursts in on you. He makes a beeline for you, presses a weapon to you, fires.

When do you escape? In the second or two it takes the intruder to reach you? When do you fight back? What does it mean to "fight back"?

What do you recall? The kicking-down of the door? The gleam of light on the weapon's shaft? The shriek your wife, beside you, made? The sound of the weapon being discharged? The burn in your throat?

Annias and his family sat in place. Maybe Annias heard a window cracking. Maybe his eldest son saw the television screen shatter. The roof was no longer there. Maybe Lillian craned her neck, looked up into the wind, and mouthed her husband's name.

He wouldn't have been able to hear her, let alone help her. As it was, he had no luck keeping his grip on the boy sitting in his lap. There was an explosion—at least, it felt like one. The boy was gone. Annias, too, was on his way out. The rest of them followed. The whole family. At the same moment, but separately, and with no assurance of a reunion.

No time to think about struggling. No time to say good-bye.

There are so many things, Annias often reminded parishioners, over which you have no power, none at all.

At ten minutes before eight, the tornado crossed Highway 72 after destroying Isom's Orchards. It zoned in on the Old Orr House, where it put on a skillful demonstration, albeit unwitnessed, of the mechanics of demolition.

It started with a river of wind flowing over the roof. The shingles, replaced just a month earlier, would have been the first pieces of the structure to begin peeling away, like flecks of old paint, starting at the front corner of the roof, where the overhanging gable provided the wind a handy purchase. This was merely a preparatory gesture, though, a loosening of the outer layer of skin. Wind squeezed beneath and between the shingles, unfastening their light tackings with ease. The shingles spun away into the last light of dusk.

The house's many windows—ten each in front and out back, and six on each side—were quickly punched out. The masonite siding—another recent addition, chosen for its benefit of energy efficiency—was stripped away. Lightweight, and with a large surface area for the wind to grab hold of, the siding could expect to travel far before being dropped back to the ground.

Its exterior removed, the bones of the Old Orr House were now ready for dismantling. The overhanging roof, which had for so long shaded those on the porch below, created a nook in which the tornado's airflow could get momentarily trapped. With nowhere to go, the wind pushed up, lifting the roof from its southwest corner. At the same time, the decking to which the shingles had been nailed was being shorn from the rafters. This decking—one-by-eight inch slabs of rough-cut oak—was tightly secured, but could hardly resist the tornado's winds, which were tugging at it from above, and which, having entered the house, were also pushing from below. The roof lifted, got held aloft for a moment in the wind, then disintegrated.

Once the roof was gone, the unbuilding could go forward efficiently.

On the house's second floor, its outer walls, unsupported by their connection with the roof, could not stand much longer. The wall that was in the wind's direct path—the "windward" wall—collapsed inward. (This is why, despite conventional wisdom, it would have been a bad idea to take refuge in the southwest, or windward, corner of the house's basement.) The side walls, pulled by the wind flowing around the house, flamed outward, as did the furthest, leeward wall. There was nothing as romantic as an explosion provoked by the difference in air pressure between the inside and the outside of the house, as tornado enthusiasts might have liked to imagine. The reality was more brutal: a blunt expression of the sledgelike power of air moving unmeasurably fast, at speeds that would be estimated at 250 miles per hour. The second floor of the house was gone. The first-floor ceiling had suddenly, in effect, become the roof, and as such it too was swiftly shucked from its bindings with the remaining frame. Then the ground floor repeated the narrative of collapse, caving in on one end and bursting away on the other three sides. However fierce the winds produced by the tornado, the funnel itself moved along at a more stately pace. It was so broad that it could hover over the site long enough to scoop the Old Orr House's riven pieces, and all its carefully chosen and lovingly maintained contents, into its path and sweep them away. The entire process may have lasted as much as thirty seconds.

Walter fell to his knees and began throwing rubble from the pile. There was brick, wood, twisted metal, jagged triangles of glass, icicle-like glass spears and no end of glassy pebbles. There were heavy blocks of masonry that Walter recognized as remnants of the chimney. He heaved them to the side. His hands began to bleed. He was still hearing cries from the pile. He dug through torn and balled-up fabric, shreds of carpet and upholstery, crumbling plaster.

He got closer to the cries and then, after dislodging a great spill of debris, he let out a cry himself. Nancy, his three-year-old daughter, was down there. He could see her eyes looking up at him. He furiously cleared the space around her. He bent over and used his back as a lever to raise the debris that was on top of her. Then he put his hands under her arms and pulled her free.

Nancy was insensible. She wailed. She could not be quieted. She was smeared with filth and her face and arms and legs were scored with cuts. When she coughed, dirt was ejected from her nose. She clung to Walter with her small fists. He pulled her away and passed her to Maxie so he could continue digging. He heard her shrieks all the while.

Then there was another sound. Grace, the seven-year-old, was calling for her father. It turned out she was not far from the spot where Walter had uncovered Nancy. Grace, however, proved more difficult to extract. She lay pinned from the chest down beneath layers of collapsed roof. Walter did not turn to take notice of the other rescuers who were now beside him, and who formed a chain to clear the mound of debris from Grace's body. When they finally dug her out, she was limp and contorted. She remained conscious, though. She sobbed to Walter, "Daddy, I was trying to help them, but I couldn't move my legs." She was carried to the back of a pickup truck and was driven away.

Frank called for his family to take cover. Marilyn opened a closet door. The closet was packed with a laundry bin and bags of household junk. Old clothes dangled from hangers. She wedged herself in. "What is going on here?" she thought, incredulous.

Marilyn's baby, Mark, was asleep in her arms. Her mother joined her in the closet, holding two-year-old Jason. Marilyn shouted for the men to come back from the porch. They couldn't seem to get enough of looking at the storm.

Rain was pelting the roof. Interestingly, the sound seemed to keep Jason calm and to keep Mark from waking.

Then the three men rushed into the corridor. They threw sofa cushions into the closet. Frank and his father hunched on the floor. Vergil knelt in front of Marilyn, and wrapped his arms around her. They were head to head, the baby pressed between their chests.

The rain stopped. There was silence. For a moment, Marilyn considered that the storm had passed. The respite didn't last long. The silence seemed to draw a noise to it, and the noise came forward with a sudden thrust, an uproar, and kept coming. It was this noise that most upset Marilyn. She began to scream. Her screams were more abject than those that began issuing from her infant. "Oh, God, please help us." The noise came still closer, at such an overwhelming pitch, so inchoate, that soon Marilyn could no longer hear herself.

* * *

Don Lauderdale rose from the floor of First Baptist Church of Tanner and brushed plaster and glass from his clothing. He had recently taken a refresher course in first aid, and when the shrill of the storm quieted, and the only sound he heard was the bawling of those around him, he went to see if anyone was hurt. It was dark in the church. He came across a man lying in the corner under a scattering of rubble, and began digging him out. The man, badly cut, started having a seizure. Don believed he was going into shock, and tried to cover the man with his jacket and to elevate his feet. Then the man began choking. Don could tell he was swallowing his tongue. He pried open the man's jaw and dug into his throat until he got hold of the tongue and pulled it out. He lifted the man over his shoulder and headed for the door, then found the front entrance of the church had collapsed. He turned and waded through the wreckage until he found an opening in the wall. He carried the man through.

The van in which Don had arrived was nowhere to be seen. He had no doubt that it had been carried off by the wind. He turned and saw a man sitting placidly behind the wheel of a brown station wagon, as though he were waiting for Don to arrive. Don approached the wagon and laid the injured man in back, then directed the driver, a stranger to Limestone County, to the hospital in Athens. As they made their way, Don stared fixedly at the driver.

"Where did this man come from?" Don wondered. "How could he have driven through the storm?" The answer struck him at once. "God puts his angels around us. Oh, I'm not saying the man wasn't human. But he came to us in our need. A person can understand these things once he accepts the Lord as Savior, and believes there is a Heaven and a Hell."

F5

Walter was reeling. He was desperate to find the rest of his family. His property had become a small mob scene, crowded with indistinct faces, its waste lit by the random glare of headlights. There was the sound of a chainsaw's grinding and of the sputtering of a front loader's engine. A group of men surrounded Walter, put their arms around him and tried to draw him away from the work that was being undertaken. He would comply with the strangers, then suddenly let out a shout and rush back toward the destruction.

Walter's nephew, Jerry, had a vague sense of the clamor above and around him. He lay in the press of utter darkness with his face wedged into the ground. He could barely issue a sound. His forearm seemed to be jammed into someone's throat. There was no hope of moving it. It stung, as if a piece of glass had pierced it. Water flowed across the ground into his mouth and nose. He struggled for breath. He thought he was drowning. He began to hyperventilate. He could hear voices on the other side of the rubble—he knew his uncle Walter had to be there, had to be looking for him—but he couldn't fathom why the search was taking so long. He could not stay awake.

Maxie returned Nancy to Walter's arms. Walter paced through the mud clutching her. For a time her screaming blocked out all other noise.

Then Walter heard a different scream. This time it was a rescuer. Walter rushed toward him. Someone tried to hold him back. He pressed forward. He stared down at the rubble through a web of flashlight beams.

It was hard to make out what he was seeing. Ruth was there. Sandra was there. Little Walter was there. They lay together. The chimney had caved in on them.

Walter no longer had control of himself. Maxie pulled him toward the utility truck and set him in the passenger's seat. They drove off toward Athens. Nancy squirmed in Walter's lap. Behind them, the digging went on.

Frank heard the pinging of shattering glass. Clouds of dust and dirt were swirling through the house, as though it were in flames. Then the household of objects—papers, dishes, photos, the innocuous little artifacts that lined mantles and shelves and night tables—were uprooted. The roof unfastened as swiftly and smoothly as the lid of a can. "Well," Frank's mother offered, "we are going to be all right. It's just going to get the roof."

The floor began twisting beneath Frank. It seemed as though it lifted in a single piece. He lost his balance and was upended. Then he felt himself beginning to whirl. He was aloft. He took a hard blow to the back of his head. He lost consciousness.

In the closet, Marilyn was staring into her husband's eyes. As the house began to come apart, his arms were torn from hers. He was gone. Then Marilyn, too, went airborne.

It was strange to be Marilyn. While the rest of her family, one and all, had managed to leave consciousness behind, she alone remained awake and alert, as though she were assigned the task of chronicling the family's journey. Indeed, her awareness seemed heightened and disconcertingly precise. She saw her mother's meat locker barreling past. Beneath her, she saw her car, an orange Volkswagen Beetle, tumbling end over end like a toy. She saw the last faint crack of daylight closing on the horizon. The anxiety that had preceded the tornado's impact was gone. She was calm. Flying was not a problem. The blaring noise with which the tornado had announced its arrival had been absorbed in a hush. It was not, of

April 3, 1974, approximately 4:30 PM Eastern time. A tornado descends and approaches Xenia, Ohio.

One hour later. Another tornado. This one is seen crossing the Ohio River towards Cincinnati.

Taking cover as Second Tanner approaches Lawson's Trailer Park,
approximately 7:40 Central time.

"Best Dressed": Donnie Powers,
Ardmore High School Yearbook, 1974.

Felica Golden, 1974.

Frank Orr and his nephew, Jason McBay, who was born while Frank was in Vietnam. 1972.

Marilyn Orr and her future husband, Vergil McBay, c. 1969. In the background is the house in which the extended Orr family was staying on April 3, 1974.

Jason McBay, 2, and Mark McBay, 6 days old, at their grandparents' house. Wednesday morning, April 3, 1974.

Frank Orr's 1974 Chevrolet El Camino.

The Green Family, c. 1973. Lillian, Annias, and children Ananias, Jr. ("Rabbit"), Titus, and Amos.

Best Friends: Rabbit and Amos Green at play.

"Mister Buddy": Sheriff Buddy Evans, far right, and the Limestone County Sheriff's Department, mid-to-late 1960s.

The sheriff of Limestone.

Tetsuya Theodore Fujita, "Mr. Tornado," featured in *People*, 1977.

Near Tanner Crossroads.

Lawson's Trailer Park.

Seen from above:
Limestone County, Alabama.

The McGlocklin family,
c. 1973. Walter, Ruth,
and children Grace,
Nancy, Walter, Jr.
and Sandra.

The McGlocklin house.

Walter McGlocklin's Dodge
Rambler wagon.

Seventh-most admired man: George Wallace is handed a list of the dead.
Limestone County, April 5, 1974.

Twenty-seven per cent approval: Nixon in Xenia, April 9, 1974.

course, as though Marilyn did not recognize the gravity of her situation. She began to ponder what might happen when she returned, as she must, to the ground. She was suddenly overwhelmed with sadness. "The people I love most in the world are dying," she thought.

In the bewildering unelectrified night that settled on Limestone as its second tornado of the hour passed through, the bodies of Annias and his family, lying in the ravaged peach orchard just below Highway 72, would barely have entered the view of passersby, who would have had to strain to see the tooth of a wall—belonging, formerly, to a hall closet—that was all that was left of the little rented house.

Annias lay in the dark earth wondering when help would arrive. He could not move. He could not hear a sound from any member of his family. He did not know where they were. He did not know how he would ever reach them.

Shortly after leaving home with his wife and fourteen-year-old son, Annias's landlord, Joe Isom, had been stopped by an Athens policeman and warned of further storms. He had parked his truck beneath an overpass on Highway 31 and waited until the skies calmed down, then returned to the orchard uneasily. Along the way, he stopped in on his parents. Their house had been pushed from its foundation, and was half dangling above the ground, like a boat out of water. They were terrified but unhurt.

Joe went on, driving to the peach orchard first. As soon as he arrived, he could see that his crop was lost. As he walked toward the field of snapped and uprooted peach trees, a neighbor appeared and warned Joe that his house, which he had abandoned a half-hour earlier, was in bad shape. That wasn't the end of it, though. Joe stared through the darkness of the orchard toward his tenant's house. There was nothing to be seen.

Marilyn fell back to earth. It was a gentle landing, as though she had been set down, rather than dropped. Debris continued to fall around her. She felt she must have traveled a great distance. She could see a highway far off, lit by passing cars. The air was cold. She fixed her gaze on a large oak tree. It was stripped of leaves and its trunk was bare. Only when she tilted her head did it occur to Marilyn that the tree was not standing upright, but lay stretched across the ground. She could not get her bearings. She gathered that the highway she spotted must be Nick Davis Road, four miles from her parents' house, but the idea of it made no sense to her. "I'm trying to recognize the landscape," she thought, "and there is no landscape."

She wondered where her children were.

She tried to move but winced and realized she was trapped. She sized herself up. One leg was buried in the ground. The other was bent crookedly upwards. Behind her, something hard and sharp was braced against her spine. It began to rain softly. She was convinced that she and her family would not be found until morning.

Then she heard a howl. She knew right away it came from Jason. At least that meant he was alive. She looked around for him and caught sight of her father limping over wreckage in a daze. Soon another voice cried out. It was her mother. She was moaning. She called out that she had Jason—she had held onto him by his clothes—but that they were buried. Marilyn's father had just tripped over them. She was in pain.

Marilyn felt a presence behind her. She craned her neck and saw her baby boy, Mark, covered in dirt. She could barely reach him.

F 5

Still, she twisted one arm free, strained backwards, and managed to pull him toward her. His orifices were packed with mud. She pushed her fingers into his mouth and dug out the mud in bits. He let out a cry. Then, suddenly, he stopped crying.

In the pulses of lightning, Marilyn made out Frank's shape. He was hovering over Vergil's chest, pressing his mouth to Vergil's. Finally, Vergil looked as though he were coughing up dirt. "Oh, God," Marilyn pleaded, "let me have him back."

Frank stood up in the rain and shouted that he was going in search of help. He set off for the road. It was a half mile away across a field littered with debris. He struggled to remain conscious. When he reached the road a man approached him. Frank recognized M. Y. Dauthit (the same man for whom Annias Green's family had sharecropped). Frank pointed toward the destruction. "Help my family," he said. Dauthit grabbed Frank and pushed him toward a car. He told the driver of the car, "Take this boy to the hospital. He's bleeding to death."

Joe Isom ventured further into the peach orchard followed by his wife, Jo Ann, who was a licensed practical nurse at Athens–Limestone County Hospital. It didn't take long before she spotted two of Annias's children, Titus and Rabbit, unsteady, but sitting up in the mud. It was too dark to see the extent of their injuries, but both boys appeared to be in trouble. When Jo Ann lifted Titus's head, his hair moved. It was as if he had been scalped. Rabbit had a deep gash in his forehead, and could not respond to Jo Ann's questions. Amos lay nearby, altogether inert.

Lillian was a bit further out in the field, flat on her back. When Jo Ann got to her, Lillian's chest was heaving and her breath was irregular. She was grunting. Her clothes were plastered to her and seemed to be choking her.

"Do you know who I am?" Jo Ann asked.

Lillian nodded. Jo Ann asked whether anyone had been in the house aside from her family.

Lillian struggled to reply. "No," she whispered. "Only us." Then she managed to mouth to Jo Ann, "My babies?"

Annias could hear activity in the distance. He called out and got no response. At one point he thought he saw someone lean over him, then walk away. He believed he had been left for dead.

Perhaps an hour after his family was taken to the hospital, Annias was located by rescuers. He had been stripped naked by the storm. When rescuers lifted him he cried out in pain. It took several people to carry him to Highway 72. The road was clogged with traffic and debris. An overturned piece of farm equipment blocked two lanes. There were no ambulances to be seen. Finally the Isoms, whose own house had been dragged sixty feet to the edge of Highway 72 before disintegrating, flagged down a passing hearse. It was from People's, one of Limestone County's two black funeral homes. Jo Ann climbed in beside Annias. She would ride with him to the hospital and then go to work. Annias asked weakly about his wife and children. Jo Ann told him they had been taken to the hospital. She could offer little more.

In the community of East Limestone, four miles northeast of the cluster of destruction that included the homes of Frank Orr, Don Lauderdale, and Annias Green, a sixty-five-year-old widow named Lorene Ricketts shared a well-kept frame house with her thirty-nine-year-old daughter, Mary Frances. Mary Frances worked as a cashier at Winn Dixie supermarket in Athens. Wednesday, her day off, was devoted to running errands with her mother. The women had stopped by the beauty parlor and done their grocery shopping

F5

and finished their rounds in Athens by visiting an elderly relative in a nursing home.

As they had left the nursing home late in the afternoon, an attendant remarked, "It sure is windy. I believe it's gonna come up a storm."

Back home, Mary Frances had turned on the television and watched H. D. Bagley's ominous broadcast. Sure enough, it wasn't long before the electricity in the house was knocked out. Mary Frances turned on a battery-powered radio, and heard warnings of a second tornado headed toward them.

The phone rang. It was Lorene's daughter-in-law, urging her and Mary Frances to join her in a neighbor's basement a few miles away. Lorene didn't want to go out. She was tired. She had lived long enough to know that the surest thing one could predict about a storm was that it was bound to pass. Besides, she said, "The radio is saying that nobody should get on the road."

Lorene then looked out her kitchen window and saw a storm cloud—"the most awful color you've ever seen, just black, blue, red, orange, a little of everything"—rolling toward the house. She and Mary Frances crawled beneath Lorene's antique cherry bed. They did not stay in place long. They heard a popping sound, as though the nails that held the house together were being pulled from their nestings.

Then they flew. Mary Frances was aware that she was spinning. "Lord, have mercy," she thought, "will I ever hit the ground?" She did, coming to rest the distance of a football field from her starting point. Her mother, on the other hand, plotted a different course, and landed 300 yards away, down a wooded ravine.

When the storm passed, relatives sped over to check on the women. Their cars, parked along the side of the road, signaled other cars to stop, and soon the field was full of helpers and spectators,

185

catching brief glimpses of each other through the lightning. Mary Frances was found by her brother, James. "I'm hurt bad," she said. One side of her body had been crushed, and part of her left ear had been cut off. "Go find Mother," she urged.

James could hear his mother's moans, and used the sound to navigate through the field. She was in agony. Her right leg had been snapped at the thigh and was turned towards her head. The bone came through the skin. She was losing blood. Her clothes were twisted around her waist, and she was covered with pellet-sized wounds. A half dozen men joined James. One removed his shirt to use as a sling to carry Lorene to the road. It was a long way to go, uphill, through foot-deep mud. Sometimes one of the men slipped, or stumbled over debris. Lorene was taken by car to Athens Hospital, where she was put in a hearse—as in Annias Green's case, it was the only available vehicle—and moved thirty miles to Huntsville Hospital. Beside her in the hearse lay a child who had been found at Isom's Orchards with a mortifying head wound.

Searchers continued to scour the nearby fields for more victims. One of them came across a body. It was a young man. His skull seemed to have been split, and in the words of one who saw him, "his brains were coming out the back of his head." He was, at the very least, unconscious. He was probably dead. He was big, and it took a concerted effort to move him from the field. No one knew who he was. Perhaps he had something to do with the crushed car by the side of the road.

Disaster:
An Interlude

Destruction is an event; death is a fact; disaster is a state of mind. Disaster strikes and the world continues. It only feels like the end. Disaster is not global—not yet, at least. It is, however, public. It requires broad participation; it requires an audience.

Disaster lends itself to the hyperbole of uniqueness, to the claim that its scale, its effects, and the misery it produces defy precedent; but it is never new. The word has classical origins. "Dis," a Latin prefix, indicates brokenness; "astron," in ancient Greek, points to the stars. To undergo a disaster, then, is to be separated from a guiding star; or, alternatively, to waken in a shattered cosmos; or, perhaps, to fall under the spell of a malign influence. It is difficult to imagine a society, however primitive, without a vocabulary for disaster and an inclination to use tales of disaster to ritualize its fears of downfall.

Disaster is in us. Myth, history, and the daily news, alike, are predisposed to it. One says: "We live in disastrous times." It may be so. But it would be challenging, too, to find a moment inhabited by human beings that was not touched by disaster. Disaster is reality, intensified.

Take, for instance, the first months of 1974. On February 1, a fire breaks out in an office building in São Paulo, Brazil, killing 189 people, including fifty who choose to escape the flames by leaping from windows. Two weeks later, fifty Egyptians are trampled at a soccer stadium. Then, on February 22, 157 lives are lost when a tugboat capsizes off the coast of South Korea.

Fire, earth, water: disaster's home turf.

Air, too: On March 3, a DC-10 crashes into a forest outside Paris, killing 346. It is, to date, the largest death toll in aviation history. But flying, in 1974, remains an accident-prone activity. In mid-March, a pair of smaller crashes, closer to home, in the mountains of California, occur on consecutive days: On the first, a plane transporting thirty-five skiers slams into a hillside; on the next, a charter with thirty-six passengers, mostly members of the cast and crew of the ABC show *Primal Man*, fails on takeoff.

Before 1974 is done, other, more lavish disasters will come: In Honduras, Hurricane Fifi, triggering landslides and flash floods, will kill at least 10,000 people; in Pakistan, a December earthquake will take some 5,000 lives; and, in ever-embattled Bangladesh and India, seasonal flooding will carry away thousands more.

No use looking ahead, though. April has barely begun.

A venerable strain of magical thinking sees natural disaster as an expression of—or retribution for—human failings. It is not simply a powerful low-pressure system that brings on the biblical Flood. Perhaps the modern mind is too sophisticated to attribute the wrath of nature to any but natural causes. But guilt by association has a powerful irrational appeal. Events related by nothing more substantial than coincidence are nonetheless related. Synchrony is the logic of disaster. Timing is everything.

It is April 3, 1974. An obscure body called the Congressional Joint Commission on Internal Revenue Taxation issues the results of its investigation of President Nixon's tax records. Nixon, it is disclosed, underpaid personal income taxes to the tune of $432,787 during the years 1969–1972. The details of the report suggest that the president—whatever else his vices and virtues—suffers from something as humiliatingly banal as mere greed. In 1970, when his income was $262,943, Nixon laid out a total of $793 in federal tax; the following year, he paid $878. To reduce his tax burden, Nixon claimed such deductions as the cost ($5,391.43) of a masked ball thrown for his daughter, Tricia; repairs to an ice machine ($432.84); the cleaning of a bathroom rug ($22.50).

The tax scandal cannot come at a worse time for Nixon. His Watergate-related troubles are spiraling out of control. On April 3, Ed Reinecke, lieutenant governor of California, is indicted by the Watergate grand jury for lying to a Senate inquiry; in a separate courtroom, the prosecution rests its case in the trial of former Attorney General John Mitchell and former Commerce Secretary Maurice Stans on charges of conspiracy, obstruction of justice, and perjury. It is only a matter of time until the storm reaches the president himself. In this context, the news of Nixon's tax irregularities, unrelated to Watergate, comes as a particularly debilitating blow. Unlike murky questions of political conspiracy, the burden of paying income tax is easy enough to understand. Even Nixon's supporters begin to abandon him. Robert Michel, a Republican congressman from Illinois, remarks, "He gambled and lost, and now he has to pay the piper." Nixon, according to his aides, will make good on his tax bill, though the expense will leave him "almost totally wiped out."

At the heart of disaster is the reversal of fortune, which must be sudden and comprehensive, though not total. Witnesses must remain standing, if for no other reason than to pass on the story. The moments prior to disaster slip into the inaccessible past. The changes it wrings are accompanied by the terrible, clarifying knowledge that its seeds have been drifting in the everyday air all along.

It is April 3, 1974. A package arrives at a San Francisco radio station. It bears an audiotape and a Polaroid color photograph of Patty Hearst, who has by now spent two months in captivity, blindfolded and locked in a dark closet, according to previous communications. The photograph shows Hearst posed in front of a banner painted with a looping, many-tendrilled emblem: the "seven-headed cobra" by which the Symbionese Liberation Army identifies itself. Hearst wears an expression that can be taken for either determination or vacancy. Her knees are bent and her legs parted. She points a submachine gun at some imaginary target off-camera.

When the news is announced, the nation is stunned. "Until her abduction," writes *Newsweek*, "she seemed an almost ordinary child of the '70s—an open, easygoing California girl given to jeans and sandals, Paul Simon records and touch-football games."

That view of Hearst is now blown apart. To the public, Hearst is no longer a victim, but something altogether more compelling. The disguise of the girl-next-door no longer fits. A secret interior violence has been exposed. The audio tape, on which Hearst's voice sounds flat, calm, and a touch irritated, is even more disturbing than the photograph. She claims to have undergone a conversion. "I have changed—grown," she announces on the tape, addressing her fiancé, Steven Weed. "I've become conscious and can never go back to the life we led before." Further, she says that she prefers to remain with her "comrades" in the SLA, fighting "for my freedom and the freedom of all oppressed people." She denounces her mother for her ruling class sensibilities and calls her father "a corporate liar" who would "kill me if necessary." She even decides to trade in her family's estimable name for that of a revolutionary role model, a lover of Che Guevara's named Tania. "Patty Hearst" is no more.

"I don't believe it," Hearst's father tells reporters. Her mother adds, "Only Patty herself in person can convince me that the terrible and weary words she uttered came from her heart." A friend observes, "It simply isn't her. Patty saw her future in a home with Steve. He'd be a professor and she'd be a mommy—and they'd nestle quietly together in the exurbs of academe."

Reversal of fortune. Synchrony. A lost star.

Even the most carefully contrived ceremonies of decorum are subject to disruptive forces. Call it the spirit of the day.

The 1973 Academy Awards show runs late into the evening of April 2, 1974. It is a tame, dull affair, straining to avoid any repetition of what *Time* calls the "spectacular flame-out" of last year's event, when Marlon Brando, winning as Best Actor for *The Godfather*, sent to the podium a surrogate named Sacheen Littlefeather, draped in a beaded doeskin dress and wearing long ponytails, to refuse the Oscar on his behalf, in protest of the indignity done to Native Americans.

Once again, though, the evening achieves memorability only when its etiquette is breached. It comes at the tail end of NBC's live broadcast. As David Niven introduces Elizabeth Taylor to deliver the award for Best Picture, a fit and slender 33-year-old advertising agent named Robert Opal scurries across the stage of the Dorothy Chandler Pavilion, flashing a peace sign with two fingers, and sporting not a shred of clothing.

Robert Opal, the streaker: He is what people are bantering about, in offices and coffee shops across America, on the morning of April 3.

The fad will quickly flame out, but while it lasts, streaking is, perhaps incongruously, among the most talked-about topics of 1974 (it even spawns a chart-topping single, "The Streak"). It is a peculiarly revealing lens through which to take in the moment. The sensation has spread throughout the country after a few isolated instances in winter. College students, in particular, revel in it. Five hundred and thirty-three University of Maryland coeds organize themselves into a naked chain-dance along the side of U.S. Highway 1; dozens of buttoned-down cadets at the U.S. Military Academy, in West Point, shed their uniforms and go on parade; students at the University of Pennsylvania organize a "Streak for Impeachment." By March, streaking has moved beyond the ivory tower. A passenger on a transatlantic Pan Am flight sprints up and down the aisle in the buff, a Wall Street bond trader drops his business attire in the financial district, and a meeting of the Michigan House of Representatives is interrupted by a visitor clad only in boots and a ski mask.

Streaking, remarks *Time*, is "the sort of totally absurd phenomenon the nation needed after a winter of lousy news." Social commentators are enlisted to parse the behavior. Yale psychiatrist Robert J. Lifton sees streaking as "a challenge to authority and a mockery of authority." Marshall McLuhan describes it as "a form of assault," but adds, "It's an art form, of course. All entertainment has elements of malice and power in it."

It is no disaster, streaking. But in its lighthearted way, it too is a spectacle of reversal. It asks to be liberated from stale habits of being. It posits a triumphant, if brief, return to the rule of nature and of pure sensation. At Syracuse University, eighteen-year-old Rob Sedwin, wearing only sneakers and a watch, takes a run for it, then reflects, "Today was a good day to let yourself go. You feel like a flower taking off its winter clothes."

Meanwhile, the Oscar for Best Picture goes to *The Sting*, a whimsical film of the sort often described as a "caper," set in a sepia-toned version of 1936, and featuring Robert Redford and Paul Newman as a pair of none-too-malicious con men. Ah, the movie would have us recall, times were simpler then. It is not the year's only exercise in nostalgia to be received with favor by the Hollywood establishment. *Paper Moon*, another comedy of the Depression, makes ten-year-old Tatum O'Neal the youngest Oscar winner in history, and *American Graffiti*, which manages to render 1962 in the burnished hues of a long-lost world, wins multiple nominations. In turbulent times, nostalgia is a vacation from the present moment, a form of fond forgetfulness.

Of course, no one is eager to be reminded that the preeminent youth drama of the previous decade had, until very recently, been screened not in drive-in theaters but on the nation's television sets, nightly, from real locations in Southeast Asia.

By 1974, no Hollywood film has yet dared to tackle the subject of Vietnam head-on. That doesn't mean that representations of epic devastation and suffering have failed to pervade popular culture—only that such anxious matters have been deflected onto the canvas of the year's defining genre, the disaster film. Hollywood's trend toward sumptuous disaster has been in the offing for a while. *Airport*, set in tumultuous high altitudes, was a hit in 1970; *The Poseidon Adventure*, about a tidal-wave-borne calamity at sea, earned more than $140 million since its 1972 release. Now, however, disaster is coming into its own. "In Los Angeles," *Time* reports, previewing 1974's attractions, "the Big Quake finally happens, sundering the foundations of the giant Hollywood reservoir" (*Earthquake*). "In San Francisco, the world's tallest building, a 136-story glass tower, explodes in flames" (*The Towering Inferno*). "Vast armies of ants relentlessly eat their way across the great southwest desert" (*Phase IV*). "Billions of giant bees swarm malevolently through the steel canyons of New York City" (*The Swarm*). "And somewhere underground the survivors of nuclear warfare find their cavernous retreat invaded by hordes of vampire bats" (*Chosen Survivors*).

In Hollywood's disaster script, many anonymous people must die, and a few hardy souls must be spared. Collective punishment and mass suffering are the restorative norm, as strands of good and evil are untangled and returned to their designated domains. As far as questions of personal or political liability are concerned—that would disturb the show. Disaster in 1974 is a creaky confection, bloated with barely credible special effects, and cast with minor celebrities and aging stars who plod through their roles in mannequinlike postures. Some are marked for heroic sacrifice, others for cowardly or heroic survival; no need to sweat the details. "You don't want to have to spend too much time explaining personality in a disaster movie," remarks one studio executive. Indeed, any character in a disaster movie who risks affinity to an actual human being would imperil the pleasures of the genre, which are predicated on bearing witness to turmoil from a protective distance, and resting assured that death is for other people, on the other side of the screen.

It is 1974. Don't look away. Evel Knievel, thirty-four years old, of Butte, Montana, plans to steer a rocket-powered vehicle across a mile-wide canyon in Idaho. Viewers get to pay—Knievel hopes to sell $11 million worth of tickets—for the odds-on prospect of watching a man die. As entertainment, it is an ambitious step up from Knievel's workaday stunt of launching himself on a Harley-Davidson motorcycle over cars, buses, and, on one occasion, a pair of contestants in a Las Vegas boxing ring. "I'm the comic-book hero in real life," he tells columnist Pete Axthelm. "In a phony world, I stand for something simple and direct. I love life, but I know that you have to take chances to make it worth living." Axthelm describes Knievel as "the strangest folk hero that Americans have ever adopted," and points out that the proposed stunt in Idaho is "nothing more than a stark contest between life and death." The contest is also one that will prove deflatingly anticlimactic, as Knievel accidentally discharges from the vehicle during takeoff, disappointing 1.5 million viewers on closed-circuit television. "It is chilling," Axthelm writes, "to wonder whether this man has conceived the ultimate modern 'sport.'"

Modern or not, a brush with death is good theater.

On the other side of the country, a young Frenchman, Philippe Petit, is preparing his own test of the limits of survivability: surreptitiously stringing a cable between the towers of the newly opened World Trade Center, and traversing the 131-foot gap between the buildings, at a height of 1,350 feet. "You must struggle against the elements to learn that staying on the wire is nothing," Petit, a poet of daredevilry, writes. "Whoever does not want to struggle against failure, against danger, whoever is not prepared to give everything to feel that he is alive, does not need to be a high-wire walker." The skyscrapers, widely derided by architects and urban planners, remain mostly untenanted as New York City—the quintessential site of the decade's social and economic malaise—hovers on the verge of bankruptcy. "Anything that is giant and man-made strikes me in an awesome way and calls me," Petit explains. The canyon between the two towers is a wind tunnel; the buildings have been engineered to withstand gusts of up to 140 miles per hour. Petit is determined to walk through that wind. "I who hope to give the greatest gift a high-wire walker can give," he writes. "To die on my wire." (Early on the morning of August 7, Petit would accomplish the feat, crossing back and forth between the towers eight times. Charles Daniels, a Port Authority police officer who is sent to the roof of one of the towers to apprehend Petit, says, "Everybody was spellbound in the watching of it.")

Nineteen seventy-four in America, half in love with death. The darkest theological questions become the stuff of mass consumption. "What is it like to die?" asks Raymond Moody, who is nearing completion of a study of "near-death experiences," to be published the following year as a spectacular bestseller called *Life After Life*. Moody, a psychiatrist, has compiled testimony from a rare category of patients: those who have ventured across the boundary of life—being declared dead before resuscitation, or coming close to death in the course of injury or illness—while managing to return to provide a report on their experiences. The similarities among such accounts are remarkable, Moody finds. The dying person tends to be overcome with serenity and to win release from pain. The moment of death often unfolds in consoling silence, though reports of loud noise— buzzing or ringing—are not uncommon. "People have the sensation of being pulled very rapidly through a dark space of some kind," Moody notes. "I have heard this space described as a cave, a well, a trough, an enclosure, a tunnel, a funnel, a vacuum, a void, a sewer, a valley, and a cylinder."

Entering this funnel, the dying person "may find himself looking upon his own physical body from a point outside of it, as though he were a 'spectator.'" Time slows down. Memory is heightened. Often a dying person will find himself accompanied by loved ones. Occasionally he suffers pangs of sadness, contemplating those he is leaving behind, and his unfinished business in life.

"What is perhaps the most incredible common element in the accounts I have studied," Moody writes, "is the encounter with a very bright light."

It is a soothing thought, the verifiable afterlife. It comes at the right moment. Vietnam has been an unredeemed anguish. Then there have been the entwined afflictions of the Cold War, and the generation gap, and the energy crisis, and the blight of American cities, and the slow downfall of a president. But there are better times to come. There is a very bright light shining on the end of days.

Triage

A t one minute before eight, Spencer Black's secretary called WJMW from Civil Defense and was immediately put on the air. "Well, right now we're in an 'all clear,'" she offered. "But this is temporary."

"All right," said Mike Davis, in the studio, sounding exhausted. "Let me tell you what we're going to do. We're going to hear this little tune from Johnny Carver."

Hey, pass me by, if you're only passing through.

Spencer's voice suddenly came blurting over the radio. He was seething. So many people had taken to the roads to gawk at the damage, he said, that rescue crews were being hampered in their efforts to reach victims. "We want to tell the people in the county here that hasn't been affected by this storm, that's not in any danger or that has people in the county, to please for godsakes to stay at home! We've got more people on the road than we can do anything with, we've got people that's injured, we can't get enough people in to do anything. We've got people hurt everywhere!" He rattled off a half-dozen sites of destruction in the county, then said, "It's actually skipped and hit everywhere, and we haven't actually found them all yet."

Mike asked whether it was true that an "all clear" advisory had been issued by Civil Defense.

"As far as I know," Spencer said, adding, "I've been so confused I haven't had any time to look at the bulletin."

It was 8:10 PM. "Right now," Mike told listeners, "we have a temporary 'clear,' meaning that right now we're in pretty good shape. But we can't promise you anything."

Athens Hospital had never been faced with such a rush of incoming patients. The facility held eighty-eight beds, with a small emergency room that could be cordoned off with drapes to accommodate five patients. On an ordinary night, the hospital was supervised by a single registered nurse, assisted by a handful of licensed practical nurses, with one member of its staff of ten doctors—most of them general practitioners—on call. James Black, head nurse on the night shift, acknowledged that the facility was "not really an up-to-date hospital." (One county official used to refer to it as "Infection General," and said, "I wouldn't let them put a Band-Aid on me.") The sorts of trauma cases with which Athens's staff were practiced were almost always the work of car wrecks, mishaps with farm machinery, or falls, and such patients did not arrive by the dozen. Two weeks earlier, Nurse Black, motivated by the opening of Brown's Ferry Nuclear Plant, had put his staff through its first disaster drill. A command center was set up, a head count was taken, and mock decisions were heatedly made about which patients to discharge in order to clear beds. Then the staff established a makeshift triage area. "It was a small-scale run-through," Black reflected. "It wasn't like an actual disaster at all."

Black was now standing in the midst of something quite different, struggling to direct human traffic. Patients were being unloaded from ambulances and hearses and the backs of pickup trucks, and hauled to the emergency room in the arms of family members, or on stretchers, or on boards. They were ragged and filthy, their expressions blank; some had had their clothes torn off; some arrived with scraps of bloody clothing tied into crude tourniquets. People came in with compound fractures, lacerations, and abrasions so severe they looked like burns. Some had hundreds of pellets of glass sprayed beneath their skin. Some had been hit by flying objects and others had themselves been sent flying and slammed into walls or floors or through windows. A few of the least fortunate had received penetrating wounds—one man came in with a tree limb protruding from his chest; another had been thrown onto a fence post.

Soon the floors were slippery with mud and blood. Patients overflowed the emergency room and spilled out onto the sidewalk; relatives and friends pushed into a waiting room, crying out for news of those with whom they had lost contact; still others crowded the hospital out of a simple desire for safety from the storms. Nurse Black unlocked the door to a disused passageway and had the seriously wounded carried there and laid on the floor; he drove nails into the wall from which to hang bags of intravenous fluids. Other less critical patients were shuttled to a storage area in the hospital's basement.

Annias Green's younger brother, Willie, lived in the west end of Athens. When Willie saw televised reports that tornadoes had crossed Highway 72 east of town, he and his wife, Frances, headed for Isom's Orchards. As soon as he arrived, he knew something serious had happened. The peach trees that had surrounded Annias's house stood like bare pegs. About the only trace of the family he could find was Annias's pickup truck, which stood straight on end in the soil near the fence line of a pasture. Willie walked toward it. Along the way he stepped across the truck's engine.

Willie and Frances took off for Athens Hospital. A half mile from the entrance, they ran into a logjam. Scores of vehicles were converging on the entrance. Willie left his car behind and walked through the snarl. There was a crush of people, too, at the hospital. While Willie tried, in vain, to find someone with information about his relatives, Frances drifted into a dim room where bodies were laid out awaiting identification. It was very quiet in the room. Frances was afraid to step forward.

A moment later she found Willie and told him that she had seen Lillian.

Frank Orr couldn't understand why he had been taken to the hospital, though his confusion might have been related to the head wound he had sustained, for which he received forty stitches. "My scalp was hanging over my right ear," he observed. He might have admitted, too, to a bit of difficulty walking, since his lower back bore the tattoolike imprint of a two-by-four—nail heads and all—which had cracked a vertebra in his spine. The injection he was given seemed to have dulled his discomfort, though, and put everything into tolerable perspective. He slumped in a chair, dozing on and off, waking only to tell anyone who would listen that they had to find his parents, his sister and brother-in-law, and their babies. At one point, he was shaken awake, and advised that he had to move because another tornado was coming. "I've had enough," he murmured. "Give me more pain pills." He was led into a dark corridor, and reclined on the floor alongside bodies wrapped in blankets.

Not far away lay a beautiful teenage girl, looking like a wild creature, barefoot in a torn dress, her face framed by long, matted hair.

F5

One of her legs had been nearly severed; a foot remained attached only by a thin cord of tendons.

Wind makes its own expansive jurisdiction. "First Tanner" and "Second Tanner"—as the consecutive Limestone tornadoes would come to be called—remained well-formed and vigorous when they crossed out of the county, headed, ultimately, for Tennessee. Both continued to take a toll in lives and misery. In Madison County, neighboring Limestone, "Mrs. Howard Truitt thought the night was over when the first twister plowed a path to her home, then leaped over it at the last minute," according to the *Huntsville Times*. "Before she could recover, the second twister demolished her home. Neighbors found her crawling across the street, deep in pain and bleeding."

Even as First Tanner and Second Tanner dissipated, new storms began coming through, plaguing rescuers and prolonging fear and disarray. Darkness heightened the plight of residents. Every scrap of cloud seemed to be aswirl, and funnels appeared wherever people looked. Hence Buddy Evans's office reported the sightings of sixteen tornadoes during the evening, while Spencer Black stood by the more restrained figure of five tornadoes on the ground and an additional fifteen "cruising the skies overhead."

Walter McGlocklin elbowed his way through the crowd at Athens Hospital, holding three-year-old Nancy, and screaming that he had misplaced his other girl. He had seen her, he said. She had been dug out. Her name was Grace. She had to be here somewhere.

He approached incoherence. No one at the hospital knew a thing about his missing daughter. In Limestone's small world, though, word had already begun to spread about the carnage at the McGlocklin house. Walter was led to an examining room, given a

201

sedative, and admitted to the hospital, briefly, for shock, though he would have no memory of any such thing, and would soon bolt from the building, his daughter in tow, to continue his search.

Willie Green wandered the halls of Athens Hospital calling out his brother's name. He stepped over bodies. It was hard to recognize faces. People looked as though they had been pulled from a murky trough. Finally, he heard his own name being called. He looked down and saw a child sitting on the floor. It was his ten-year-old nephew Amos.

Amos was animated. He wanted to chat. There was a big blast, he told Willie. Willie nodded. "How's my Mama and Daddy?" he asked. Willie paused. He told Amos that his mother was in the hospital. In a way, it was true. Then he went on to promise Amos that he would find his father and brothers soon. Amos didn't want Willie to leave. He prattled on about the NBA playoffs, which were under way. The Knicks, Amos said, had gotten down by two games to one to the Baltimore Bullets. Still, he was sure they would make a comeback.

Soon after Brother Fred Lackey rode out the tornado in the ditch at Lawson's, the sheriff took him aside with the news that help was needed outside Athens, on Highway 72. Brother Fred rounded up the men from his church and headed there. Arriving, they walked through a dark field of rubble above the highway. Soon they came upon several people lying in a tangle of debris. They set to work digging them out. The first person they freed was a woman, who now sat in the mud, head down, covered by a rescuer's jacket. Brother Fred recognized her as one of his parishioners, Marilyn McBay. He knew she had just given birth. But there were no children to be seen anywhere.

Brother Fred and several other men linked arms to fashion a

"pack saddle," and hauled Marilyn toward the road. She was dazed. "Brother Fred," she asked, "what in the world are you doing here?" He inquired after her children. She told him that while she had been trapped, two strange men had appeared and removed the boys. "They promised they weren't going to let go of my babies until they had them in the hospital," she said. She could offer no further information about the men. For all Brother Fred could tell, she might have been delusional. She could not account for Frank's whereabouts, or for the condition of the rest of her family. She could not even say whether she was in pain.

Brother Fred returned to the wreckage. He found Marilyn's mother in a grievous condition. The lower half of her body had been crushed. Brother Fred and another man moved her across the field slowly and painstakingly, and left her at the side of the road. Then they went back once more to attend to Vergil, who remained on the ground, partly pinned beneath a heap of debris. He was not breathing. He was cold. Brother Fred forced his jaws open and blew into his mouth. After ten minutes, he still couldn't detect a breath. One of the men from church came up to him and said, "It's all right, Brother Fred. He's dead."

Suddenly, another man appeared out of the darkness, carrying an ax. He hacked away at the debris until he managed to pry loose a door. He and Brother Fred pulled Vergil free, hoisted him atop the door, and carted him to the road. They saw an ambulance idling there with no driver in sight. They pushed Vergil in. Brother Fred hesitated, then got behind the wheel. Years earlier, as a college student, he had had a part-time job as an ambulance driver. Now he drew a deep breath, and took off in the direction of Huntsville.

By the time Don Lauderdale found his way back to the Old Orr House—his wife and children remained in downtown Athens, at

First Baptist—rescuers had moved on from Highway 72. The road was packed, instead, with a parade of curiosity seekers. Necks craned through the open windows of cars; horns honked arrhythmically; insults were shouted at passersby; bottles, concealed in brown bags, were furtively emptied, then tossed to the side of the road. Among those whose families and property were unharmed, a spirit of unseemly elation had taken hold, combining elements of Mardi Gras and the Fourth of July, as though the passage of the tornadoes had unbound them from the strictures of law, order, and, in some cases, compassion.

Don's demeanor was, of course, in no way festive. He strode towards the remains of his house in a stupor. The totality of destruction was nearly hypnotic. "You would think there had to be something left of the house," he sighed. "But no." He could not dwell on it. He managed, too, to keep at arm's length his memories of a previous disaster—the house fire, more than thirty years earlier, in which he had lost his father. He walked up his long drive, passed the two enormous oaks that had framed the view of his house from the road, and which were lying, uprooted, on the ground, then made his way around the barren rectangle of the cellar above which his home had risen. He might as well have been looking at the surface of the moon. He turned away and began walking through fields along the path the tornado had followed. The ground was as littered with junk as a salvage yard. Still, he could identify nothing of his own.

After stumbling on for a half mile, he found himself in a clearing that evoked a familiar sensation. It took him a moment to realize it was the spot from which Frank Orr's house had been blown away. He reeled around. Everything was disfigured. How, he wondered, could anyone have survived?

He hobbled back to the highway. When he got there, an ambu-

F5

lance pulled up. By this point he was numb to surprise, and took it in stride when he saw Brother Fred in the driver's seat. Brother Fred told him he had just returned from bringing Vergil to Huntsville. He had come back to search for more injured. "How does it look for Vergil?" Don asked.

"Not good," said Brother Fred.

Don climbed in the ambulance. "Take me to him," he said.

At 8:50 PM, yet another powerful tornado, originating in Mississippi, crossed into central Alabama, journeying over the next two hours to Limestone's doorstep, 102 miles away. The track it incised along the ground was so graphic that it could be picked up by satellite photograph. It particularly afflicted residents in and around Guin, Alabama, population 1,500, taking at least twenty-three lives there. "There's nothing left of Guin but its name," one report announced. Then the tornado entered the dense wilds of the 180,000-acre Bankhead National Forest in an area known as Rabbit Town, descending into river gorges, spreading itself through valleys, and picking trees off steep-sided hills. At times the path it hacked through the woods was a mile wide. Twenty million board feet of pine and hardwood were felled. The tornado went on to the outskirts of Decatur, cutting electrical power to the city. By the time it crossed the Tennessee River and entered Limestone, most of its violence was spent, though it looked fearful enough, its funnel swirling low in the sky on its way to Huntsville.

Willie had no luck locating Annias and his two other sons at Athens Hospital, and decided to leave his wife with Amos and search elsewhere. As he left the hospital, he saw a hearse parked by the entrance. Beside it, he caught sight of Annias, stretched out on the sidewalk. Two men were lifting him back into the vehicle.

It was not quite as bad as it looked. Willie rushed over and learned that Annias was still alive, barely. Athens Hospital, though, was refusing to take more patients. The driver was going to have to bring Annias to Decatur. Willie got into the hearse to ride beside him.

Annias was groggy and disoriented. He didn't talk much on the way. "I'm doing all right," he told Willie. His appearance suggested otherwise. His limbs were splayed—there was no telling how many broken bones he had—and he was bleeding from his head. He could not move his arms or legs. His breathing was faint. His eyelids would drop shut and then suddenly flutter open. "I'm just wondering about my wife and boys," he muttered. Willie offered vague words of reassurance.

The hearse slowed down. Willie heard the driver honking and cursing. They were stopped at a roadblock. The sheriff had closed Highway 31 to Decatur, and no one, not even the injured, was getting through. The driver rattled across the median and turned around. With every bump in the road, Annias groaned, until after a while he fell silent. Back on Highway 72 in Athens, the hearse was stopped once again. This time it was prevented from making its way to Huntsville. Willie was beside himself. The driver suggested there was only one option left: tiny Jackson Memorial Hospital, a facility served by a single doctor, in Lester, Alabama, on the Tennessee State line.

Willie had doubts about whether Lester could treat someone with Annias's injuries. Some attention, though, seemed better than none. Willie realized, too, that by the time they got there, any attempt at care might be unavailing. Annias had lost consciousness. Willie sat alongside him, grasping his hand, and worrying about the fate of Titus and Rabbit. Before long, the rainswept road was deserted.

F 5

Halfway to Lester, Willie felt the car pull sharply over to the side of the road.

"What's going on here?" he asked.

The driver told him that he thought he had seen another tornado coming. He was getting out of the hearse to take a look.

A few hours earlier, when Ralph Padgett heard over a police radio in his house that a tornado had hit Lawson's Trailer Park, he suspected that the coroner's services might be required. "I didn't imagine there'd be another tornado, though," he said. "And another, and another." He got in his car and headed toward Lawson's. Along the way, he crossed paths with Second Tanner. "I stopped the car and made a run for a ditch. I saw a woman and two children standing by a store at Tanner Crossroads, and pulled them down with me. I got so much glass sprayed in my butt I doubt I'll ever dig it all out."

Shortly afterwards, Ralph found Buddy Evans, who had evidently had a rough go of it himself. His clothes were torn, and his face looked like that of someone who had just had a bar fight. He was organizing a house-to-house search for victims. Even with the assistance of a small corps of volunteers—men who were typically called on for such tasks as directing traffic during parades—Buddy knew he didn't have enough manpower to clear roads or to dig through rubble looking for survivors. He decided to enlist prisoners—those he deemed trustworthy—to the effort. He assigned a pair to Ralph, to assist in collecting the dead. Ralph set out for the southern end of Limestone, near the river, with his prisoners in the backseat of his car. Along the way, he stopped a few times so the men could clear tree limbs from the road. He wasn't afraid they would take off into the night. "They weren't some kind of desperadoes," he said.

Limestone's first deaths occurred not far from the river. A pair of elderly widows, Nobie Ruffin and Rosie Maclin, who lived a few hundred yards from each other, had decided to ride out the storm together, and had debated whose home was more suitable for the purpose. They chose Ruffin's. It was a bad call. The house they left empty was undamaged by the storm. Ruffin's, on the other hand, left little evidence that it had ever stood. It took hours to find enough traces of the two frail women to provide the basis for an identification. "Rosie Macklin [sic], c/f, age 87," recorded Ralph's notes. "Field on Beulah Bay Road. Companion: Nokie [sic] Ruffin. Internal injuries. Mrs. Macklin was a victim of the tornado."

A mile away, at Walter McGlocklin's house, a large search party was still sifting through the rubble. Buddy's wife and brother-in-law were there to help out, and had a hard time speaking of what they found. "My brother-in-law came back all in pieces," Buddy remarked. "He kept saying, 'It's the worst thing I've ever seen. The kid crying, Walter screaming like that.' I shouldn't have sent him over there." Without any ceremony, Ralph wrote, "Walter James McGlocklin, Jr. Age 2. Tornado victim. Companion at time of death: mother and sister."

Back on Highway 31, at the cinder block shell of the Apostolic Pentecostal Church, twenty people had been hurt. Among them was a mentally retarded man named Herman Lambert. Lambert had been in his trailer at Lawson's when it overturned. He had then been escorted from the trailer park to the ostensible safety of the church by his brother, the church's pastor. When Second Tanner hit, the church's ceiling came down on him. He was added to the coroner's list of the dead.

At 10:24 PM, still another tornado materialized in the bottom corner of Limestone, headed for Huntsville. This one made it to the city. At

10:40, staffers at the National Weather Service field office, housed at Huntsville Airport, ditched their posts when they saw the tornado coming at them. Moments later, some of the thousand soldiers receiving training at the U.S. Army Missiles and Munitions Center and School on the Redstone Arsenal spotted the cloud, spiraling through the saddle between two hills and advancing toward them. According to reports, "There was little more time than to move to the bottom floors of the multistory barracks and drop to the floor." Ninety-eight buildings on the base were damaged or destroyed, along with five others in the adjoining Marshall Space Flight Center. One combat veteran described the scene as "an air raid without bombs."

The tornado left Redstone Arsenal and tore through an elementary school, a trailer park, a Cadillac dealership, and an International House of Pancakes, where twenty customers cowered beneath their booths. It trounced the Parkway City Shopping Center, on whose construction Annias had labored in the days after he left M. Y. Dauthit's farm, and hit a movie theater where Bill Dunnavant's younger brother, Ron, had escaped the inclement weather earlier that evening, enjoying the 7:30 screening of *American Graffiti*. Then the tornado headed toward Huntsville Hospital.

Don Lauderdale and Brother Fred braced themselves as they passed the lights of a police car. All the way to Huntsville, they had been hearing calls over their vehicle's radio reporting a stolen ambulance. They looked at each other and kept going. The police, apparently, were otherwise occupied.

It was storming again. Brother Fred jerked the steering wheel and crossed the median, into the oncoming lanes, to avoid crashing into debris. As they neared Huntsville, Don looked back through his window and caught sight of a funnel cloud bearing down on them. He didn't bother to question the likelihood of what he was seeing.

Rather, he screamed for Brother Fred to pull the ambulance beneath a highway overpass. "That one was close," Don said. "I'm almost getting used to it."

At Huntsville Hospital, according to Brother Fred, "It was a chaotic scene, and very morbid—there were a lot of people with limbs torn off, and some small children who had been killed." He passed through a waiting area and saw bodies on the floor. At first he thought they were crying in pain. Then he saw they were holding hands, praying that no more tornadoes would come through.

Don found Vergil unconscious in a cubicle in the Intensive Care Unit. He was still lying on the door on which Brother Fred had removed him from the field. His head was swollen. There was no time for decorum. While Don stood by, a doctor picked up a drill, bore a hole in Vergil's skull, and inserted a tube to drain fluid.

Don recoiled. He left the enclosure and sought fresh air on the ambulance dock. There, a policeman was calling for anyone with knowledge of first aid to lend a hand. The hospital was receiving wave after wave of tornado victims. "Each time a group of injured was rolled into the emergency treatment area after a tornado struck a specific sector of the county," the *Huntsville Times* would report, "only a few minutes would lapse before someone would yell that yet another funnel cloud had been spotted over the area." The hospital had run out of both blood—more was said to be on its way, under police escort, from Birmingham—and space. At the beginning of the evening, only six of its 400 beds were available. "To alleviate the situation," the *Times* reported, "hospital administrators moved patients in the psychiatric ward from their rooms."

Don stood on the dock unloading victims onto stretchers. "There were bodies all over," he said. "They were stacked up on the sidewalk. Nurses told me, 'If they're moaning, get them first.' Some of them didn't have legs—I saw one person whose leg had been strapped to his torso for safekeeping."

As Don observed, "You would not believe how mangled a human body can be. One ambulance drove up, and when I opened the door blood poured out. Another vehicle came, a pickup truck, and there were dead bodies sitting up in back."

At one point, a man came through dragging the body of his son, a tall, strapping teenager. "Help me," the man said. "He got thrown from his car. I think he's broken his neck."

In Lester, Willie Green's attention was divided between fear for his brother's life and distress over his two as yet unaccounted-for nephews. Willie's wife arrived to join him. She was still shaken by her earlier glimpse of Lillian. Willie bent down and touched Annias's shoulder. "I'm going off to look for your boys," he said. He knew that Annias might not be alive the next time he visited. He turned from his bedside and left for Huntsville by way of back roads.

When he arrived, he found Hunstville Hospital in a furor. An alarm had sounded amid reports that yet another tornado was sweeping through town. According to the *Huntsville Times*, this latest storm was said "to be heading right up Governors Drive toward the hospital." Staff furiously herded patients toward the inner core of the building, away from windows. Willie followed the crowds streaming through the hospital entrance. "Electrical power snapped," wrote the paper, "lights flickered, and darkness made the gory emergency room scene even more unbearable." Then word circulated that the warning was a false alarm. "Someone yelled an 'all clear,'" the *Times* continued, "and persons crept slowly from small rooms and corners on the main hospital floor. But in seconds, an ambulance driver coming to a screeching halt outside the emergency room door shouted that a funnel cloud was 'right overhead.' The scrambling scene of persons running to shelter again was repeated."

Willie found himself winding through the Intensive Care Unit. To his amazement, he came upon Rabbit and Titus there, each lying on a gurney. Both boys were clinging to life. Rabbit's head was wrapped in a bloody bandage, and one of his lungs was punctured. Doctors felt he would not survive surgery. Titus was in even worse shape. The back of his head was cracked open; his vital signs were waning. In his case, there was no choice but to go ahead with desperate measures. He was being prepared for brain surgery.

At eleven, as the latest tornado skidded past Huntsville Hospital and out of town, it ascended the steep hillside of 1,600-foot Monte Sano, or "Health Mountain," whose woods had housed a sanatorium at the end of the nineteenth century. In 1974, much of the mountain was a state park, and the rest featured some of Huntsville's most luxurious homes, several of which were about to be destroyed.

Curiously, the tornado picked up speed after cresting Monte Sano, and seemed to have recharged its energy as it sheared a path down the other side. This happened in spite of a long-held piece of folk wisdom maintaining that tornadoes could not climb mountains. Indeed, reports of the mountain-climbing tornado were met with initial skepticism and attributed to overheated imaginations. Fortunately, weatherman H. D. Bagley was available to separate fact from fancy, for he lay crouching in a ditch just below the peak of Monte Sano, having fled Channel 19's hilltop studio when he saw the whirlwind coming.

Toward midnight, Coroner Ralph Padgett received a message that the governor of Alabama was insisting all victims be identified by daylight. "There was no way," he said. "I was running around like crazy. There was a lot of confusion. Some of the bodies had three or four inches of mud on them. You couldn't tell what house they came from, because so many houses were gone. And some had had the clothes blown off them."

Just east of Tanner Crossroads, Mary Elizabeth Smith, 45, had been home alone Wednesday night. Her husband, Clifford, was working at Brown's Ferry Nuclear Plant; her children were grown. She had been on the phone with her daughter when, seeing First Tanner cross through a nearby field, she believed the danger to have passed her by. She was not banking on Second Tanner. As her husband would remark, "When I came home, I had no more home, and I knew that my wife was there. Her car was there, blown 300 or 400 yards away, but the house was gone. She wasn't there and I knew that she must be gone." Her body was not recovered until deep into the night. She had been carried far across the road, into Strain and Son's Nursery. Some locals claimed to have seen a horse standing near the body. No one knew whom the horse belonged to, or how it had gotten there. It refused to move.

Northeast of the Smiths' house, on Lindsay Lane, passing rescuers heard cries in a field. In time they discovered the source of the cries—an infant girl, who had survived the tornado. The child's caretakers—her grandmother, Louise Cain, 51, and Cain's son Thomas, 19—were dead.

It wasn't much more than a mile from there to Isom's Orchards. "We just got through getting some people out of a house—what was a house—out there," an ambulance driver told a reporter, pointing to the site where Annias had lived. "I don't think one of them is going to survive. Nobody knows how many people are injured or dead," the driver continued. "It's total confusion."

Annias's story would go otherwise unreported in local papers. The *Decatur Daily* would, however, run an article on the losses suffered by his landlord. "Completely wiped out," the headline would say, going on to describe the damage done to the Isom's peach trees.

Don remained in Huntsville hoping for word on Vergil's condition. He wandered back up to Intensive Care, and saw a group of doctors and nurses conferring. They motioned for him to come over. "Is it Vergil?" he asked.

A nurse brought him to a cubicle where a body lay covered by a sheet. She pulled back the sheet. Don turned his head away. When he regained his composure, he examined the face. "Oh, my Lord," he said. "That's not Vergil."

He found Vergil down the hall. One side of his body was paralyzed from his head injury. A lung had collapsed. He was breathing through a tube that had been inserted in his trachea. But though he remained in critical condition, he was stable.

As Don recovered from his shock, he paused to glance at a child being wheeled past him. Even through the child's mass of bandages, he seemed familiar to Don. Finally he recognized the boy as Titus Green, one of the sons of his neighbor across the highway. "It looked like he had been whacked with a machete," Don said. Titus was about to get a steel plate inserted in his skull. Don asked a nurse about the boy's condition, and was told, "That boy has more stitches in his little body than anyone has ever received at Huntsville Hospital."

Soon afterwards, Don ran into Brother Fred, looking bereft. Brother Fred asked Don to come with him. He explained that the bodies of a young woman and an infant were awaiting identification. So many bodies had been brought to the hospital that a makeshift morgue had been opened. "It did not contain the carpeting or other 'comforts' which attempt to soften the blow of death," the *Huntsville Times* commented. "This morgue was cold, with cold steel tables leaving an ugly but vivid impression." The two men were led through the morgue and stood over the draped outline of a corpse. Its feet protruded from beneath the covering. On one toe a tag reading "Marilyn McBay" dangled from a string. Brother Fred warned Don that, according to nurses, the body had been impaled.

"Brother Fred, that's my niece," Don cried. "I don't think I can do this." He turned away.

There was silence. Then Don heard Brother Fred's voice. "This can't be right," he said. "There is a poor young woman lying here. But it's not Marilyn."

Don was overwhelmed. He began to tally up the evening's improbably close calls. He and his family had been elsewhere when their house was destroyed. He had made it through two tornadoes—once on the floor of a church, once in a stolen ambulance. Twice he had been called on to confirm the deaths of loved ones, and both times he had been spared the agony. "It's the providence of God," he said. Standing in the morgue, though, in the midst of a roomful of the night's unclaimed victims, his gratitude was tempered with grief.

Marilyn had been placed along with her parents in the back of a delivery van, headed for Athens Hospital. She was frantic. It was as though the reality of the night was announcing itself to her at last. She had been separated from her husband, and when she had last glimpsed him he was lifeless. Her mother, too, was in terrible shape, unable to move or speak. As for Frank, he had disappeared.

One matter, though, frightened her most: Where were her children? How could she have handed them to strangers?

At Athens Hospital, she lurched from the van, cornered a nurse, and demanded to know whether any babies had been brought in. The nurse stared at her in her mud-caked nightgown.

No, the nurse said. No children.

Marilyn called out her question to the room. People turned to regard her. Many of them, too, had survived the storm. None had seen her children.

The hospital had no room to take her and her parents. "Not unless you're dying," she was told. She pointed out that it was possible her mother was, indeed, dying. They were turned away nonetheless.

The van got back on the road toward Decatur. Somehow they made it through. "It took a lot of time, though," Marilyn said. "At Lawson's, the road was blocked. I could feel the van crossing back and forth across the highway. Then, when we finally got to Decatur General, we were turned away there, too."

The van then proceeded to ill-equipped Baugh-Wiley-Smith Hospital, also in Decatur. By now Marilyn was desperate to find her children. No one seemed to be listening to her. She was taken to an examination room, where she received stitches in her head, and then was left alone. Each time a nurse passed by, Marilyn repeated her inquiries about Jason and Mark. "I was sitting there, cold, wet, shaking," she said. She believed the entire calamity had been her fault. Had she not been staying at her parents' house with her children, her parents and Frank would have had time to leave, and the house would have been empty when the storm hit. Vergil would have been with her, in Athens. And she never would have made the mistake of letting go of her babies.

Suddenly a young girl walked by, wearing the striped coat of a volunteer. The girl was carrying a bundle. "What have you got there," Marilyn called out.

"It's a little boy," the girl said. "He's lost his mother."

Marilyn tore open the swaddling. It was Mark. "He was just cuddled up, wearing a diaper, with a bandage on his forehead."

Jason was not far away. He had a gash in his leg, but it had been so plastered with mud that he hadn't lost much blood. Still, he had been sedated. "He was pretty traumatized," Marilyn said. "He was carrying on so badly they couldn't get him to stay in bed. They took him to the administrator's office, and he finally fell asleep in a big chair."

As the night wore on, Buddy Evans called the state capital in Montgomery and asked that the National Guard be deployed. "The looting started right away," he said. "You'd be surprised how people will do that. I caught some loading up their car at a store that was damaged. Others were going to damaged houses and just grabbing anything they could." Some residents began patrolling their property, wielding shotguns. "I was amazed," Ralph Padgett added, "at the crap people would steal—tin and copper and bits of wood. Of course, if they could find better stuff, they'd take that, too. People's coin collections. Their guns. Their clothes."

Ralph's work lasted through the night. As dawn approached, he had identified eight bodies, and recovered another six, as yet unnamed. He knew the final count of the dead would be higher. As he drove through the sundered county, calling on damaged houses, he found people huddled in storm shelters, refusing to emerge, refusing to believe the storm was over.

At a desolate farm on Copeland Road, at Limestone's eastern edge, a family had been blown across the county line. Ralph retrieved them. There were four bodies. "Ternessa Carter," he recorded,

"Age 5. Internal injuries. Companion: Father—Mother—Brother—all victims." "They lived up a field," Ralph said, "and the storm carried them and their house away. They were stuck up in trees. Buddy's prisoners helped me get them down, and then we got them loaded. There was no ambulance. We were hauling bodies in a funeral hearse. It was so muddy, we probably ruined that Cadillac hearse. For all I know, it was the first time blacks had ever been put in a white hearse in Limestone County."

Accompanied by his daughter, Nancy, Walter had left Athens Hospital as though in a dream. It was pitch dark by now, and very quiet. The sky was full of stars. The streets were abandoned. Walter would not allow himself to recall the images he had seen at home, or to think of Ruth or Sandra or Little Walter. He turned his full attention, instead, to his remaining child, Grace. He knew she must be alive. He was certain that as he was being hustled from his home, Buddy Evans's wife—where had she come from?—assured him Grace would be fine.

Walter made his way to the Electric Department and retrieved his truck, which he had left at work at the outset of the night's troubles. It had been a long time since then.

He began driving. Closed roads didn't disturb him. If he couldn't make his way through, he'd make his way around. Nancy slept on the seat next to him. He was going to find Grace.

He went to Decatur and searched every room of both hospitals in town. Grace was not there. Walter's nephews, Steve and Jerry, who were being treated in Decatur for lacerations and, in Jerry's case, a shattered leg, had not seen her, either. He went on to Huntsville and scoured the eight-floor hospital top to bottom. He went outside to gather himself and returned to look again, this time making sure he stopped at the morgue. He went back to Athens Hospital once more. He could find no sign of his daughter.

Dawn was breaking. Walter did not welcome daylight. He was not about to return "home"—not to sift through the wastes of his family's life, or to make a frustrated attempt at salvage, or to take snapshots of his Rambler station wagon, which was perched, absurdly, in the tops of a pair of oaks a hundred yards from the driveway. He was not ready to go back there. Not just yet.

Daybreak

The morning after the tornadoes, a general practitioner of medicine named Stanley Hand, who had spent the night tending to patients in the emergency room at Athens Hospital, woke with an urge to take in the ravages from a different vantage point. An experienced pilot, he drove to Athens airfield, on the north end of town, and rented a Cessna. The skies were clearing over north Alabama and the air was cool and temperate. It was a fine day for flying.

He rose to an altitude of 3,000 feet, where he was granted a panoramic vista. "It looked as if somebody had come across the earth with a giant bush hog," he said, referring to the huge cylinder of rotating blades that farmers used to clear their fields. A half-mile-wide path had been slashed across the landscape. "At the hospital, everybody had said the tornadoes turned and twisted and changed directions, but flying over it, the path was just as straight as an arrow," he observed. He headed southwest and identified the point at which the wreckage began, in Lawrence County, some fifty miles from Athens. Then he dropped to a thousand feet, turned around, and allowed himself to retrace the trail of damage at a leisurely pace. It was not hard to follow. It was like examining the length of a patient's scar. "Trees were flattened out. Houses were flattened out. You'd see the spot where a house had been, you'd see the foundation, and then the material that came out of the house was thrown in a pattern like a flame from a candle." He flew over the Lawrence County settlements of Parkertown, Mount Moriah, and Langtown, which were in ruins, and in which sixteen people had been killed. "Trees looked like they'd had their leaves picked, and most had been broken down to the ground," he said. "The trees that were left standing had all kinds of things hung in them, everything from refrigerators to bedsheets and mattresses."

The doctor followed the path up the southern edge of the Tennessee River, crossed the vast pool of dun-colored water, and found the spot where the tornado had resumed its course on the other bank, in Limestone, near Bridgeforth Landing. (He often went duck hunting there.) For a while he could see a second line, running parallel to the first, where Second Tanner had set down in Limestone; but soon the two tracks closed in on each other, then touched, and then overlapped, forming a single broad path. Down below, house after house stood in eerie fragments, blots on the spring ground.

He flew over Highway 31, whose median was scattered with overturned vehicles, and along whose sides people could be seen, in skittering motion, trolling through debris. Soon the landscape took on a sameness, like a reel of film moving in a continuous loop: windblown farmland; clusters of blasted homes and outbuildings; overturned cars; splintered woods; windblown farmland.

The entwined paths of the Tanner tornadoes proceeded uninterrupted into the Appalachian foothills. He flew over the wreckage while bodies were still being recovered and animals were still being buried in muddy pits. "I followed it on into the hills," he said, "and followed it into the mountains, and then it must have lifted, because I couldn't track it any further."

Dr. Hand had been in practice for twenty-five years, and knew more than most people about the fragility of life. Still, looking down on the torn-apart houses and compacted cars and storm-tossed trees, he had a newfound respect for human resiliency. "I really wondered how in the world anyone survived," he remarked.

The April 4 edition of the *Athens News Courier* had been sent to press before the evening storms of April 3 broke out. As a result, Athens's Thursday morning paper was blithely out of sync with the community it covered, like a dispatch from the unrecoverable past. "Two Athens ladies are opening a new beauty salon on U.S. 31 south of here," it reported. The salon would be called the "Kutie-Kurl." A photo on the Sports page showed an Athens man named David Christopher proudly displaying "a lunker-sized largemouth bass that he landed during a recent fishing trip on Elk River." A lengthier item announced that Tanner High—grazed by a tornado Wednesday night, and kept open as a refuge for displaced people—had named its choices for class speakers in the upcoming graduation ceremony.

A few grimmer pieces of news, too, were allowed to reach the *News Courier*'s readers on April 4. A two-inch wire service report told of a "racial fracas" at a high school in Mobile, far south of Limestone. "Theodore High School has had numerous fights between black and white students during the past two years," the item noted. Closer to Limestone, an account was provided of the indictment of three men for the murder of a black preacher, Edward Pace, in the town of Gadsden. The Ku Klux Klan was believed to have targeted Pace for suspected membership in the Black Panthers.

By and large, though, the dominant tone of the April 4 edition of Limestone's daily news was one of civic-minded optimism—the sort of spirit that had seemed to characterize the county, at least in its official version of itself, only a day earlier. Primary elections were coming up in a month, and the *News Courier* strayed from its usual practices by devoting its front page to a rousing political endorsement. "Give Wallace Best Victory," the headline encouraged, referring to Governor George Wallace, who was not only the state's most famous standard-bearer, but who had become a national celebrity. As an independent candidate for the presidency in 1968, Wallace had carried five states; in 1972, he had his sights set on the Democratic nomination, and had already won the Florida primary, when he was shot five times by a would-be assassin, and paralyzed. At the time, a Gallup poll showed him to be the seventh most-admired man in the United States, just ahead of the Pope. "George Wallace ought to be given a third term as governor of the State of Alabama," the editorial began, "not because we are sorry for him because he was shot and is an invalid, but because he has been a good governor. His accomplishments, and they are many, clearly make him the best governor Alabama has ever had." The editorial did not cite, as features of Wallace's distinction, his long and vigorous crusade on behalf of segregation, or the many instances of his past defiance of federal civil rights laws. Instead, it focused on Wallace's improvement of state parks and roads, and his role in making Alabama "the hottest spot in the country for new or expanding industrial plants."

"The attempted assassination of Wallace as he campaigned for the Democratic nomination for president is one of the tragic moments of our nation's history. Only a man of Wallace's stamina would have survived."

Spencer Black had stayed at the Civil Defense office through Wednesday night, and into Thursday, sustaining himself on coffee and NoDoz pills when his energy waned. After daybreak, he drove out to eyeball the damage. From within the confines of Civil Defense, the tornadoes had seemed strangely abstract. Now, the repetitive sight of battered houses and farms became numbing. It was hard to fathom how the mess would ever be cleaned up, or how Limestone would manage to recuperate. Down by the Tennessee River, Spencer steered off the road to examine the carcass of a cow whose bottom jaw had been pulled from its head. "For some reason, that's what brought it all home to me," he said.

He remained at work through Thursday night, setting up a disaster relief center at the National Guard armory. There were cots for those who had lost their homes. Guardsmen cooked meals. By Friday morning, truckloads of donated clothing began to arrive. At first Spencer was touched by the concern of people from around the country. Soon, however, the task of managing the donations became a hindrance. "In a disaster," he observed, "people's hearts run away with them, and they look in their closets and see they've got a lot of junk stored up. It makes them feel better to give it away. They get to take it off their income tax. You cannot imagine the truckloads of clothing that came in here. We had to burn a lot of it. Let me tell you—unless a disaster victim is naked, he doesn't want something that some stranger has thrown away."

At noon on Friday, Spencer headed home for the first time in three days. "Funny thing. Exhausted as I was, when I lay down in bed I couldn't sleep. My wife had to run to the doctor and get some pills to knock me out."

Willie Green returned to Lester on Thursday morning, full of apprehension. Thankfully, Annias was still alive, but he remained in a wretched state. A garish scar curled down from his temple and extended behind an ear, and the few parts of his body that were not covered by casts or dressings were swollen and discolored. A nurse recited his list of injuries: concussion, cracked ribs, broken collarbone, shattered ankle. One of his shoulders had been torn from its socket, and rested limply beside him. "It almost broke my arm off," Annias remarked, weakly, as he went in and out of consciousness.

There was more. Annias's spine had been fractured in several places, and it was believed that his spinal cord had been severed. He was paralyzed. He would never walk again.

In his haze of painkillers, Annias remained unaware that he could not feel his body. "The God I serve is able," he told Willie, seeing his brother's expression. "I've got a power working for me."

Willie told Annias about finding Amos in Athens, and said that the boy had been chatting away as if nothing had happened. The news was a comfort to Annias. Willie tried to offer assurances that Rabbit and Titus were getting good care in Huntsville and would be out of the hospital in no time.

One further question hung in the room. Willie hoped that it would not be voiced. But Annias, despite his fog, remembered to ask. "Lillian?"

Willie was at a loss. "Well, I think she's at Athens Hospital, but I'm not entirely sure," he said. "I'll tell you just as soon as I've got more information."

When Walter opened his eyes on Thursday morning, he found himself on the sofa at his mother's house. He couldn't remember getting there. Nancy was asleep in her grandmother's bed. It was too soon for Walter to consider the course that his life would now take. Instead, he immediately set out to resume his search for Grace. He drove back to the hospitals in Decatur, Athens, and Huntsville. He paid no attention to the ruins outside his car window. There were National Guardsmen on the road. Cars drove infuriatingly slowly, their drivers gaping out their windows. He wondered if Grace were out there, lost. He glanced across the railroad tracks in the direction of his house, then quickly turned away. It was a cruelly sunny day.

Walter was nothing if not practical. He determined that he had to exhaust all possibilities in looking for Grace. This meant stopping in at funeral homes. Of course, he was relieved that she did not turn up at the first stop he made. Nor was she at the next funeral home. Much of the rest of his family was there, though. He was taken to view their bodies. In turn, he identified Ruth, Sandra, and Little Walter. They no longer bore much resemblance to the loved ones he had left the day before. The undertaker advised Walter to keep their caskets closed at the funeral service. Reluctantly, Walter agreed. He continued searching for Grace, though he was running out of places to look.

By the next day, he was coming unhinged. He contacted rescuers who had been at his house after the tornado. In the pandemonium of the moment, Grace seemed to have slipped away. No one could account for her whereabouts. In despair, Walter drove back to Huntsville, then talked his way past a guard and onto the grounds of the Redstone Arsenal. There was a military hospital there. He struggled to explain his predicament to the staff. Finally, a passing doctor overheard him, and told Walter that during Wednesday night's confusion, an unnamed girl had, indeed, been brought to the Arsenal in critical condition.

It was Grace. She was asleep. She had suffered a crushed pelvis. Walter was told she would have to remain in the hospital for weeks. She would be in a body cast long after that, too. Then it would be time to see if any of her injuries were permanent.

On Thursday afternoon, Governor Wallace began a busy slate of appearances at disaster sites.

Wallace had already been scheduled that day to embark on a

statewide campaign trip. The tornadoes, though, allowed his political stops to assume an official purpose. "The governor just doesn't think it is appropriate to be going around looking for votes in a time of disaster like this," his press secretary, Billy Joe Camp, announced Thursday morning. Wallace set off to visit sixteen counties (only half that many had suffered tornado damage), putting on display his unique gift for personalizing the suffering of his constituents. "I know about things being fine one minute and something altogether different another," he remarked to a crowd in Huntsville, not needing to spell out his meaning. One woman whose home had been destroyed grabbed Wallace's hand. "I pray for you, too," she told him. "I pray you can walk again some day." Wallace responded, "You just keep praying for me and I'll keep praying for you."

Prayers and goodwill accounted for the better part of what Wallace had to offer, since the state had few tangible resources to deliver to those who had lost their homes, and was relying for help, instead, on churches, private charities like the Red Cross, and the federal government, including five-percent loans from the Farmer's Home Administration, and trailers from the Department of Housing and Urban Development to shelter the homeless.

At one point, the governor's helicopter set down at East Limestone Public School, just down the road from the spot where a group of houses had been destroyed and a pair of teenagers blown from their car into nearby fields. Surrounded by local politicians, Wallace shouted through a bullhorn to an audience of seventy-five. Nearly alone among political appointees, Spencer Black declined to attend the event. "It's a political showboat," he said. "It doesn't help a bit. We need people working, not parading around shaking hands and getting their picture taken with somebody who had their kid killed. It's bull crap."

F5

* * *

On Friday morning, Willie stopped by Athens Hospital to visit Amos, who had been kept there for observation. He found the boy talkative and in good humor. Willie was relieved, too, that Amos was not probing too deeply about his mother's whereabouts.

Later that afternoon, though, when Willie returned to the hospital, Amos was no longer in his room. Willie was told he had been taken to Huntsville for further tests. Willie was perplexed, but not alarmed.

He drove on to Huntsville. He found Amos right away. The boy greeted him and began speaking in the same easy manner with which they had conversed a few hours earlier. Something seemed different, though.

"Uncle," Amos suddenly blurted out, "I can hear you, but I can't see you."

Willie was dumbfounded. He asked nurses what had happened. Apparently, he was told, an X-ray had revealed a splinter of wood lodged in Amos's brain. A physician in Athens had attempted to extract the object. The procedure had left Amos blind and paralyzed.

Willie asked why such an operation had not been left to a specialist. He received no answer.

Down at Lawson's, Paula Marbut, who had watched the first Tanner tornado crossing the Tennessee River, returned with her family to find, as she suspected, that her home was gone. "We saw where we had lived, and it looked like we'd been bombed," she cried. "Wedding rings, family pictures, birth records, everything was lost." Then she corrected herself. "Actually, I found one thing—the Bible my father had left me." In the field behind Lawson's, some of her neighbors were burying dead pets. Paula's poodle, Cocoa, leapt out of the rubble when one of her sons walked by. Her children rejoiced.

Within a few days, though, the dog started having seizures caused by a head wound, and had to be put down.

One afternoon, as Paula sifted through the scraps of her home, she felt a tap on her shoulder. It was a man in a suit. "The governor would like to talk to you," he told her. Paula was led to a car idling on the side of Highway 31. A window was rolled down. "The governor shook my hand and told me that he was glad I had survived," she recounted, "and that if there was anything he could ever do for me, I should let him know." Then he and his staff drove off.

"I had looked in that window and seen him, and seen what he had lost," Paula said. "I couldn't think about my own losses anymore."

On Saturday, while her husband and three sons remained in critical condition in separate hospitals, a funeral was held for Lillian Green at Macedonia Primitive Baptist Church, where under better circumstances Annias usually took the pulpit. The grief of those in attendance was extreme. "It wasn't like an old person's funeral, where you could accept the death," said Willie. Lillian was thirty-one. Most of the reflections offered about her concerned her love for her family, which was said to be boundless. No one knew how her paralyzed husband was going to manage to take care of himself, let alone his sons.

Willie decided it was finally time Annias was told the truth. He was afraid to be the one to break the news, though. He suspected that, in some way, Annias must have sensed Lillian's death, but had not had the strength to pursue the question. After all, he was in traction, heavily sedated, and rarely emerging from sleep. Willie asked an uncle, Samuel Crutcher, who was also a preacher, to speak to him. The two men entered Annias's room with a doctor.

F5

Samuel was blunt. "Nephew," he told Annias, "your wife has been killed."

Annias seemed to have half-expected the words. He turned his head away and wept, for five, ten, fifteen minutes. Finally he turned back to Willie and Samuel. "The Lord gave her to me," he said, "but she doesn't belong to me. She belongs to God." Then he went to sleep.

There was another funeral that morning. Three pine caskets of differing lengths—the smallest not much more than three feet long—lay before the pulpit at Tanner Church of Christ. The sanctuary could not hold all those who had arrived to mourn the McGlocklin family. Walter had to be helped to the small graveyard beside the church where the family was lowered into the ground.

Walter had wanted to have Grace brought to the funeral. Her doctor cautioned against it. "If she were one of mine," the doctor suggested, "I wouldn't let her know anything just yet. She's got to get herself straightened out first." When Grace asked after her mother and siblings, Walter told her that, like her, they were in the hospital getting well.

Walter and Nancy stayed with his mother for a few more days. Then Walter rented a house in Decatur. He told his nephew Jerry he would be unable to look after him any longer. When Grace was ready to come home from the hospital, a month later, Walter steeled himself. "What could I do? I had to tell her that her mother and brother and sister had gone to Heaven."

Walter was tormented with guilt. He had left his family unprotected during the tornado, and he didn't know how his two surviving daughters could forgive him. "If I'd been home, I would have done the same thing Ruth did—get down by the chimney—and then I'd be the one that was dead." But that hadn't happened, and that was the problem. Moreover, "I was afraid Grace would hold it against me, not letting her go to the funeral," Walter said. "But I don't reckon she did."

Much to his bemusement, Spencer found that he was being celebrated as a hero in the press. Buddy and Ralph Padgett were similarly praised; the *Decatur Daily* suggested that Limestone's death toll "could have been much worse if not for the heroic efforts" of the pair, and made the slightly exaggerated claim that the sheriff "single-handedly evacuated persons in the Lawson Trailer Park area just before twister one hit." Local media appeared to have taken on a dual role in the days after the disaster, running multi-page spreads of photos with captions like "Nothing Left," "Searching the Ruins," and "Falling Apart," and offering testimonials to the prowess of local officials. "Friends in need are friends," ran a headline in the *News Courier*, extolling the efforts of ambulance drivers, road crews, National Guardsmen, law enforcement, and, above all, Civil Defense, which "in all probability . . . saved the lives of many." Spencer and his helpers "tracked the killer twister and the situation would have been worse if a thorough watch had not been kept."

Spencer's own appraisal of his performance was more circumspect. "I was so caught up in it that I forgot I didn't have much sense what to do. All I really remember is being on the phone all night, going back and forth with the radio station, just like we were calling a football game."

Spencer knew, too, that much of the boosterism of the press reflected a desire to tamp down the community's anguish. He had done what he could on Wednesday night, but he had a realistic sense of what had gone on. He saw that a single factor, above all else, had been responsible for preventing a broader disaster: luck.

F5

Nobody wanted to admit it, but sheer, dumb luck spelled the difference between life and death. It was lucky, Spencer acknowledged, that many residents had been at church as evening fell, or the tornado would have found occupied some of the empty houses it destroyed. The ground at Lawson's, in particular, would have been thick with bodies. Spencer himself was lucky that reports of tornadoes destroying the Clements community, where his family was sheltering, turned out to be wrong. Several families, like those of Annias and Walter, whom Spencer had known since childhood, had been unlucky, to be sure. But when Spencer considered the potential consequences of the tornadoes driving a lane through the center of Athens—they didn't miss by much—he knew that he had reason to be grateful. Limestone's morning-after assessment—seventeen dead, according to Spencer's preliminary count, 200 injured, 140 houses wrecked, 57 mobile homes trashed, and the unfortunate but acceptable loss of 18 tractor sheds, seven chicken houses, two grocery stores, two churches, a service station, and "an undetermined number of animals"—could seem like a tally of good fortune given the brutality of the storms.

Suffering was relative, after all. Limestone's greatest stroke of luck may have been that its residents, many of them inured to hardship by long experience, tended to be uncomplaining, accepting of ill tidings, and among the least likely people to agitate for handouts. Spencer counted forty-seven families with nowhere to turn for housing after the tornado hit, and, as he put it, "These were not wealthy people." By and large, too, the homeless didn't have insurance, had lost what few possessions they had, and lacked relatives nearby to take them in. Luckily, such people could be offered shelter for a while in a new housing project that had just been completed outside of Athens; luckily, too, it wouldn't be long before some of them would move on to other counties with more to offer.

* * *

On Monday, April 8, four days before his twelfth birthday, Rabbit emerged from his coma in Huntsville. He had confounded doctors. His injured lung had been drained of fluid and his breathing restored to normal, but he had continued to regain consciousness only briefly, before slipping away for lengthy spells. Now, suddenly, he was alert and responsive. He was moved from Intensive Care to a standard hospital room.

The room had a radio. Rabbit tuned in WEUP, which was Alabama's first black-owned and -operated radio station, and which specialized in broadcasting news about the black community. It was during one such report that Rabbit heard that the family of Pastor Annias Green had had its home destroyed by Wednesday's tornadoes, and that Lillian Green had been buried over the weekend. Rabbit could not believe the report. It seemed as though the radio announcer must have been talking about another family.

His uncles Willie and Samuel visited him soon afterwards. Rabbit asked about what he had heard on the radio. Samuel confirmed, as gently as possible, that Rabbit's mother was dead. The uncles did not, however, tell Rabbit how seriously his father and brothers were injured. He had just lost his mother, they reasoned. A little at a time.

Two days later, Willie arrived at Huntsville Hospital to find relatives leaving Amos's room in tears. Over the previous days, since his arrival from Athens Hospital, Amos's condition had declined steeply. He had stopped speaking or responding to voices. He seemed to be moving further and further away from life. Willie could not bear to see the boy's deterioration. He paced outside the room. Moments later, a doctor emerged and told him Amos had died.

Willie returned to Lester with Samuel, who told Annias the difficult truth. Once again, Annias sobbed inconsolably for a time, and when he stopped he announced once more that it was not his role to question God. This time, though, he seemed to have withdrawn far into himself.

By the end of the week, Titus, who was recovering well from surgery, was moved from Intensive Care into a bed next to Rabbit. It was good for Rabbit to have his little brother beside him. It was a particular comfort to be together when Samuel came and sat with them and told them that Amos was gone.

A few weeks after the tornadoes, Spencer received a call from Chicago. A scientist wanted to come to Limestone to investigate the tornado's damage, and asked Spencer to show him around. "I traveled with Dr. Fujita for two days," Spencer related. "I had no idea what he was doing. We'd be driving along, and suddenly he'd get all excited and make me stop so he could go out into a field, put a tag on some tree that was blown down, or an axle that got twisted, or some piece of a house. He'd take a picture, then take a picture from another angle. On and on it went." By now, much of the debris had already been carted to the county landfill, but Fujita was intrigued by minutiae that were imperceptible to Spencer. "It was pretty boring. He told me he was doing some kind of study, but to be honest, it didn't mean a thing to me. I knew families that had had deaths, had lost everything, and here was some guy taking pictures. I thought to myself, 'Who cares how fast the wind was?'"

Spencer brought Fujita to Brown's Ferry Nuclear Plant. The tornadoes had landed east of the plant, but Brown's Ferry had nonetheless gone into an automatic shutdown sequence, triggered by damage to the 500 kilovolt lines carrying power to substations throughout the TVA grid. Fujita told Spencer that the reactors were built to withstand winds of more than 300 miles per hour. "He said that if winds that strong went right over the nuclear plant, though, the cooling towers could be sucked dry. That could cause a meltdown. He liked thinking about that kind of thing.

"I was glad when he was gone," Spencer added. "We didn't have a lot to talk about. I could hardly understand a word he said, and I suppose he couldn't make me out too well, either."

After two weeks in the hospital, Rabbit went to stay with Annias's parents, who lived in a housing project in Huntsville. A week later, Titus joined him. Both boys returned to finish the school year in Tanner. An uncle would pick them up each morning for the thirty-mile trip. When they passed Isom's Orchards, on Highway 72, the boys would fall silent.

It was not until the first Saturday in May that Rabbit and Titus were taken to Lester to visit their father. The moment he saw them, Annias broke into tears. The boys had never seen their father cry before. It was upsetting. The family did not discuss the deaths of Lillian and Amos, though the subject weighed on everyone's minds. Annias, still in great physical discomfort, tried his best to offer the boys words of encouragement. He told them that God would look after them.

Late in the afternoon, the family turned on the television in Annias's room and watched the Kentucky Derby. It was the hundredth running of the race, and Churchill Downs was marking the occasion with plenty of pageantry. More horses than ever—twenty-three— were crowding the field, and more spectators—over 164,000—were squeezed around the track. It was a glorious spring day. A horse called Cannonade won by more than two lengths over Hudson County. The unfortunate Flip Sal pulled up lame.

As the hours of the visit wore on, sadness overtook the room. The boys could not quite grasp the meaning of their father's paralysis, and Annias himself refused to discuss it. But the boys knew that their lives would be changed. They had lost everything in the storm— every stitch of clothing, every schoolbook and family photo. Where would they live? Who was going to cook them dinner? Who would bring them to Little League games, and take them shopping for school clothes? Annias had never performed such tasks before. Rabbit began to take in the depth of the family's predicament. "Daddy," he said, "what are we gonna do?"

Annias could not answer him.

SUPEROUTBREAK TORNADOES OF APRIL 3-4, 1974
148 TWISTERS IN 24 HOURS
From the FINAL ED. COLOR MAP by T. Theodore Fujita, The University of Chicago

EPILOGUE

Mysteries of
Severe Storms

I n a moment your life changes. It's that sudden. The moment is over. It was so quick it might as well not have happened. You ought to be able to forget it, or to pretend it gone. You don't know why it happened to you and not someone else. And since it happened to you, why did you survive it? Others didn't.

It's as though something was revealed to you inside the tornado, something you need to know in order to go on, in order to get out the other side of it. But for the moment you can't recall what it is. So you go back there, back inside it, you feel the wind trying to pull you apart, you go back and tell yourself: This time pay attention to every detail.

You wake in pain. You can't move your leg. You see it at the other end of the bed, under the hump of the sheet, and it doesn't seem to have anything to do with the rest of you. In any case, the leg might not be yours for long. You hear the doctor whispering to someone in the shadows of the room. "I can't promise she'll keep it," he says. You close your eyes.

Sometime later, you wake in pain again. Your father is sitting beside you. He takes your hand. You turn your head and catch your reflection in a basin near the bed. It is not you, really, but some ugly, beaten, sorrowful new version of you.

You are afraid to ask about the boy who was driving. Afraid even to *say his name if that means he must be answered for. You would rather not know.*

Your father tells you that he and your mother went out looking for you during the storm. When they passed the compacted Mustang, your mother went hysterical, fainted, had to be taken home. Your father lied to her and told her it wasn't the same car, all the while praying to himself that if you and the boy were in bad shape, the Lord would take you quickly and not make you suffer.

Well, here you are anyway.

At first, the extent of the outbreak of April 3 was hard even for Ted Fujita to grasp. A few dozen tornadoes was one thing. Damage in two, three, even four states lay within the realm of the possible. But as the day wore on and Fujita began collecting teletype printouts from the National Weather Service, it became clear that the breadth of the outbreak and the scope of its violence went beyond anything in recorded history.

Even as tornadoes continued to land, Fujita saw the opportunity for a research project like none other. He started scrambling to assemble a team to map the outbreak, document the damage, and employ the F-scale to quantify the impact. He chartered aircraft, called a dozen meteorologists to his lab, handed out stacks of topographical maps, and portioned out the midsection of the country to teams of researchers. The work needed to get under way immediately, before cleanup efforts removed too much evidence.

Fujita did much of the surveying himself. For a time, he was accompanied by a twenty-three-year-old named Julian Sereno, who held a degree in geography from the University of Chicago, and whom Fujita had hired nine months earlier to assign F-scale ratings to thousands of twentieth-century tornadoes. ("The job was excruciatingly boring," Sereno said.) Together, the two flew over Mississippi, Alabama, Kentucky, Tennessee, Georgia, North Carolina, West Virginia, and Virginia in a four-seat Cessna 410. Fujita sat alongside the pilot, and Sereno perched behind him, handing him maps, pencils, and film. "I had thought of him as a sort of absent-minded professor," said Sereno, "but once we were in the air, that all changed. He navigated the entire way. He could look down and read every feature of the topography, every trace of damage." Many tornado paths were marked by signposts of flame and smoke, as people on the ground burned debris. Fujita also looked for "white wood," which was visible in freshly cracked trees. He could sometimes see the paths of two or three tornadoes at a time, unfurling across the landscape like parallel highways, then hitting abrupt dead ends.

"Fujita seemed to know all there was to know about flying," Sereno remarked. "He would have the pilot bank the plane so he could go in low and get pictures from the precise angle he wanted. The wing would be way up, and suddenly the treetops would appear right beneath us, and it would seem like we were in free fall. Then Fujita would say the word, and the pilot would pull out of it. He never flinched. He seemed a lot more knowledgeable about flying than the pilot."

The survey produced mounds of data, and Fujita and his team began work on the most detailed and sophisticated study of tornadoes that had ever been undertaken. Fujita's sense of tornadoes was growing increasingly nuanced. On the basis of damage patterns, he described tornadoes changing speed along their paths, accelerating and subsiding, momentarily lifting and then setting back down with renewed violence. He produced evidence of phenomena that had long been thought to be the stuff of fancy, like tornadoes with a pair or even a trio of funnels, or families of tornadoes spawned from a single storm and traveling together. He studied photographs of scallop-shaped marks in a field in Illinois, and intuited that the marks were produced by multiple, tiny, intense vacuums—tornadoes within tornadoes, which Fujita saw as primary agents of destruction. (Such microtornadoes might explain why two people sitting side by side could be thrown in different directions.)

Flying over mountainous terrain in West Virginia, Fujita took particular note of a seemingly unremarkable sight: a stand of trees that had been felled in a flaring, starburst pattern. The pattern indicated that wind had blown straight down, and fanned outward on contact with the ground. The image reminded Fujita of damage he had seen thirty years earlier, in Nagasaki. For the time being, though, the meaning of the association remained elusive.

The outbreak had excited public interest in tornadoes, and Fujita embraced his role as the definitive chronicler of the event, speaking enthusiastically of the day's mythological proportions. "Extraordinary tornado outbreak of 3 April 1974 may be called the 'Jumbo outbreak,'" he wrote in the journal *Weatherwise* in June 1974, even before all the data were in, "because the combination of the year 74 and the 3rd day of April or the 4th month of the year, results in the numbers 747 which designate Jumbo Jet." (Later, Fujita settled on the name "superoutbreak," which seemed to have a better ring to it.)

Indeed, by the time he completed the tally from his survey, the results described an eruption of nature that might be expected to occur once every 500 years. During a seventeen-hour period, 148 tornadoes had careened across thirteen states and a Canadian province. The cumulative paths of the tornadoes covered 2,584 miles. Along the way, some 335 people were killed and more than 6,000 injured. Twenty-seven thousand families sustained property losses, which were estimated, conservatively, at $600 million.

F5

It was not just the number of tornadoes, but their severity, that was astonishing. In the entire decade of the 1960s, Fujita noted, nine tornadoes qualified as F5, characterized by winds believed to approach 318 miles per hour and guaranteeing destruction on an epic scale. Within five hours on April 3, a half-dozen F5 tornadoes hit. The sites of punishment included Brandenburg, Kentucky; Depauw, Indiana; Xenia, Ohio; Cincinnati's suburban neighborhood of Sayler Park; Guin, Alabama; and Limestone County, which had the distinction of playing host to an "incredible" F5 and a "devastating" F4 within a half hour and a half mile of each other. The six F5 tornadoes alone accounted for more than a third of the day's deaths.

Fujita observed, further, that while an average year brought a total of ten F4 tornadoes, twenty-four such tornadoes stormed forth during the daylong superoutbreak. In such a context, the day's thirty-five F3 tornadoes could appear almost to be an afterthought, though on an ordinary day a single F3 would be more than sufficient to inflict notable suffering on a community. Fujita broke down the effects of the tornadoes in a dizzying range of categories—by age and gender of victims, time of day of death, and location in city, town, or rural district. He found that 74 percent of the day's victims perished in houses or buildings, 6 percent in their vehicles, 3 percent while seeking shelter, and 17 percent in mobile homes. To top off his illustration of the day's unparalleled doings, Fujita produced a striking and elegant graphic of destruction: a map of the center of the United States, riddled with 148 red diagonal slashes marking the tracks of the tornadoes. His was a vision of a nation menaced by nature.

For a scientist of Fujita's bent, the day offered abundant material, and he did not hesitate to recognize the richness of the event. "The last night of the survey," Fujita's assistant, Sereno, recalled, "we were in Louisville, at a restaurant. Suddenly, Fujita said that he wanted to propose a toast to tornadoes. I looked around the place and I said, 'You really shouldn't do that. People died around here.' So he stopped. He was a very restrained man. But you could tell how excited he was by what had happened."

The disaster briefly provided the nation a diversion from its post-Vietnam, late-Watergate doldrums. The morning after the outbreak, Vice President Ford directed Air Force Two to fly low over Xenia, Ohio. "The destruction, the devastation is unbelievable," he told reporters. "I have never seen tornado damage where it just literally tore apart buildings. It made matchsticks of them." Ford continued on to Cincinnati, where he attended the baseball game between the Reds and the Atlanta Braves. On his first swing of the season, Hank Aaron hit a home run into the stands behind left-center field, tying Babe Ruth's record.

Aaron may have laid claim to the part of the nation's attention that could be trained on heroes, but Xenia, with its cratered downtown, its dense concentration of casualties, and its convenient proximity to the media centers of Cincinnati and Columbus, stirred the reservoir of pity. The town's image of affliction was only augmented when its neighborhoods were set upon by looters ("Like vultures, the looters continue to pick at the bare bones of shattered buildings in Xenia," reported the *Daily News* in nearby Dayton), and when, to top off the wretchedness, a pair of National Guardsmen—among hundreds sent to Xenia to provide security—were killed in a suspicious fire in a gutted furniture store. "I feel heartsick that men gave their lives to protect junk," said the store's owner.

With the media's gaze trained on the disaster, President Nixon seized the moment to flee the hostile setting of Washington and make an unannounced visit to Xenia, accompanied by dozens of reporters, and finding no shortage of opportunities to convey his sympathy for survivors of the tornado. "It's the worst disaster I've ever seen," he commented, with a blunt sense of the superlatives required on such occasions. During his two-hour stay, he met with local officials, stopped by a relief center, promised to expedite aid to rebuild the city, and remarked, "Xenia has suffered physically, but it has not suffered spiritually." Although a few hecklers greeted his motorcade with calls for impeachment, most of those lining Xenia's debris-choked streets seemed grateful for the attention. "You will make it," Nixon assured a man at a Red Cross shelter. "You will make it as well as Henry Aaron who hit that home run. . . . Wasn't that something?"

Xenia would soon learn, though, that disaster stories have short runs in the crowded national consciousness, and that the town would imminently be left to "make it" on its own. After a week, coverage of the tornado and its aftermath disappeared from the national press as surely as if there had never been a superoutbreak at all. Xenia emerged from the oddly exultant glow of the calamity to take on the tedious and lonely work of digging out. It did not all go smoothly. By the time Bob Hope made an appearance in Xenia at a Christmastime fund-raiser, the town had grown divided against itself. Many locals groused that the town's leaders were exploiting the opportunity provided by the tornado to condemn older properties and push through a sweeping urban renewal plan. The residents of the older homes, mostly low-income workers, learned that raised voices could not stop wrecking crews. Ten blocks of houses adjacent to the business district were razed. A few years later, a new shopping center, complete with a sprawling parking lot, was erected in the heart of town.

Being alive is not what it used to be. Felica stays in the hospital seven weeks. Surgeons reattach the tendons of her left leg, but her recovery is plagued by complications. She has more surgery—skin grafts to replace infected tissue. These, too, are slow to heal. She is wan and demoralized.

Some of her ailments are more difficult to explain. When she thinks of the world outside the hospital room—her home in Wooley Springs, her school, the little grocery store in Coffee Pot and Donnie's parents behind the counter—she panics. She can't breathe, she can't move. It is as though she left her parents' house that Wednesday night, climbed into the red Mustang in the rain, and never got out. She shuts her eyes to calm down, and eventually she falls asleep. But even then the respite is temporary. She begins to dream. "It's always the same moment," *she says.* "I'm in the car. Donnie is next to me. There's the lightning. There's the pressure against me. Rocks are flying, hitting me in the face and body. The cloud is coming. It gets closer. Then it hits. That's when I wake up. Every time. At that moment."

In the middle of May, she is allowed an afternoon's furlough from the hospital. She is brought to Ardmore High to attend the graduation ceremony. She sees Donnie standing across the gym. He is surrounded by friends and is surprised to see her. He has visited her in the hospital, but here he is, back in his element, and Felica appears suddenly, like a stranger. She feels awkward. She needs help walking. She has put on some weight from being bedridden. She is pale.

Everyone at school has been talking about Donnie's crazy luck: found in a field and taken for dead, dumped unconscious at Athens Hospital, diagnosed with a broken neck, put in a hearse and sent to Huntsville. His father, riding along, thought he was delivering his son's corpse to the morgue.

But Donnie came back, and he did it in typically charmed fashion. After spending two days in a coma at the hospital, he opened his eyes, asked where he was, and said he felt worse than the morning after a big game. Within a few days, he went home—to all appearances, not much

worse for the wear. He even drew closer to accepting the football schol-
arship to Ole Miss.

Now, on graduation day, he stands among his classmates, wearing
a wide blue tie beneath his robe, his hair brushed sideways in an attempt
to cover the portion of his scalp that was shaved in the hospital.

He walks over to Felica and offers her his yearbook. She leafs through.
Other girls have scrawled "Love ya" to Donnie across their photographs.
Felica borrows a ballpoint pen. "Donnie," she writes,

> I just don't know how to begin. We have had some great
> times and some bad times. But mostly good ones. You have
> really brought some sunshine into my life. Without you I
> really wouldn't be anything. Even though I have only been
> knowing you for 1 year and 2 months I feel as though I have
> known you all my life. I hope you finally believe me when
> I tell you that "I love you."

She continues,

> It is so great to be able to just sit and think of all that me and
> you have gone through together. I really hope that we can
> go through a lot more just so that we are together.

What else is there to say? Who else but Donnie could understand what
has happened to her? She doesn't have the words for it yet, though. In-
stead, she goes on,

> Next year when your gone it is going to seem so terrible not
> being able to meet on our radiator at lunch break. I'm really
> going to miss you. . . . So be good and please let's don't try
> to tackle another tornado O.K.? Even if we don't make it in

the future (which I hope we do) I still wish the best of luck to you.

Love you,
Felica

Then one of her sisters drives her back to the hospital.

In Limestone County, spring was always a time for renewal: crops in the fields, flowers in gardens, family reunions at Easter, the annual ritual of floor-to-ceiling house cleaning. This year, the overhaul was more total. Hundreds of residents had to cut down damaged trees, replace shattered windows, repair roofs, build new barns. Some had help from insurers. Some received charity from churches, friends, and strangers. A group of Mennonite volunteers arrived in Limestone and went to work rebuilding homes, accepting only food and shelter in return.

Among those whose property had been damaged, there was an unfortunate subgroup whose homes were a total loss. To be sure, these people had reason to be grateful for their lives, but their gratitude was tinged with the loss of everything that reminded them of who they were. Even after most found some kind of temporary shelter, usually at the homes of relatives, other subtler dimensions of their circumstances became apparent as the hours and days passed. The documents with which they could prove ownership of insured goods had been destroyed. Children cried for favorite toys. Teenagers lost their notebooks and school supplies. All of the small, often overlooked comforts of memorabilia—jewelry passed down from a grandmother, an heirloom coin collection, a father's army uniform, wedding photos—were gone. Routines and long-established habits were thrown off. Home was gone.

It was not a question of the modesty or the grandeur of one's prior lifestyle. "The night of the tornado, I made the remark that I'd never live in a mobile home again," said Paula Marbut, whose place in Lawson's Trailer Park had been reduced to shambles. "Be careful what you say!" With six children to look after, Paula had no choice but to get back on her feet quickly. "Mr. Lawson went in there with tractors and cleared our lot, and there I was—back in the same spot two weeks later." Most of the other residents of Lawson's, which was two-thirds destroyed, also returned. Despite their losses, and despite the loss of faith in the safety of their homes, it turned out that they had less mobility and fewer options to start fresh than they might have imagined. They needed to remain close to their jobs and families, and few had much in the way of savings. They were, after all, living in twenty-five-dollar a month housing for a reason. Paula took some comfort from the addition of a communal underground storm shelter in the rebuilt development. "I was really nervous after I moved back," she said. "Whenever the winds got high, I'd gather the kids and go to the storm shelter. I didn't wait for any warnings. We'd carry our dinner down there."

Of course, those whose primary losses had been material could, with time, afford some philosophical reflection on what they had suffered. By the vagaries of good timing, they had survived. Don Lauderdale, whose lavish house had been obliterated, knew how much worse it might have been. "I found one pair of shoes and some scraps of a dining table, and that was it," he said. "Had my family been at home, that would have been scraps of us that were left behind." He remained in awe of the storm's power. "We had a beautiful house, and we had just worked hard to remodel it. I'd be lying if I denied that I was proud of it. But I knew as clear as day that my family had been spared by the power of God." This was not to say that Don was pleased with his insurance adjuster, who, he came to believe, had taken advantage of his rattled state by imposing on him a settlement that far undervalued his losses. "He'd say, 'This is the best you're going to get,' and I was in no mind to argue with him."

Don's wife and family stayed with relatives for a time, while Don moved into a trailer on his property, provided by the Department of Housing and Urban Development, and supervised the construction of a new ranch-style house. The place he built was modern and up-to-date, but it never felt the same to him as the Old Orr House. Eventually he and his wife soured on the place, moving to a smaller house on a historic street in the center of Athens.

Recovery came more haltingly to those who also had injuries, or injured loved ones, to nurse. In many respects, Marilyn McBay was among those who had fared much better than might have been expected. She had found the children she lost hold of during the tornado, and her husband, Vergil, had come back from the brink of death. But Marilyn's lot was not easy. Vergil remained in the hospital for a month with swelling in his brain. He had double vision, was paralyzed down the right side of his body, and had a serious lung infection caused by soil that had been blown into his respiratory tract. Even though he was young and strong, it would be a long road until he was to return to health, and he would have to accept living with some permanent, if mild, impairments to his mobility. Nonetheless, Marilyn and he decided right away to resume construction of the house they had been building next door to her parents. (Work on the house, which had been nearing completion on April 3, would have to start again from scratch.) The familiarity of the surroundings outweighed Marilyn's unease about returning to the site of the disaster. "I'd never lived anywhere else for any length of time," she said. "No matter what happened, I still thought of that land as the safest place for me."

Some weeks after the tornado, Marilyn watched as neighbors arrived at the site of her parents' property with a bulldozer, dug a hole the size of a backyard swimming pool, and buried the rubble of the house in which she had been raised. It was like attending a funeral for a house and a childhood. Afterwards, Marilyn wandered to the woods at the back of the property, stepping over downed trees, and found a few reminders of her past: shreds of her wedding dress, some torn and muddied photographs, bent kitchen utensils. There was not much more. She picked up a Tupperware container that had sewing needles driven through it by the winds of the storm. It struck her as an appropriate symbol for what her family had gone through.

Her brother Frank left the hospital after a week. "I came out of there with a pair of blue jeans, a shirt, and a pair of shoes. I'd ask myself, 'Where are my good jeans?' and then I'd remember, 'Man, they're gone.' First you've got to get yourself a place to sleep, then you need a change of underwear, and then you take it from there." Still, Frank had a job to return to, at Monsanto, and he was strong-willed. With his parents' house gone, he was motivated, finally, to build a place of his own, next door to the one Marilyn and Vergil were building. It would take months to build, of course, and in the meantime he signed up for the loan of a trailer from HUD. He shared the accommodations with his father, Bobby. "That didn't work out too well for either one of us, the bachelor living," Frank remarked. The two men bickered a good deal, and Frank's father seemed disoriented, failing, at times, to take in what had happened. "He'd say, 'I'll be back in a minute—I've got to get something from the basement,'" Frank recalled. "Then he'd walk right back in, with this strange look on his face, and say, 'I've got no basement.'"

Indeed, Marilyn was worried about their father. He was anxious and depressed, blamed himself for his family's predicament, and could not decide whether to rebuild, or how to get on with his life. She had never before known him to be like this. "I'd come up the drive and see that little trailer sitting on a bare patch of dirt, hooked up to this one utility pole they'd brought in," Marilyn said. "Daddy would be sitting inside, looking so sad, like that was all that was left of his life. He was lost not knowing what would happen with my mother."

Frank and Marilyn's mother, Joyce, was in the worst shape of anyone in the family. She had a shattered pelvis and had sustained nerve damage. For a while it was unclear whether she would live; then, for months, there was uncertainty about whether she would walk again. She stayed in the hospital for four months, and when she got out she lived with constant, debilitating pain. She tried to return to her job in Huntsville, but was forced to retire on disability. Sometimes it was small discomforts that most brought home the painful facts of the turn her life had taken. "My mother was a person who always loved shoes," said Marilyn, sadly. "She used to have so many different pairs, and was always shopping for new styles. Now the doctors told her she had to wear these flat, ugly orthopedic shoes. It made her feel different about herself. Somehow, the shoes were the thing that bothered her most."

Civic life went on without missing a beat. However widespread the outbreak had been, for the great majority of people, even in Limestone, the tornadoes had been an inconvenience at worst. For a few, it had been a remarkable, death-defying enterprise. On May 7, a month after his wild night, Buddy Evans won the Democratic primary election for Limestone County sheriff by a wide margin.

On the same ballot, Governor George Wallace captured more

than three-quarters of the vote in Limestone, en route to a land-slide victory in the general election.

Where Civil Defense was concerned, residents of Limestone were quick to abandon their casual stance toward tornadoes. "After April 3," Spencer Black noted, "you didn't have to say much about severe weather to get people to pay attention. That day really set up the fear of tornadoes in this county." A self-congratulatory federal government report on the outbreak, prepared by the National Oceanic and Atmospheric Administration, concluded that "preseason planning and preparedness, education, and dissemination of information, the outstanding performance by National Weather Service staffs . . . and the dedicated and superb job of the broadcast media in relaying weather information to the public resulted in saving thousands of lives during the April 3–4 outbreak." In Limestone, though, there had been nothing systematic about who lived and who died. In some cases, it had been a simple matter of whether someone in a tornado's path had his radio tuned to Spencer and the King Country Rover's intrepid Bill Dunnavant. Following the outbreak, though, residents scrambled to protect themselves from further storms, like people who quit smoking after a neighbor's death from cancer. "To be honest with you," Spencer said, "I would have loved to have been in the business of putting in storm shelters after April 3, because it seemed that everybody started getting one. I'd have been a millionaire." Limestone received additional tornado protection in a roundabout way, as TVA installed four dozen sirens within a ten-mile radius of newly opened Brown's Ferry Nuclear Plant between April and August 1974. Spencer realized that the sirens, which were intended to provide warning in the event of a release of radiation or other malfunction at the nuclear plant, and which could be heard over a range of three miles, provided an excellent system for alerting residents to the threat of severe weather.

Soon enough, the blare of the sirens was taken as seriously in Limestone as air raid sirens in war zones.

By the following March, though, the presumed safety of high-tech Brown's Ferry would be called into question, when workers at the nuclear plant accidentally set fire to cables running from the generator's control room to the reactor. The public was not initially informed of the episode. Later, the facility's superintendent "did concede that the amount of radioactivity rose in the immediate area of the fire," according to local papers, but it was not until months had gone by that the Nuclear Regulatory Commission revealed that "the fire . . . was spreading on the reactor building side of the wall." An alarming number of the plant's safety measures had failed, and the reactor had had to be shut down manually. It stayed shut for more than a year, and by the time it reopened, confidence in the facility had been undermined. By the mid-80s, Unit One went offline indefinitely. "There's no other way to put it," Spencer said. "We just about had a meltdown here."

As debris was trucked off, houses restored, and broken bones slowly healed, other, less visible scars remained. Although the dimensions of the disaster were most easily measured in casualties, it turned out that survival was not always a simple proposition.

Walter McGlocklin, who had been called away from his son's second birthday party to help reset downed power lines, and who had unwittingly left his family to confront a tornado on their own, struggled to endure the storm's aftermath. "My world was torn to pieces," he said. He was left alone with his two small daughters, Nancy and Grace. "Grace was in a body cast for a long time, and when they took it off, she had to learn to walk all over again. It was hard on her. She would start crying, and I'd have to say, 'Now come on there, take another step.'" Walter, too, was forced to relearn many aspects of daily life. He went back to work at the Electric Department, but devoted himself to homemaking the rest of the time. It was a constant struggle. Not only did he lack the skills that had seemed to come so easily to his wife, Ruth; his attempts at being a mother, as well as a father, to his girls, were emotionally harrowing.

"I learned to give them baths and to feed them," Walter said. "Cooking wasn't so bad—I could open a can, I could fry potatoes. But learning how to wash the clothes was another thing. I went to a store in Decatur and got enough clothes so the girls had something different to wear every day of the week. Then, each Sunday, I'd go to the Washeteria and clean everything to get us through the next week." His grief, and that of his daughters, surfaced frequently. "The hardest thing was when the girls would go crying for their mother and brother and sister," he said. "It happened a lot. Me, I never drank, I've never been on dope, but I would get to feeling sorry for myself when they cried like that." He paused to collect himself. "I thought about shooting myself more than once."

For months, Walter carefully avoided returning to his ruined property. Then one day his daughter Grace startled him by saying that if he installed a storm shelter, she and Nancy were ready to move back home. "That's why I decided to build back the house," Walter said. "Their mother had worked hard to help me pay for it, and nothing was going to keep me from leaving it to my children." He toiled on the house over two years of evenings and weekends. When it was done, it was identical to the original, brick for brick. "I thought that even if I didn't live much longer, at least they would have a home."

The tornadoes of April 3 brought Walter and Annias Green to a common place of sorrow and hardship. Annias stayed in the hospital for three months, during which time his faith in miracles was, to some extent, confirmed. "When the time came," he said, "I was walking—barely, but that was more than the doctor was expecting. I got out of the hospital on Saturday, and the next day I went to church and thanked God." He was hardly in high spirits, though. "Everything was gone. I had two boys who needed me, but I realized that, in a way, I had always had someone else taking care of me. My wife had looked after all the family's needs. She had protected me." He moved the family into an apartment provided by HUD, and reacquainted himself with Rabbit and Titus. "I said to them, 'We've got to depend on each other. I depend on you. Every morning, I'm going to get up and fix you breakfast, and if anything's on your mind, I want to know about it.'" Like Walter, Annias found that learning to manage the routines of household life was painful. His mother and other relatives helped out, but Annias, hobbled as he was, was intent on being self-sufficient. Before long, "I bought a cookbook. I sat down and studied it just like I would study a fishing magazine or the Bible. I'd make a roast beef, or pork chops, or chicken. I found a cake that came in a box, and you just added milk and baked it."

He worried about his boys constantly. Rabbit, he said, "was so attached to his mother. He gave up a lot when he lost her. I think he was lonely for some time. Probably I should have gotten him some therapy. But I didn't know that at the time, and he didn't really show that he was hurting." Annias relied on prayer to relieve his own grief. But his sons often found him in tears, and his sadness could make him seem more remote than ever. He even had fleeting thoughts of suicide. "I always tried to keep my sorrow close to me. I prayed that somehow I would find inner strength."

December 20, 1974. Seven months after the tornado. Felica, a tenth-grader, returns home from the last day of classes before Christmas vacation. She has much to accomplish in the next few hours. She has to

F5

make sure that her hair—which is now cut straight, in bangs, across her forehead, and which has, despite all her efforts to dye it blonde, settled into a reddish tint ("Donnie loves redheads," *she confesses)—is perfect. Her sisters help with her makeup. Then, finally, they stand around her as she puts on the white gown her mother has made for her. The dress is anything but form-fitting. Its bulky pleats extend to the floor, covering even her shoes, and its neckline exposes just a tiny triangle of flesh beneath her throat. Still, she is radiant. She heads off to Wooley Springs Baptist.*

Enter Donnie, strolling down the aisle of the church in a broad-lapelled blue suit striped with thick herringbone. His hair covers his ears and forehead. His father, Calvin, his best man, is waiting for him.

"After the tornado," *Donnie says,* "I just didn't want to let Felica out of my sight. I was afraid of losing her." *He has turned down his football scholarship, and spent the summer after high school graduation working at a Coca-Cola bottling plant in Huntsville. His only long-term plan is to stay close to Felica.* "I started wanting to marry her so bad," *he admits. One night in July, he picked Felica up—he had bought a new car by then—and took her for a long drive. He pulled over at a quiet spot.* "Open the glove compartment," *he said. When she looked inside, she found a ring. Felicia, still just fifteen, needed her parents' permission, as well as their signatures on the marriage license. She and Donnie agreed that if her parents opposed her, she would tell them she was prepared to run off with Donnie.*

It did not come to that. Since the tornado, her father's health, always fragile, has been failing rapidly. He wants to live to see his youngest daughter wed. He has made her promise to finish school. "I promised," *Felica says,* "but I don't think he really believed me." *Now he stands at the altar, facing her. He lifts her veil, and performs the ceremony.*

Before the new school term begins, Felica and Donnie move into a small apartment at the back of Powers Grocery, in Coffee Pot. Donnie works full time in his father's store. Felica helps out in the store, teaches piano lessons, and continues in tenth grade, keeping up good grades. In the eyes of the school, Donnie is now her legal guardian. He has to provide her with handwritten notes to excuse any absences. He has to sign her report card.

At times, Donnie finds himself driving by the site of the accident over and over. Although he is back to his old state of fitness, as opposed to Felica, whose leg still bothers her, he too continues to be haunted by the tornado, as though he were still behind the wheel of the Mustang, and has still realized, too late, what he has driven into. Each time someone says the word "tornado" he sees the storm cloud coming toward him.

"Sometimes Felica and I would be sleeping," *says Donnie,* "and we'd hear the wind coming around the corner of the store, and we'd be scared to death. If there was thunder, I couldn't stay in place. I'd need to run and get in someone's basement right away." *Others don't notice. He still seems to be the same gregarious, confident, easygoing football star. But he knows he is going through the motions. He is, as he puts it,* "weather-scared."

Three months after getting married, Felica and Donnie drive to Birmingham, where Felica's father is receiving a kidney transplant. While they are there, they learn that a tornado has hit Coffee Pot. "We left that night to come home," *Donnie says.* "There wasn't much damage to the house, but the trees around it had been demolished and—I don't know, I lost it. I cried like a baby. I thought, 'This can't be happening again.'"

Could anything be gained from the tornado outbreak, other than an appreciation of the annihilating power of natural forces? Fujita was on the verge of coming up with a comprehensive vision of airborne violence. His life had been marked by an obsession with prizing out the minute facets of destruction. But he was still one piece of evidence short of completing his puzzle.

The evidence would come a year after the superoutbreak, on the afternoon of June 24, 1975, and it, too, would be deadly. Eastern Airlines Flight 66, en route from New Orleans, crashed while attempting to land at New York's Kennedy International Airport. All but twelve of the 124 passengers and crew on board the Boeing 727 were killed. Most of the survivors were critically burned. (Among the dead was Wendell Ladner, a player for the New York Nets of the American Basketball Association, who was known as "Wonderful Wendell.") Scattered thunderstorms were passing over the airport at the time of the crash, but a spokesman for the Federal Aviation Administration reported that the conditions were "not particularly adverse for an experienced airline crew."

Indeed, Flight 66 made its final approach to the airport smoothly and with routine ease. Suddenly, though, at 400 feet, the plane lost speed. Fighting to remain airborne, the pilot accelerated rapidly. The plane went out of control, clipping a row of lights 2,400 feet from the runway, nearly flipping over sideways, and incising a 340-foot track in the ground. It broke apart over busy Rockaway Boulevard in Queens, littering the road with fiery debris.

Fujita, at the height of his fame following the superoutbreak, was invited to weigh in on the crash. He analyzed the flight data recorders of several planes that had landed prior to Flight 66, as well as pilot reports and local weather conditions. As always, he pieced together the scattered bits of data into a three-dimensional picture of air in motion. Then he took a leap of imagination. He connected the crash to the image of starburst-shaped damage patterns that he had held in his memory since visiting Nagasaki thirty years earlier. It was an image that had been freshly evoked the previous year, when he flew over a forest of trees uprooted during the superoutbreak. Now, he surmised that the distinctive patterns of damage had been caused by "rare downbursts" of wind that "descended near the ground and burst out violently." Such winds, he argued, were too small—perhaps a few hundred yards in diameter—to be detected by radar, but were capable of producing explosive effects. Flight 66, as he saw it, had been unlucky enough to cross paths with a downburst. As the plane attempted to cross through the wind, Fujita reasoned, it encountered a sudden shift from a headwind to a tailwind, which cut off the airflow over the wings, and caused the plane to plummet.

Fujita's suggestion rang true to aviators, many of whom wrote to him of having struggled with unexpected bursts of wind. Meteorologists, though, brushed aside the theory, claiming that it was based on scant data, and represented the height of conjecture. Some even accused Fujita of simply giving a new name to such well-known phenomena as the thunderstorm downdraft and "gust front," thereby claiming credit for long-established ideas.

"The criticism led to several sleepless nights," Fujita commented. Indeed, he was wounded by the response, adopting a defensive posture towards his critics, and believing that the controversy, which would drag on for years, confirmed his maverick status. With some grandiosity, he likened himself to German geologist Alfred Wegener, who had proposed the fundamentals of continental drift theory in the 1920s, only to have his work rejected by his hidebound contemporaries. "In Winter 1930," Fujita noted, "desperate and disappointed on his lifetime work on the drift, Wegener undertook an expedition in Greenland and was found dead in snow and ice."

Fujita went on to spend more than a decade marshaling evidence in support of his model. In 1991, he received a letter from a reviewer of his work acknowledging the "professional jealousy" of the meteorological community. For Fujita, vindication was finally on its

F5

way. The downburst theory was coming to be regarded "as one of the major, rapid payoff, success stories in the atmospheric sciences," according to James Wilson and Roger Wakimoto of the National Center for Atmospheric Research. Strategies for contending with downbursts were made standard parts of pilot training, and as the emerging technology of Doppler radar was refined, not only was the existence of violent small-scale winds verified, but, as Wilson and Wakimoto wrote, Fujita's insights "benefited the whole of society. . . . There is little question that many lives have been saved."

By now, though, a decisive changing of the guard was taking place in meteorology. Fujita's methods, which depended above all on conceptual thinking, aided by superior skills of draftsmanship and scrupulous attention to diverse detail, came to seem outmoded. Instead, computer modeling and space-based technology drove new research. By the early '90s, the University of Chicago scaled back its once-renowned meteorology program, and Fujita was forced to retire at age seventy.

Although he had long promised his wife, Suzuki, that they would resettle in Japan when he retired, when the time came he insisted that he needed to remain in the United States to continue his work. He began assembling a lifetime of materials into a highly unusual, privately published book, entitled *Memoirs of An Effort to Unlock the Mystery of Severe Storms During the 50 Years, 1942–1992.* The memoir was organized in the form of a scientific paper, and was replete with charts and diagrams. (It cost $113.56 to print each of the 1,130 copies.) Throughout, Fujita strained to maintain a tone of scientific objectivity, and hinted at wistfulness only infrequently. "Although I regret that I had no chance to orbit around the earth in a manned spacecraft," he wrote, "I was fortunate to have flown repeatedly over and around thunderstorm tops by high-altitude research Lear Jet."

In his last years, he suffered from constant and mysterious pain. Doctors attributed his condition to complications from diabetes, but Fujita was not convinced. He undertook an extensive study of his own vital signs, charting some of his results in his memoir, but was unable to alleviate his suffering. "Anything that moves I am interested in," he had once remarked. He died on November 19, 1998.

Thirty years after the tornado outbreak, Limestone County is a changed place. Highway 72, which runs through Athens, is lined with shopping plazas anchored by large national retailers, like Wal-Mart, Lowes, and Staples, while Athens's tree-lined downtown square is often deserted. Even longtime residents satisfy their hankerings for cornbread and dumplings at Cracker Barrel, and with the shuttering of most small eateries, Limestone's remaining farmers and its many retirees are apt to take their morning coffee at McDonald's or Waffle House. Athens has its own exit off the interstate highway, around which an alternate village of motels and convenience stores has grown up. (The county has even begun allowing the sale of beer and wine.) Indeed, as Limestone has prospered—its population increasing by three-fourths since 1974, its income and educational levels rising impressively, its health care services being greatly modernized—the area has attained a measure of anonymity that could make it seem virtually indistinguishable from any number of towns or suburbs in the country. Limestone's low real estate taxes have made it an appealing bedroom community for people with jobs in Huntsville, and the twenty-five-mile stretch between Athens and Huntsville is a near-unbroken sprawl of development. Much of Limestone's beautiful, gently rolling farmland has given way to subdivisions, retirement villages, and golf courses. (There is also a maximum security penitentiary.) For most of those traveling through, there would be little to indicate that Limestone is anything but a generic stopover.

But of course, something did happen here. There are few reminders of it. Land has no memory, wind has no memory, and it does not take long before actors in distant dramas retreat into the privacy of the unremembered past.

The past has not yet vanished entirely, though. Just a few turns off Limestone's main routes, cotton is still being planted in the fields, cows still graze in pastures, and people who have been reared in the county, along with generations of their families, are living out their days. They are aging, but they have not moved away. Limestone is the world they know. Few are wealthy and none is famous. Like people in out-of-the-way places anywhere, they have stories to tell, if anyone stops to ask. Out of a collection of their stories—some of them contradictory, some mythologizing, some told only with great reluctance—a world can seem to emerge.

In a severe windowless bunker near Athens–Limestone County Hospital, Spencer Black continues to hold sway over Limestone's modern Emergency Operations Center, where Civil Defense, now called Limestone County Emergency Management, is located. The single inconspicuous entrance is always locked, and visitors are screened by camera before being admitted. It is the type of structure in which one might imagine hazardous materials being stored. Inside, its walls are plastered with maps of evacuation routes, and a command center, with posts for local, state, and federal officials, stands at the ready. Spencer, looking hale and full of swagger, comes and goes on his own schedule. "I built us one of the best EOCs in the nation," he says, proudly. "This place is full to the gills of emergency equipment." Computers monitor all of the county's gas lines, fire hydrants, and emergency communications, and a mobile command post is on its way. Doppler radar has made for vast improvements in predicting and tracking severe weather, including tornadoes, and although Limestone has been hit with twenty tornadoes since 1974, including an F4 in 1995, there has been only one tornado-related death in that time. Over the years, Spencer has had his own setbacks—he has suffered two heart attacks and developed diabetes—but he looks as though he is far from ready to pack it in. However unlikely, he has succeeded in becoming the longest-serving Civil Defense Director in Alabama's history, and masterfully works the system to Limestone's advantage. "Ever since September 11, Homeland Security has been handing out all kinds of money," he says, "and I'm making sure we get a good share of it."

Spencer's counterpart in maintaining Limestone's security back in 1974, Buddy Evans, stepped aside from official duties years ago. In 1978, he ran for a fifth term as sheriff. "I didn't campaign at all," he says. "My heart wasn't in it anymore. The guy who ran against me—he was a good fellow, but he wasn't sheriff-ing material. He got himself a big hickory stick to walk around with, like the sheriff in that movie *Walking Tall*. People bought that stuff. I got beat." Buddy spent the next three years at the State Alcohol and Beverage Control Board in Montgomery, continuing to pursue drug dealers and moonshiners, then returned to Limestone for good. Since his pension from his years as sheriff amounts to $560 monthly, or, as he puts it, "enough to pay your light bill," he and his wife returned to public life, this time as restaurateurs. The first place they opened was called Catfish Inn, and it was so successful that they have added a second restaurant, on a dusty road across from a cotton gin, that is considered Limestone's best stop for barbecue. Buddy opens the place most mornings, and stays to man the register and to greet customers through lunch. But that takes all the energy he can muster. His health has gone into decline. He has had a pair of knee replacements, a hip replacement, prostate cancer, and multiple strokes. For a time, he lost his eyesight. And he is frequently crippled by severe back trouble and arthritis. "It was from all those nights lying on the ground in the snow and ice, staking out whiskey stills," he says. His memory comes and goes. During good spells, he can still project the command of the man who ran Limestone for sixteen years. His time as sheriff was the high point of his life. "I never felt that being sheriff made me powerful," he remarked. "It was just good work, and I like to think I was good at it."

Looking back to the night of tornadoes in 1974, Buddy remarks, "It was the worst thing I ever dealt with. It was a booger. But Limestone—well, we've got the best people anyplace. We look after each other. If I was going to live anywhere, it would be right here. Which is where I'll be until the day I die. Which won't be long."

Each person has his own disaster, and each his own survival. After the tornado, well-heeled Don Lauderdale, who had been laid off from his job in aerospace just a week earlier, was not only homeless, he was out of work. He eventually landed a job at Dunlop Tire, in a neighboring county. "It wasn't as much money as working at Redstone Arsenal, and it wasn't the same excitement," he admits. "But how could I have any complaints?" He stayed on the job until retiring at fifty-five. Then he and his wife threw themselves into their new passion, missionary work. They have traveled to more than twenty countries in Africa, Europe, and Central America. "I've been faithful to the Lord," he says.

He is sitting on a porch swing in the shade of a summer day, wearing a golf shirt, chinos, and loafers. A granddaughter plays nearby. He sips from a Pepsi, and allows himself to get lost in the past. "One thing that I had always wanted to do," he remarks, "was to go to the land of Israel. I used to have an old Bible in which I marked the Biblical cities I planned to visit. I thought I'd take that Bible with me if I ever got to Israel, and use it the way you use a guide book. Well, naturally it got blown away in the storm with everything else." In 2000, Don finally made his pilgrimage. "I thank the Lord for letting me get there." A year later, in December 2001, he made a different kind of journey, venturing to New York City for the first time. His purpose was to visit the site of the World Trade Center after the attacks of that fall. "I'd seen it on television, but I had to get a close-up look," he says. He goes silent. Finally, he reflects, "It's been a long time now since I've thought about that tornado."

Not far from the spot where Don's beloved Old Orr House stood, Frank Orr can still be found, in jeans and a T-shirt, doing chores around the house he built for himself after the storm. Frank married in the early '80s, and had a daughter who is now grown, though she still lives at home. He quit Monsanto long ago, and went to work in a General Motors assembly plant in Spring Hill, Tennessee, an hour-long commute from Limestone in each direction. When GM cut 1,500 jobs at the factory late in 2005, Frank had enough seniority to stay on. The situation is precarious, though, and his best hope is that his job might last until he is ready to retire. He spends most of his free time in his large and meticulously organized vegetable garden. "It's a hobby," he says, bashfully. "It's like riding a motorcycle. I just enjoy going out there and playing in the dirt." He is still tall and gangly and seems less like a middle-aged man than a kid fresh out of the army, wandering away every so often, only to return a few minutes later, smelling of cigarette smoke.

The tornado, Frank insists, belongs to another lifetime. "It's just a thing that happened. In that way, it was like Vietnam. It wasn't

F5

good or bad. It happened. It couldn't be avoided." Still, he admits, "I dream of my parents' old house"—the one he was in when the tornado struck—"all the time. The lights go out and I'm back there, walking through every room. It's not a dream about the tornado. I might be dreaming that I've overslept and need to get to work—something ordinary like that. But whatever it is, the dream is always happening in that house."

He steps outside, and looks across some fields, as though he were paying attention to something just beyond the edge of sight. Three dogs run up to him, and he jostles with them affectionately. "There's one thing I know," he laughs. "I've got these dogs here, and the minute they start acting funny, I'm headed to the storm pit. If you want to learn about tornadoes," he says, as the dogs surround him, "keep an eye out for these guys."

Frank's sister Marilyn still lives next door, too, in a house decorated throughout with American flags. Marilyn has never stopped pondering why the seven members of her family at home on the night of the tornado survived. "I felt myself dying during the tornado," she reflects. "There was no way we should have lived. The only way I can think about it is that God's hand was around us." She doesn't seem entirely satisfied by the explanation, though, and the matter still gnaws at her. Though it was long ago, the tornado divided her family's life into "before" and "after." After the tornado, her mother failed to recover her former health, and lived in pain until dying of cancer in 1993. Marilyn's father, too, never regained his confidence in himself, and remained convinced that he had let down his family that night. In 1995, Marilyn's father also died of cancer.

Now, past age fifty-five, Marilyn has found that the steadiness of having spent her life in a single place, surrounded by extended family and longtime friends, is still not enough to keep life's larger mysteries at bay. In July 2004, her son Jason, who was two years old in 1974, and who got through the tornado with a bad gash on his leg, tumbling through the air in his grandmother's arms, took his own life. Marilyn is suffering his loss terribly. "My son hurt so bad that he thought all he could do was to die. That's the hardest part to live with. I have so many questions. I just have to live with not knowing the answers. Still," she says, "I believe he's okay now."

Scars and debris. Walter McGlocklin points to the stump of a white oak tree in front of his house. "It's been there since April 3, 1974, when the tornado knocked the tree down," he explains. The wood of the stump dried out long ago and has hardened in the sun. Walter stares at it. "The pain doesn't go away. The Bible tells you that you're not supposed to question God, but I have surely wondered why God let it happen. My wife was a good person. And those two little ones, my boy and my girl, they were too young to be accountable. So why would the good Lord take them away? It's a shame."

He walks into the living room of his house. The furniture sags, the air smells musty, and a display case is cluttered with mementoes. Walter reaches for one, a framed photo, faded almost to white with age. "This here is my little boy," he whispers. He struggles to continue speaking. "Someone found it in the mess, and I did my best to fix it up. It's all I've got." He studies the photo. Little Walter would now be in his thirties. His features are soft and delicate. He is locked in time. "He looks like me, doesn't he?" Walter says, as though to himself. "That's what people tell me."

Although Walter eventually remarried, he confesses to having found little solace over the years. The night of the tornado remains fresh to him, and he continues to replay his actions, as though he might somehow alter the outcome. "If I hadn't been called into work, I would have been right here," he repeats. "I would have been right here with all of them, at the fireplace. It probably would have been me that had gotten killed. If it had been me instead of my wife, she could have done a better job raising the children than I did. I tried my best, I did. But she was their mother."

As the years have passed, the stress of work and worry have taken a toll on Walter's health. He has had a severe stroke, which damaged his vision and paralyzed one side of his body. Slowly, he has recovered, and, never having known idleness, has kept himself busy with errands and housework. Often, he looks after the young children of his daughter, Nancy, who has gone back to school to pursue a master's degree in psychology. And he regularly tends to the graves of his wife and two children.

"There's not a day goes by that it doesn't come back to me," Walter says. "I'll be out in the yard, working, and I'll look up, and I'll have a vision of that little redheaded tomboy, Sandra, just about to round the corner of the house. She was five years old, was all, back then. She'll run right over to me and say, 'What are you doing now, Daddy?' "

Annias Green lives just a few miles from Walter, on a quiet country road, in a small house he shares with his second wife, Sara. He became acquainted with her shortly after the tornado. Sara was a young widow then. In Limestone's tight-knit black community, it was not surprising that she knew members of Annias's family, and hearing of his situation, she had paid him a visit in the hospital. Slowly, a relationship developed and deepened. Annias was fiercely protective of his surviving sons, Rabbit and Titus, and even after he and Sara had a child of their own together, he refused to remarry until the boys were grown. (The arrangement caused some consternation among members of Annias's church.) He was also highly sensitive about the memory of his late wife. Over the years, he rarely, if ever, spoke of the night of the tornado, or of his losses. He went back to work at the Laborers' International Union, Local 366, where he became manager before retiring in 1995, and he continues to preach at Macedonia Primitive Baptist Church, where he is senior pastor.

He is proud of how his sons have turned out. Titus, the youngest, lives in California and works as an undertaker. Ananias, Jr.—still known as Rabbit to family back in Limestone—joined the Air Force at eighteen. He remained in the service for twenty-two years, rising to the rank of senior master sergeant, and earning two college degrees along the way. After retiring, Rabbit settled in Atlanta and became an investigator with the Drug Enforcement Agency. Married, with three children of his own, Rabbit has managed to make his peace with the storm that took his mother and his brother Amos. He still has a long scar on his forehead, a daily reminder of what he went through. "The tornado is a part of who I am," Rabbit says.

Despite Annias's reticence, there is little doubt that he, too, carries the tornado within himself. Now in his mid-sixties, he has put on some weight, walks stiffly from his old spinal injuries, and carries himself with a reserved dignity. He also has about him an air of loneliness. "It's not my business to question God," he considers one night, sitting on a sofa in his living room, the television playing in the background, and the walls hung with framed prayers. "I lost a child—it's like losing a piece of yourself. More than ever, I had to learn to depend on the Lord. I couldn't try to make sense of it on my own. I would have lost my mind. I studied Job, and I saw what he had endured. I didn't seek explanations. It can't be explained."

Since retiring, Annias is free to go fishing any day he chooses. As always, he prefers to go alone. His reluctance to revisit memories of the tornado has become nearly absolute. When the subject is raised, he lowers his voice, and begins speaking in rapid, agitated tones. He cries, then turns away. "It's still a little tender," he says, recovering himself. "I think I've fared better, not talking about it. Maybe now that I'm getting old it might be a good time to talk a little bit. But once I share it, and get it all out, that's going to be all the talking there is for me."

Sara appears in the doorway of the living room, and Annias immediately falls quiet. Hard as it is for him to talk about the past under any circumstances, it is particularly difficult when Sara is nearby. It is clear that he doesn't want to wound her by bringing up his feelings for his former wife. But after a moment of discomfort, he glances over at her. He seems tired, and his eyes are cloudy. Sara looks back at him with great concern and affection. "It was important that I met someone who helped me recover," Annias says. "I couldn't live with a dead person. I had to find a way to come back to the living. I had a good marriage back then, and later I met Sara and I have a good marriage now. I've been heavenly blessed. I've got no bitterness. I just hope and pray that if Sara dies, I can die along with her."

November 14, 2005. The skies over Limestone County are filmy gray. The air is sticky. Trees list in the gusty wind. Tornado warnings are in effect for adjacent counties.

Felica and Donnie Powers sit in the living room of their spacious Athens house, where they moved in 2004, after selling the convenience store they had taken over from Donnie's parents in Coffee Pot. They are looking over some reminders of the old days: an Ardmore High School yearbook, circa 1974, its pages buckled with moisture and stuck together; Donnie's class ring, with its dull aquamarine stone; the slender band of a "promise ring," which looks as though it could have fit on a child's finger; an inch-long wooden peg, kept in an old pill bottle, which worked its way out of Felica's foot a year after she was injured in the tornado.

After many years, Felica and Donnie have finally stepped out of the past, out of the moment that nearly brought them to their deaths. It was a moment each of them has relived over and over, as though time had stopped with it. All of their fears seem to have been contained in it. In it, too, they found each other.

Of course, life has gone on all the while. They have raised two children. Donna was born in 1977, four months after Felica graduated from high school, and Donnie, Jr., followed three years later. "You can guess who named them," Felica says. (Donna now has two children of her own.) Donnie is forty-nine. He is still tall and garrulous, but his athlete's frame has softened. He retired from the Limestone County Board of Education after thirty years—twenty of them as a bus driver, and the final ten as director of transportation and maintenance for the school system's fleet of ninety school buses. "I always loved to drive," he jokes. Now, he finds himself at another moment of transition, exploring his options for the years to come. He is mulling over entering county politics. In the meantime, Felica has become a school bus driver, too. "It's the family business," she notes.

Tornadoes are the family business, too. They have come to stand for all the sudden uncertainty that can disturb Felica and Donnie's sense of safety and order. Once, in May 1988, Donnie was transporting a group of second graders back from a field trip, when the weather turned unexpectedly ugly. Rain swept the road from visibility. The windshield fogged up. A teacher stood beside Donnie wiping the glass as he drove on. "I turned my head," he recalls, "and I saw a funnel. There was nothing I could do. I could feel the bus shaking. I pulled beneath an overpass. There were forty kids on board. One of them was my own son. I told the kids to get beneath their seats." The children screamed and cried. Donnie was seized with a familiar fear. "The thoughts came right back to me," he says. "But I had to stay calm." In some ways, the experience helped him

F5

to expunge the memories of April 3, 1974. The tornado passed. Donnie made his way slowly back to Limestone. "When we pulled up to the school, the parents were cheering."

Listening to Donnie tell the story, Felica shifts uneasily in her chair, and glances out the front window. The sky has a peculiar yellowish tint. In a few minutes, she must leave home, drive into the storm on her afternoon rounds, and deliver a busload of children to their families. She turns back to Donnie. "I think there must have been a reason we went through the tornado," she ventures. "I've done a lot of deep thinking on it over the years. Maybe it was to bring us closer together."

"You know," Donnie adds, "sometimes I think we were saved so that we'd be able to tell our story to others."

He begins browsing through wedding pictures. "We looked so awful!" Felica cries, in mock horror. "Put those away!" But she, too, pauses to take in a photo of the two of them getting into a streamer-covered car to leave for their honeymoon. She remembers how they had stopped for burgers at Krystal's on their way out of Limestone, and how, checking into a hotel that night in Huntsville, they were forced to return to Limestone to retrieve their marriage certificate, without which the clerk would not give them a room. "We must have known that if we could withstand the tornado, we could get through most anything," she says. "And we pretty much have. We've had our little ups and downs, but we've always worked through it. Donnie?"

He is now absorbed in his high school yearbook.

"Donnie," Felica teases, "are you looking at your old girlfriends again?"

"There's the head cheerleader," he points out. "Just look at her. It's been so long I'd almost forgotten, but there were some fine looking girls in that class."

Felica leaves for work. From elsewhere comes the sound of a child's cry, and Donnie steps from the living room for a moment, returning with his drowsy two-year-old granddaughter, Mallory, in his arms. He sits down in an armchair, cradling her.

He turns on the television and studies the Doppler radar images on the screen, the patches of various shades of green, the yellows and oranges, the unnerving specks of red. A law enforcement scanner squawks in the background. When Felica is out on the road, Donnie has a habit of listening to the scanner for accident reports.

A half hour later, the phone rings. Donnie picks it up quickly. It is Felica, calling from the bus. She has just heard tornado sirens blow, and she is scared. She wants to know what to do. Donnie speaks calmly, in a serious tone. "You've got to be strong, Felica," he says. "You've got kids on the bus. You get those kids home, now. You can do it."

He sits back, stroking his granddaughter's hair, a look of distraction on his face.

Before long, his granddaughter drifts back to sleep. The skies outside are darkening. There is silence and thunder and rain on the windows. Donnie looks toward the empty street. "You come on home, now, Felica," he says.

Notes

F5 is a book of memory, and memory is an ambiguous force. The challenge of reconstructing a swiftly passing, violent moment from the point of view of those who lived through it, let alone those who did not, turned out to be far more complicated than I had expected. As meteorologists who study tornadoes recognize: Anything that moves makes for a difficult study.

It might have been possible to describe the events of April 3, 1974, on the basis of documentary evidence alone, and I have done my best to get hold of as many such sources as I could. These are mostly drawn from newspapers, magazines, meteorological journals, and a few compilations of photographs and news accounts. My attempt to examine the human and psychological dimensions of the disaster, however, relied crucially on interviews with survivors, their family members, and witnesses, especially in Limestone County, Alabama.

For most people with whom I spoke, the experience of April 3, 1974, was both indelible and remote. Many had not addressed their memories in years or decades. A number of interview subjects had lost consciousness during the storms; for others, grief and trauma continued to effect their ability, or willingness, to recapitulate the details of that day. Yet this book would not have been possible without their participation.

It has been my intention to tell the story of April 3, 1974, with literal accuracy, while striving to capture the texture of the disaster as it has been preserved in the memories of the survivors. This book is predicated on the belief that fact and memory are deeply entwined. While I have worked, where possible, to gather multiple accounts of particular scenes, I have been careful to respect the memories of those people whose stories figure prominently in the book, and to give their versions of events primacy. As a result, this book records, and indeed values, certain impressionistic accounts that were offered to me, and lets stand a few inconsistent details—presenting, for example, a number of conflicting descriptions of the physical appearance of the same tornado. After three decades, the reality of a tornado, it seems to me, is indistinguishable from the memory of it.

I struggled with the problem of how to make use of the words of those who spoke to me many years after the fact. I decided, finally, to allow myself to be guided into the past by those I interviewed: setting the book on the eventful day, but inserting the voices of memory into the events being reconstructed. Unless otherwise noted, all dialogue in quotation marks in this book was spoken to me between 2003–2006. None of the words of my interview subjects have been altered, other than to standardize grammar. Material quoted from WJMW-AM, in Athens, Alabama, is from a verbatim transcript of that evening's broadcast.

Complete bibliographic information for books can be found in the Bibliography that follows these notes. Newspapers, periodicals, web sites, and ephemera are cited only in the notes.

FORECAST

15. *a fourfold increase in the price of oil*: *Collier's Encyclopedia 1975 Year Book*, p. 58. For data on day-to-day events and trends of 1974, I found that such frequently scorned sources as Encyclopedia Year Books and almanacs were invaluable—as accurate, and often as insightful and lively, as the dominant news sources on which I relied, which included *The New York Times*, *The Chicago Tribune*, *Time*, and *Newsweek*.

16. *"a worldwide rash of kidnappings"*: *Reader's Digest 1975 Almanac and Yearbook*, p. 143.

16. *"throwing a few crumbs"*: SLA recording, February 21, 1974. Cited in *Historic Documents of 1974*, p. 248.

18. *One could also start the story*: The description that follows of the meteorology of the outbreak is boiled down from many sources. Some of these would be accessible to a reader—like the author—with limited background in meteorology. These include: Theodore Tetsuya Fujita, "Tornadoes Around the World," in *Weatherwise*, Vol. 26, p. 56–83, 1973; Fujita, "Jumbo Tornado Outbreak of 3 April 1974," in *Weatherwise*, Vol. 27, p. 116–126, 1974; Fujita, "New Evidence from April 3–4, 1974 Tornadoes," in Preprints, *Ninth Conference on Severe Local Storms*, American Meteorological Society, p. 248–254, 1975; Fujita, "Graphic examples of tornadoes," in *Bulletin of the American Meteorological Society*, Vol. 57, p. 401–412, 1976; Robert F. Abbey and T.T. Fujita, ""The Tornado Outbreak of 3–4 April, 1974," in Edwin Kessler, Ed., *The Thunderstorm in Human Affairs, Vol. 1*, p. 37–66; F.P. Ostby and Allen Pearson, "The Tornado Season of 1973" in *Weatherwise*, Vol. 27, p. 4–9, 1974; Allen Pearson and F. P. Ostby, "The Tornado Season of 1974" in *Weatherwise*, Vol. 28, p. 4–11, 1975; and James F. Purdom, "The 3 April 1974 Tornado Outbreak" in *Weatherwise*, Vol. 27, p. 120–121, 1974. The best descriptive account of the outbreak is in a Natural Disaster Survey Report produced by NOAA in 1974, *Widespread Tornado Outbreak of April 3–4, 1974*, available online at *www.april31974.com* and elsewhere.

To understand the outbreak as best I could, I enlisted the help of a young meteorologist, Adam Clark, who acted as my mentor on matters tornadic. In assisting me, Adam pored over a good deal of technical research on the outbreak, which formed the basis of the explanations he offered me. These technical sources include: C. Church, C. Morris, and J. Snow, "Some Synoptic Aspects and Dynamic Features of Vortices Associated with the Tornado Outbreak of 3 April 1974," in *Monthly Weather Review*, Vol. 103, p. 318–333, 1975; S.F. Corfidi, J. J. Levit, and S. J. Weiss, "The Super Outbreak: Outbreak of the Century," in Preprints, *22nd Conference on Severe Local Storms*, Hyannis, MA, American Meteorological Society, 2004; Gregory S. Forbes, "Three Scales of Motion Associated with Tornadoes," U. S. Nuclear Regulatory Commission Techical Report 0363, 1978; T.T. Fujita, "History of Suction Vortices," in *Proceedings of the Symposium on Tornadoes*, Texas Tech University, p. 78–88, 1976; L.R. Hoxit and C. F. Chappell, "Tornado Outbreak of April 3–4, 1974: Synoptic Analysis," *NOAA Technical Report*, 1975; J.D. Locatelli,

M. T. Stoelinga, and P. V. Hobbs, "A New Look at the Super Outbreak of Tornadoes on 3–4 April 1974," in *Monthly Weather Review*, Vol. 130, p. 1,633–1,165, 2002; and D.A. Miller and F. Sanders, "Mesoscale Conditions for the Severe Convection of 3 April 1974 in the East-Central United States," in *Journal of Atmospheric Sciences*, Vol. 37, p. 1041–1055, 1980. The raw meteorological data that formed the basis of Adam's analysis of the outbreak came from archived storm reports at the Storm Prediction Center, Norman, OK (*www.spc.noaa.gov/climo/historical.html*).

19. *One tornado derailed a boxcar*: Thomas Grazulis, *Significant Tornadoes, 1880–1989, Volume II: A Chronology of Events*, p. 547. I am deeply indebted to the work of Mr. Grazulis, whose exhaustive documentation of tornadoes was my source for many details of historic tornadoes. The two-volume *Significant Tornadoes* can be difficult to find; I would refer readers to the website *www.tornado project.com*, run by Mr. Grazulis's company, for further information and resources.

20. *As Allen Pearson, director of the National Severe Storms Forecast Center*: the quotation is from the question-and-answer session following "Meteorology in the Year 2001," a speech delivered by Pearson at the Midwest Research Institute in Kansas City, MO, on June 30, 1977, p. 13.

23. *"in detecting tornadoes"*: Pearson, "Meteorology in the Year 2001," p. 8.

23. *"the harm done by such a prediction"*: Army Signal Corps, "Report of the Chief Signal Officer of the Army, 1887," p. 21; cited in Marlene Bradford, *A History of Tornado Forecasting*, p. 44.

23. *"The longer I am in the business"*: Pearson, p. 14.

24. *At 4:19 AM*: NOAA, *Natural Disaster Survey Report 74–1: The Widespread Tornado Outbreak of April 3–4, 1974*, p. 13.

LIMESTONE: WEDNESDAY MORNING

In addition to interviews I conducted in and around Limestone County, I relied a great deal on microfilm copies of three area newspapers to provide me with a sense of what issues were locally important in 1974, and what national and international news was reaching the people of northern Alabama. These newspapers were the *Athens News Courier*, the *Huntsville Times*, and the *Decatur Daily*.

25. *the county's 41,699 residents*: for this, and other demographic information, I use the most timely data from the United States Census Bureau, which was compiled in 1970. This data also formed the basis of a March, 1975 economic development report, "Limestone County Comprehensive Plan," prepared by Top of Alabama Regional Council of Governments (TARCOG), which provides the best available snapshot of economic and social conditions in the county in 1974.

26. *weekend screenings at the Hatfield Drive-In*: from the *Athens News Courier*, April 4, 1974.

26. *The forecast in the local paper*: the *Athens News Courier*, April 3, 1974.

29. *By 10 AM*: NOAA, *Natural Disaster Survey Report 74–1*, p. 14.

30. *"I lost a lot of hard earned money here"*: this quote, and the summary of the April 1 storm provided in the following paragraph, come from the *Athens News Courier*, April 3, 1974.

31. *In a county in which nearly half the black population*: U.S. Census Bureau, 1970. Precise figure is 47.8 percent.

32. *"Fishing Time"*: *Athens News Courier*, April 3, 1974.

33. *In 1805, an adventurer named John Hunt*: Hunt's quote is recorded in Robert Henry Walker, Jr., *History of Limestone County*, p. 5–6.

34. *The tribal Chief warned*: Ibid., p. 7.

34. *two dollars an acre*: from a 1998 compendium, *The Heritage of Limestone County*, p.2.

34. *Its people were more poor than rich*: U.S. Census Bureau, 1970.

35–6. *an article in* Life *celebrated Acrilan*: "The Reign of Chemistry," in *Life*, January 5, 1953.

36. *one of twenty-two residents of Limestone to die in Vietnam*: *The Heritage of Limestone County*, p. 27.

38. *class of 1961 voted him "Class Clown (by far)"*: from *My Alma Mater*, a pamphlet on Clements High School by Gatha Crowson, self-published, no date of publication provided. This item was found, among other arcana, in the Limestone County Archives, in downtown Athens.

44. *There, students drew water from a well*: these details are from Charlotte Fulton, *Etched in Limestone, Volume 2: Living and Learning in Old Limestone County*, p. 98–99.

44. *Teachers in Limestone's black elementary schools*: from "Report on Community Survey" published by Athens City Schools, 1939, no page numbers provided.

Notes

44. *40 percent of Limestone's residents*: U.S. Census Bureau, 1970.

45. *John Tanner, a five-time mayor*: John Thomas Tanner, *A History of Athens, and Incidentally of Limestone County, Alabama, 1825–1876*, p. 8. I am grateful to Faye Acton Axford, Limestone's dedicated local historian, for providing me with a copy of this rare document. Ms. Axford graciously gave me a tour of Limestone during my first visit there. She died in July 2004.

45. *With the fourth highest number of killer tornadoes*: combining data from a number of sources, Grazulis, in *Significant Tornadoes, Volume I*, p. 20, counts 237 killer tornadoes in Alabama between 1880–1989, resulting in 888 deaths.

45. *In April 1936, a tornado rode through*: the Limestone, Tupelo, and Gainesville tornadoes are described in Grazulis, *Significant Tornadoes, Volume II*, p. 259–260, with some additional details in Snowden Flora, *Tornadoes of the United States*, p. 97–98. Elvis Presley is mentioned in Keay Davidson, *Twister*, p. 74. Davidson cites Presley biographer Patricia Jobe Pierce as writing, "The tornado leveled St. Mark's Methodist Church across from the Presleys' home and flattened other shacks along the street . . . years later Gladys [Presley's mother] convinced Elvis that God saved him that day . . . because God had determined Elvis was 'born to be a great man.'"

46. *Limestone had never suffered*: all descriptions of tornadoes in this paragraph are from Grazulis, *Volume II*, p. 183, 275, 408, and p. 236–238.

50. *"The human eye"*: from NOAA Photoessay No. 2: *SKYWARN*, 1971.

51. *The proportion of county residents who farmed*: TARCOG, "Limestone County Comprehensive Plan," p. 12.

SUPERCELL

55. *It took a disaster to spur large-scale investigations*: Roscoe Braham, "The Thunderstorm Project," a speech published in the *Bulletin of the American Meteorological Society*, Volume 77, No. 8, August 1996, p. 1,835.

55. *On the afternoon of August 31, 1940*: the *New York Times*, September 1, 1940, "25 Dead in Crash of Air Transport; Lundeen is Killed," and "Lundeen Noted as Isolationist."

56. *"Early airplane pilots quickly learned"*: J.T. Lee and W.B. Beckwith, "Thunderstorms and Aviation," in Edwin Kessler, Ed., *The Thunderstorm in Human Affairs, Volume 1*, p. 125.

56. *By January 1945, as the end of World War II drew near*: Braham, p. 1836.

56. *"the vanguard of the new generation"*: Horace R. Byers, "The Founding of the Institute of Meteorology at the University of Chicago," in the *Bulletin of the American Meteorological Society*, Volume 57, No. 11, November 1976, p. 1,343.

57. *Chicago,"with its reputation for strong, innovative research"*: Douglas R. Allen, "The Genesis of Meteorology at the University of Chicago," *Bulletin of the American Meteorological Society*, Vo. 82, No. 9, September 2001, p. 1,906. The quote refers to the vision initially proposed by Byers's colleague Carl Rossby.

57. *Sewell Avery*: Byers, p. 1,344.

57. *The Thunderstorm Project*: The description that follows has three main sources: an interview with Roscoe Braham; Braham's published recollection of The Thunderstorm Project, cited above; and *The Thunderstorm: Report of the Thunderstorm Project*, published by the U.S. Department of Commerce, 1949.

57. *"to study and probe the thunderstorm"*: Byers's words, cited by Braham, p. 1,837.

58. *the planes "were built to withstand"*: Braham, p. 1838.

59. *Warm air is the fuel*: basic descriptions of the mechanics of thunderstorms can be found in any general-interest guide to weather. I often turned to *USA Today: The Weather Book*, by Jack Williams, and *National Audubon Society Field Guide to North American Weather*, by David M. Ludlum.

60. *"In its initial stage every thunderstorm"*: The Thunderstorm, p. 20.

60. *"With the continued updraft"*: Ibid., p. 21.

61. *"'The downdraft,' Byers and Braham noted"*: Ibid., p. 19.

62. *The apotheosis*: For more on supercell thunderstorms, see Thomas Grazulis, *The Tornado*; Howard Bluestein, *Tornado Alley*; Grazulis, *Significant Tornadoes, Vol. I*; Keay Davidson, *Twister*. *USA Today: The Weather Book* includes an excellent, mind-bending diagram of a supercell.

62. *grapefruit-sized hail*. I was impressed to learn that a June 2003 supercell thunderstorm hit the town of Aurora, Nebraska, with hailstones that measured seven inches in diameter, and weighed 1.7 pounds. Accordingly, in an earlier draft of this book, I included a reference to volleyball-sized hail. On reviewing the manuscript, Adam Clark commented, "this was atypical. Really, you should compare the hail size to grapefruits or softballs." Only two deaths in the United

States have been attributed to hail strikes. In 1888, however, a hailstorm killed 246 people in India.

64. *"Steadily the cloud came on"*: cited in Flora, p. 12.

65. "In a year like 1973": Frederick P. Ostby and Allen D. Pearson, "The Tornado Season of 1973," in *Weatherwise*, Vol. 27, February 1974, p. 4–9.

65. *no more than once in 1,400 years*: this figure is provided by Walter A. Lyons on p. 186 of *The Handy Weather Book*, a popular, though very useful, guide. Others present even more circumspect estimates. Grazulis, in *The Tornado*, writes that "The frequency of actual destruction of any given house in the heart of tornado alley is only about once in 10,000 to 1,000,000 years, depending largely on one's definition of the word *destruction*" (p. 9). In *Significant Tornadoes, Vol I*, p. 88–92, Grazulis surveys several studies of tornado risk. One such estimate projects that any given spot in the state with the highest tornado frequency, Oklahoma, is apt to be hit by a tornado once every 1,980 years; in Alabama, the recurrence interval is projected to be 3,510 years (p. 91).

66. *In July, 1643*: recorded in David M. Ludlum, *Early American Tornadoes*, p. 3.

66. *Rev. Increase Mather*: also cited in Ludlum, p. 4.

67. *an article in Popular Science Monthly*: cited in Davidson, *Twister*, p. 64. The author of the quote is George Clinton Smith. The following quote, from T.B. Maury, in *North American Review*, is cited by Davidson on the same page.

67. *"Many people actually believe"*: J.P. Finley, "The Tornadoes of May 29 and 30, 1879, in Kansas, Nebraska, Missouri, and Iowa," Professional Paper No. 4, U.S. Signal Service, 1881.

67. *the Natchez Weekly Courier and Journal*: cited in Davidson, p. 61.

67. *The Mississippi Free Trader*: cited in David M. Ludlum, *The American Weather Book*, p. 109.

68. *February 19, 1884*: Ludlum, p. 110.

68. *"The death-dealing funnel"*: Ibid., p. 113–4. *The Forgotten Storm: The Great Tri-State Tornado of 1925*, by Wallace Akin, is a careful reconstruction of the storm.

68. *"a jar of pickles"*: Flora, p. 82. Even as dour an observer as Sergeant John P. Finley, writing of an 1878 outbreak of tornadoes in Kansas, employed the term "freaks of the storm," noting, for instance, "Several chickens were carried . . . from one-fourth to one-half mile and entirely stripped of their feathers" (Finley, 1881, p. 28).

On the disputatious matter of chicken feathers, meteorologist Bernard Vonnegut, in an article in the October, 1975 issue of *Weatherwise* called "Chicken Plucking as Measure of Tornado Wind Speed," concluded, "In light of the fact that the force required to remove the feathers from the follicles varies over a wide range in a complicated and unpredictable way and depends on the chicken's condition and his reaction to his environment, the plucking phenomenon is of doubtful value as an index." Not incidentally, Vonnegut is the brother of novelist Kurt Vonnegut.

69. *"The hypnotic terror of witnessing"*: "My 45 Seconds Inside the Tornado," by Ira J. Braden, as told to Robert H. Parham, in *The Saturday Evening Post*, July 11, 1953. A complete account of the Waco tornado is provided by John Edward Weems in *The Tornado*.

70. *"which appeared to have five fingers"*: Grazulis, *Significant Tornadoes, Vol. II*, p. 367.

70. *Mads Madsden*: *Life*, June 22 1953.

70. *"Six savage twisters"*: the *New York Times*, June 10 ,1953.

70. *"It was 8:30 o'clock"*: *Time*, June 22, 1953.

70–71. *"Homes exploded to kindling"*: the *New York Times*, June 10, 1953.

71. *Ray Madden, a congressman from Indiana*: *New York Times*, June 10, 1953. See also D. Lee Harris, "Effects of Atomic Explosions on the Frequency of Tornadoes in the United States," *Monthly Weather Review*, December 1954.

71. *Officials from the Atomic Energy Commission*: *Newsweek*, June 22 1953, p. 29.

LIMESTONE: LAW AND DEATH

In addition to interviews with Buddy Evans, many of the details of crime in Limestone County came from scrapbooks provided to me by Mr. Evans, primarily comprised of clippings from the *Athens News Courier* and the *Decatur Daily*.

74. *Bobbie did the grocery shopping*: the *Athens News Courier*, October 19, 1967 and April 15, 1971.

74. *like a small business*: Ibid., November 27, 1968, June 12, 1970, and April 15, 1971.

74–75. *On April 3*: Ibid., April 3, 1974.

75. *In 1973, his office set a record*: Ibid., January 7, 1974; *Decatur Daily*, December 15, 1973.

Notes

76. *multiple "pignapping"*: *Decatur Daily*, January 16, 1966.

76. *Shlitz beer*: *Athens News Courier*, January 15, 1974.

76. *Limestone's first census*: Walker, *History of Limestone County*, p. 53.

76. *"It seems that the negroes"*: cited in Walker, p. 119–120.

77. *During the Civil War*: the "Sack of Athens" is described in Walker; *The Heritage of Limestone County*; Axford, Ed., *To Lochaber Na Mair: Southerners View the Civil War*; Robert Dunnavant, Jr., *Historic Limestone County*; and Theodore J. Karamanski, "Civilians, Soldiers, and the Sack of Athens," in *Illinois History Teacher*, 1997, p. 48–51. The quote of James Garfield is cited in Karamanski, p. 49; that of John Bell Hood is cited in *Heritage*, p. 2.

77–78. *Susan Lawrence Davis*: Davis's book is *Authentic History Ku Klux Klan 1865–1877*.

79. *the state rewarded the sheriff*: the *Athens News Courier*, June 12, 1970.

79. *in December 1970*: Ibid., December 16, 1970.

79. *"The sheriff, one of the best known men"*: Ibid., December 1, 1973.

80. *"an alarming growth"*: Ibid., July 17, 1974.

80–82. *In his first twenty months on the job*: interviews with Ralph Padgett were supplemented by an examination of Coroner's Inquest reports at the Limestone County Archives.

83. *Just in case*: the *Athens News Courier*, May 31, 1974.

83. *"A vote for Buddy"*: Ibid., April 24, 1974. The poem by Clyde Ennis ran on the same day.

MR. TORNADO

Unless otherwise noted, the source for all quotes in this chapter is *Memoirs of an Effort to Unlock the Mystery of Severe Storms During the 50 Years, 1942–1992*, by Tetsuya Theodore Fujita. I am grateful to Thomas Grazulis for giving me a copy of a study guide he wrote to accompany The Tornado Project production *Tornado Video Classics 2*, which includes footage of Fujita. In addition to Mr. Grazulis, several former friends, students, and colleagues of Fujita shared their memories during interviews, and I am particularly grateful to Robert Abbey, Roscoe Braham, Gregory Forbes, Joseph Golden, Leslie Lemon, James McDonald, Kishor Mehta, Julian Sereno, and Roger Wakimoto, and to

Austin Bunn for his invaluable research assistance. Dr. Fujita's son, Kazuya Fujita, responded to my questions via e-mail and also steered me toward useful resources regarding his father. I referred to several papers presented at a symposium held by the American Meteorological Society entitled *Mystery of Severe Storms: A Tribute to the Work of T. Theodore Fujita*, and published in a special issue of *Bulletin of the American Meteorological Society*, Volume 82, January 2001. (Many of these papers are cited below.) The American Meteorological Society also furnished me with a tape of a speech by Fujita, "42 Years of Research on Atmospheric Disturbances," delivered on February 24, 1988, and the transcript of an interview conducted with Fujita the following day by Richard Rotunno. *Stormtrack: The Magazine for Storm Spotters and Chasers*, published its November/December 1998 issue in tribute to Fujita, and the May/June 1999 edition of *Weatherwise* included a profile of Fujita, "Mr. Tornado," by Jeff Rosenfield.

Fujita wrote hundreds of papers, most of them brief and technical in nature. Only a dozen or so, mostly pertaining to the 1974 outbreak, are cited here. The dazzling eccentricity of his mind is most readily on display in his *Memoirs*, a book that is difficult to come by, but worth the effort.

85. *On August 8, 1953*: Fujita, *Memoirs*, p. 234–235. All citations following are from the same source, unless otherwise noted.

85. *"In comparison with the flying range"*: p. 230.

85. *"I spoke to myself"*: p. 234.

86. *"After a long sleep"*: p. 235.

86. *"my wonder island"*: p. 157.

86. *"The return trip was very tricky"*: p. 161.

86. *"adorned with two active volcanoes"*: p. 157.

87. *"when everybody became one year older"*: p. 160.

87. *"My childhood life"*: p. 159.

87. *"If I were asked to dig'"*: p. 163.

87. *"'You spent over ten days'"*: p. 164.

87. *"After working on this project"*: p. 177.

88. *Immediately after graduating*: p. 180.

88. *Nine thousand such balloons*: see, for instance, John McPhee, "The Gravel Pier," in *The New Yorker*, January 29, 1996, p. 52–60.

89. *The campaign was launched on Tokyo*: see Kenneth P. Werrell, *Blankets of Fire*, and Hoito Edon, *The Night Tokyo Burned*, among many others.

89. *"I happened to be in Tokyo"*: Fujita, *Memoirs,* p. 180.

89. *"Stacked up corpses"*: this quote was found on a website of aviation history, *century-of-flight.net,* in the section on World War II aviation covering the firebombing of Japan.

89–90. Fujita's journeys to Nagasaki and Hiroshima are described in *Memoirs,* p. 181–182.

91. *"My daily life"*: p. 185.

91. *"I thought that weather science"*: p. 185.

91. *"took a bus from Fukuoka"*: p. 188.

91–92. *After he delivered his paper*: the incident, including Fujita's purchase of a typewriter and Byers's reply, is included in *Memoirs* on p. 197–9.

93. *"found me walking down the station platform"*: p. 235.

93. *"In my childhood days"*: p. 11.

93. *"The Gross National Product"*: p. 11.

93. *"I wished I could fly over"*: p. 196.

94–96. *Fargo, North Dakota*: p. 21–26. Fujita's original paper on Fargo was "A Detailed Analysis of the Fargo tornadoes of June 20, 1957" (U.S. Weather Bureau Research Paper 42, 1960). Gregory S. Forbes and Howard B. Bluestein present an excellent explanation of Fujita's work on Fargo in "Tornadoes, Tornadic Thunderstorms, and Photogrammetry: A Review of the Contributions by T.T. Fujita," *Bulletin of the American Meteorological Society*, Volume 82, January 2001.

96. *"costing only 45 cents"*: *Memoirs,* p. 21.

96. *Years later his son, Kazuya*: The younger Dr. Fujita, Professor of Geological Sciences at Michigan State University and an authority on seismology, made this comment to me during a phone conversation in 2004.

97–98. *Lubbock, Texas*: The Lubbock tornado is described in Grazulis, *The Tornado,* which reproduces Fujita's diagram on p. 241.

p. 95. *"According to Fujita's scale"*: the precise wording of Fujita's descriptions of the damage associated with each category of tornado changed slightly since the scale was introduced. For example, an F2, or "strong" tornado, came to be called a "significant" tornado. I use Fujita's language from the mid-seventies, as employed by a frequent sponsor of his research at the Nuclear Regulatory Commission, Robert F. Abbey, Jr., in "Risk Probabilities Associated with Tornado Windspeeds," *Proceedings, Symposium on Tornadoes: Assessment of Knowledge and Implications for Man,* p. 177–236.

The vagaries of the Fujita scale have been much criticized since its adoption. See, for example, James R. McDonald and Kishor C. Mehta, "Summary Report: Fujita-Scale Forum" (2002), available on-line at *www.april31974.com* under "Fujita Scale Enhancement Project," which bluntly notes that the scale "Fails to account for variations in the quality of construction," "Is difficult to apply consistently," and "Does not yield accurate assessments when there are no damage indicators." Nonetheless, the Fujita Scale has demonstrated remarkable staying power. On February 1, 2007, the National Weather Service began rating tornadoes according to the "Enhanced Fujita" or EF Scale, which retains the ratings of F0–F5, but downgrades estimates of windspeeds. See *www.spc.noaa.gov/efscale* for a thorough discussion and links to further information.

LIMESTONE: WEDNESDAY AFTERNOON

106. *"Born today, you are possessed of"*: the *Athens News Courier*, April 3, 1974.

113. *"From the time Bob heard"*: *The Heritage of Limestone County*, p. 4. I was fortunate to have had the opportunity to meet with Robert Dunnavant in 2004, at a time when he was in failing health. The meeting was facilitated by Mr. Dunnavant's youngest son, Keith, for whose assistance I am grateful.

116. *"We just had a report from the civil defense office"*: all dialogue from the April 3, 1974, broadcast of WJMW-AM, as well as advertisements and song lyrics, are transcribed from a tape recording made that evening by Bill Dunnavant, and furnished to me for my use in this book. I give my deep thanks to Mr. Dunnavant for rummaging through his basement to locate the tape. No grammatical irregularities have been altered; I hope that readers will recognize the occasional rawness of phrasing as an element of the pressures faced by those whose voices were preserved on tape.

OUTBREAK

The major source of the timeline of the day's tornadoes is a table in Abbey and Fujita, "The Tornado Outbreak of 3–4 April 1974," in Kessler, Ed., *The Thunderstorm in Human Affairs, Vol. 1*. Other details of the overall course of the outbreak are found in the two NOAA reports cited above, "Natural Disaster Survey Report 74–1: The Widespread Tornado Outbreak of April 3–4, 1974" and "Technical Report: Tornado Outbreak of April 3–4, 1974; Synoptic Analysis." An accessible gathering of materials related to the outbreak, and links to other resources, can be found at the website *www.april31974.com*.

119. *Earlier that morning*: NOAA, "Technical Report," p. 27.

120. *Along the way, a woman came to rest*: Grazulis, *Significant Tornadoes, Vol. II*, p. 547. Grazulis gives details of 95 "significant tornadoes," rating F2 or above, that occurred during the outbreak. He also reproduces maps and photos of damage on p. 543–557.

120–121. The descriptions of the Indiana tornadoes are from Grazulis, p. 547–549, and the *Indianapolis Star*, April 4 and April 5, 1974.

121. *Steve Wilson, a police department patrolman*: "A Most Tragic Day," supplement to the *Louisville Courier-Journal and Times*, March 30, 1975, p. 6.

121. *"We're going off the air"*: Ibid., p. 2.

121. *"a Mark Twain town"*: *New York Times*, April 7, 1974.

121. *"When I looked around"*: "A Most Tragic Day," p. 4.

121–124. *Dick Gilbert*: In addition to meeting with me for a lengthy interview, Mr. Gilbert's daughter, Candy Medina, furnished me with materials vital to my description of his background and experience on April 3, 1974. These include: Gilbert's autobiography, *Just My Luck!*, which provides a transcript of Gilbert's broadcast on WHAS on April 3, 1974; a recording of that broadcast; and two articles about Gilbert, "Dick Gilbert and the unfriendly sky," in the *Louisville Courier-Journal and Times* magazine, May 5, 1974, and "10 Years, 10 Stories," from the *Louisville Times SCENE* magazine, March 31, 1984.

122. *"a definite chartreuse tint"*: *Just My Luck!*, p. 156.

122. *"Well, we do have a pretty wild"*: Ibid., p. 164–5.

122. *"As I approached the site"*: Ibid., p. 117.

122. *"I live at 500 feet"*: the *Louisville Times SCENE*, p. 4.

123. *"I don't actually physically see"*: *Just My Luck!*, p. 166.

123. *"Well, it's a spectacular sight"*: Ibid., p. 168.

123. *"about $800 worth"*: "A Most Tragic Day," p. 10.

123. *"The park was left a hideous skeleton"*: Ibid., p. 10.

124. *"The city to me"*: *SCENE*, p. 4.

124. *"My old homestead there"*: "A Most Tragic Day," p. 10.

124. *"A tornado is mindless"*: *SCENE*, p. 4.

124. *"a man was killed in his island home"*: Grazulis, p. 554.

124–5. *"neighbors found the home"*: *Time*, April 15, 1974.

125. *Karen Stott*: the *Indianapolis Star*, April 6, 1974.

125. *In Xenia*: the Xenia tornado is the most exhaustively documented episode of the outbreak. The *Xenia Daily Gazette* won a Pulitzer Prize in 1975, "For its coverage, under enormous difficulties, of the tornado that wrecked the city on April 3, 1974." (My thanks to Tom McCatherine, a reporter at the *Daily Gazette* at the time, for sharing his experiences with me.) In intervals of every five or ten years since 1974, the *Daily Gazette* has published issues devoted to commemorating the tornado. Moreover, the Greene County Public Library in Xenia maintains a large archive of outbreak-related material, and *Tornado*, by Polk Laffoon IV, the only book-length, contemporaneous account of the outbreak, is centered on a detailed description of both the storm in Xenia and its aftermath.

125. *Thomas Youngen*: *Xenia Daily Gazette*, April 10, 1974. Also recounted in Laffoon, p. 38.

126–8. *The tornado entered town at a subdivision called Windsor Park*: Laffoon provides thorough coverage of the injuries and fatalities in Xenia. All quotes in this paragraph, and information about victims in this and succeeding paragraphs, is from "Rebuilding the Rubble," a commemorative supplement to The *Greene County Dailies*, April 3, 2004.

128. *"It looked worse than a war scene"*: Ibid.

128–132. *Even the national pastime*: Hank Aaron's quest to match Babe Ruth's record received enormous coverage from print media, and is the subject of *Hank Aaron and the Home Run that Changed America*, by Tom Stanton.

129. *930,000 letters*: Hank Aaron with Lonnie Wheeler, *I Had a Hammer: The Hank Aaron Story*, p. 332–333.

129. *"Dear Mr. Nigger"*: Ibid., p. 316.

129. *"Dear Jungle Bunny"*: Ibid., p. 320.

129. *"Here I am with all these records"*: quoted in Stanton, p. 50.

130. *"Retire or die!"*: Aaron, p. 325.

130. *According to Casanova*: Stanton, p. 198.

131. *"I saw funnel clouds"*: Aaron, p. 357.

131. *At Cincinnati's Longview State Hospital*: all details from this paragraph are from the *Cincinnati Enquirer*, April 4, 1974.

131. *His wife, Karolyn*: the *Cincinnati Enquirer*, April 6, 1974.

131. *pitcher Jack Billingham*: Stanton, p. 202.

131–132. *"made me forget all about Babe Ruth"*: Aaron, p. 357–8.

132. *"It was really something"*: cited in the *Athens News Courier*, April 5, 1974.

132. *"earth tremors"*: the *Indianapolis Star*, April 4, 1974.

132. *Windsor, Ontario*: the *Toronto Globe and Mail*, April 4, 1974, and the *Indianapolis Star*, April 5, 1974.

PART TWO

Unless otherwise noted, the account of the impact of the tornado outbreak on Limestone County, Alabama, is based on interviews with survivors, witnesses, and officials; the broadcast of WJMW-AM, noted above; and articles in the *Athens News Courier*, *Decatur Daily*, and *Huntsville Times*. I am indebted, as well, to the exhaustive oral history compiled by Charles Jordan in *April 3, 1974: A Night to Remember*, which includes a section on Limestone. The Birmingham office of the National Weather Service provides data about the outbreak, and a timeline, on its website; the website of the Huntsville NWS office includes articles about WHNT-TV weatherman H.D. Bagley. Finally, a compilation of photos and articles (mostly from the *Huntsville Times*) called *April 3, 1974: The Alabama Tornadoes*, published by C.F. Boone (Lubbock, TX, 1974), is a useful summary of the disaster, and an interesting glimpse at the industry of "quickie" disaster books.

THE CROSSROADS

150. *The grander a house*: a written description of the house and its contents was provided to me by Don and Sheila Lauderdale.

152. *Spencer Black was getting besieged*: my impression, based on the recorded broadcast of WJMW-AM.

154–155. *Bloodied, his rain-soaked uniform*: my description of the debris on Highway 31 is based on multiple interviews with people who traveled the road that night and in succeeding days, rather than exclusively on the comments of Buddy Evans.

157. *"But nothing like this"*: the comments of Dunnavant in this paragraph are from an interview, not from the broadcast of April 3, 1974. The quote in the next paragraph, however, is from the radio broadcast.

165. *"I laid in a shallow ditch"*: *Huntsville Times*, April 5, 1974.

HOME

174–176. *It zoned in on the Old Orr House*: the description of how a tornado destroys a house is based on interviews with wind engineers James McDonald and Kishor Mehta, and conversations with Adam Clark. I also consulted James R. McDonald, "Tornado-Generated Missiles and their Effects," *Proceedings of the Symposium on Tornadoes*, 1976, p. 331–348; Charles A. Doswell III and Harold E. Brooks, "Lessons Learned from the Damage Produced by the Tornadoes of 3 May 1999," *Bulletin of the American Meteorological Society*, June 2002, p. 611–618; and Kai Pan, Peter Montpellier, and Masoud Zadeh, "Engineering Observations of 3 May 1999 Oklahoma Tornado Damage," *Bulletin of the American Meteorological Society*, June 2002, p. 599–610.

184–186. *a sixty-five year old widow named Lorene Ricketts*: based on interviews with Ms. Ricketts, Mary Frances Ricketts, James Stinnett, and other family members.

DISASTER: AN INTERLUDE

An interesting satire of disaster journalism published not long before the outbreak can be found in Alexander Cockburn's "Death Rampant! Readers Rejoice," from the December 1973 issue of the long-defunct *[More]* magazine. On the subject of tornadoes, Cockburn's mock instruction to journalists is, "Get a good photograph if you can. Stress malign fury and awesome strength of the twister, 'hurling cars hundreds of yards, tearing up houses.'" He goes on, "Emphasize miraculous escape of child in pram. Ask where it will strike next. Advise people what to do."

187. *the first months of 1974*: the litany of disasters that follows was drawn from *Collier's Encyclopedia 1975 Year Book*, p. 218–219, and *Reader's Digest 1975 Almanac and Yearbook*, p. 33–48.

188–189. *Nixon*: for details on Nixon's tax problems, see the cover story in *Time*, April 15, 1974; *New York Times*, April 4, 1974; *Collier's*, p. 5; and "Report on Nixon's Taxes: April 3, 1974," in *Historic Documents of 1974*, p. 235–245.

190. The notorious photograph of Patty Hearst was featured on the front page of many papers, including the *New York Times*, on April 4, 1974, along with early accounts of the tornado outbreak, and in the case of the *Times*, an article on Hank Aaron's pursuit of base-

ball's home run record. *Newsweek*'s cover story of April 29, 1974, "The Saga of Patty Hearst," provides extensive detail. A full transcript of the tape recording is included in "Hearst Kidnapping: April 3, 1974," in *Historic Documents of 1974*, p. 247–253.

190. *"I don't believe it"*: *Newsweek*, April 15, 1974, p. 37.

190–191. *Her mother adds*: Ibid.

191. *"It simply isn't her"*: *Newsweek*, April 29, 1974, p. 24.

191. *"the spectacular flame-out"*: *Time*, April 15, 1974, p. 103.

192. *Five hundred and thirty-three*: the following details on streaking are from *Time*, March 18, 1974, p. 58–59. For those who are skeptical about the high profile of the short-lived sensation, see also "Streaking: A Mad Dash to Where?" in the *New York Times*, March 8, 1974; "Streakers Off and Running on Nation's Campuses," the *New York Times*, March 10, 1974; "Streaking: One Way to Get a B.A." in *Newsweek*, March 18, 1974, p. 41–42; and numerous smaller items in the *New York Times*, including "Columbia Campus Gets Its First Gawk At 'Streaking' Fad" (March 7, 1974); "Even L.I.R.R. Pauses For a Female Streaker" (March 26, 1974); "Streaking Legalized, Calendar Permitting" (March 29, 1974); "2 Who Streaked at Vatican Are Given Time to Reflect" (March 29, 1974); and "Soviet Informs Public of Streaking in West" (March 31, 1974).

192. *"the sort of totally absurd phenomenon"*: *Time*, March 18, 1974.

192. *Robert J. Lifton*: Lifton and McLuhan are quoted in the *New York Times*, March 8, 1974.

192. *At Syracuse University*: Ibid., March 10, 1974.

193–194. *"By 1974, no Hollywood film"*: the roster of upcoming disaster films is from "A Preview of Coming Afflictions," *Time*, June 10, 1974. The quote "You don't want to have to spend too much time" is from the same article.

194–195. *Evel Knievel*: see, for example, Joe Eszterhas, "Deliver Us From Evel," in *Rolling Stone*, November 7, 1974; "Make it or Break it," *Sports Illustrated*, September 2, 1974; and Evel's $6 Million Fizzle," *Newsweek*, September 16, 1974. Pete Axthelm's column, from which I have quoted, was "The Roots of Evel," *Newsweek*, August 26, 1974.

195. *Philippe Petit*: Petit's remarks, as quoted here, are from his extraordinary book *On the High Wire*. Since *On the High Wire* was written in 1972, Petit's words refer to his view of his craft, rather than to his plan to traverse the towers of the World Trade Center. Petit's later book *To Reach the Clouds* provides a detailed remembrance of the World Trade Center walk.

195. *"You must struggle"*: *On the High Wire*, p. 86.

195. *"Whoever does not want to struggle"*: Ibid., p. 9.

195. *"Anything that is giant and manmade"*: see the website for the PBS show *The American Experience* at *www.pbs.org/wgbh/amex*. Information on an episode called "The Center of the World" features a page on Petit, and includes this quote and the one by Port Authority officer Charles Daniel later in the paragraph.

195. *"I who hope"*: *On the High Wire*, p. 110.

195. *"What is it like to die?"*: Raymond A. Moody, Jr., *Life After Life*, p. 15.

196. *"People have the sensation"*: Ibid., p. 29.

196. *"may find himself looking"*: Ibid., p. 31.

196. *"What is perhaps the most incredible"*: Ibid., p. 45–6.

TRIAGE

198. *Patients were being unloaded*: the description of the scene at Athens-Limestone County Hospital comes from multiple eyewitnesses, including two nurses, a doctor, patients, and visitors.

201. *as the consecutive Limestone tornadoes would come to be called*: the names "First Tanner" and "Second Tanner" are employed in Abbey and Fujita in "The Tornado Outbreak of 3–4 April 1974," and elsewhere.

201. *"Mrs. Howard Truitt"*: *Huntsville Times*, April 5, 1974.

201. *Buddy Evans's office reported*: Ibid.

201. *"cruising the skies overhead"*: *Athens News Courier*, April 5, 1974.

202. *"he would have no memory"*: Walter McGlocklin is listed in the *Decatur Daily* among those admitted to Athens-Limestone County Hospital. Though Mr. McGlocklin recalls searching area hospitals for his daughter, he does not recall receiving treatment. He has acknowledged, though, the possibility that there are some gaps in his memory of that evening and the following days.

203: *carrying an ax*: the man mentioned, but not named, was Jerry Dauthit, the son of Annias Green's former landlord, and an an occasional childhood playmate of Mr. Green.

205. *"There's nothing left of Guin"*: *The Alabama Tornadoes*, p. 17.

208. *Herman Lambert*: details of Mr. Lambert's death were reported to me by Paula Marbut and others. Ralph Padgett does not recall being at the scene to pronounce Mr. Lambert dead; it is possible that a sheriff's deputy had been assigned to help fill out coroner's reports.

208–209. *At 10:24*: details of the damage to Redstone Arsenal come from the *Huntsville Times*, April 5, 1974.

209. *American Graffiti*: Bill Dunnavant recalled that his brother had attended a movie that evening at Parkway City Shopping Center. *American Graffiti* was the only movie being screened at the theater.

210–211. *"Each time a group of injured"*: print material quoted in the rest of this section is from an April 5, 1974, article in the *Huntsville Times* called "Humanities of the Hospital Ease Suffering," describing the scene at Huntsville Hospital.

211. *"to be heading right up Governors Drive"*: Ibid.

212. *H.D. Bagley*: from an interview with Keith Lowhorne of WHNT, who was an intern at the station in 1974, and joined Bagley in the ditch.

213. *Mary Elizabeth Smith*: Clifford Smith's words were recorded in *April 3, 1974: A Night To Remember* by Charles Jordan, p. 289. Ms. Smith's granddaughter, Kim Wilbanks, also provided me with a detailed account of her mother's death.

215. *"It did not contain the carpeting"*: *Huntsville Times*, April 5, 1974.

DAYBREAK

221. *The morning after*: based on an interview with Dr. Stanley Hand.

223. *The April 4 edition*: all quotes in this section are from the *Athens News Courier*, April 4, 1974.

224. *The editorial did not cite*: see, for instance, *Wallace*, by Marshall Frady.

226. *He couldn't remember getting there.* Indeed, Mr. McGlocklin believes it is possible that he and his daughter Nancy slept in his truck that night.

228. *"The governor just doesn't think it's appropriate"*: *Decatur Daily*, April 7, 1974.

228. *"I know about things being fine one minute"*: *Huntsville Times*, April 6, 1974.

228. *"I pray for you, too"*: *April 3, 1974: The Alabama Tornadoes*, p. 32.

232. *Buddy and Ralph Padgett were similarly praised*: *Decatur Daily*, April 7, 1974.

232. *multipage spreads of photos*: *Athens News Courier*, April 5, 1974, for example.

232. *"Friends in need"*: Ibid.

233. *Spencer's preliminary count*: Athens New Courier, April 7, 1974.

234. *Rabbit emerged from his coma*: Ananias Green, Jr., or "Rabbit," is certain of the date in part because that night, in his hospital room, he recalls having watched Hank Aaron break Babe Ruth's record by hitting his 715th career home run.

235. *Brown's Ferry had nonetheless gone into an automatic shutdown*: Huntsville Times, April 5, 1974.

EPILOGUE: MYSTERIES OF SEVERE STORMS

242. *He chartered aircraft*: Gregory Forbes, Joseph Golden, and Leslie Lemon, all of whom went on to distinguished careers in meteorology, participated in the survey and provided interviews recounting their experiences. (Forbes also wrote his doctoral dissertation, under Fujita's direction, on an aspect of the outbreak.) Kishor Mehta was not part of Fujita's team, but performed extensive studies of the damage in Xenia, Ohio. Julian Sereno, who traveled with Fujita, is now the editor and publisher of Chatham County Line, a community newspaper in North Carolina.

244. *scallop-shaped marks*: Leslie Lemon took these photographs.

244. *"Extraordinary tornado outbreak"*: Fujita, "Jumbo Tornado Outbreak of 3 April 1974," in *Weatherwise*, June 1974, p. 117.

244. *During a seventeen-hour period*: Abbey and Fujita, "The Tornado Outbreak of 3–4 April 1974", p. 38. This article, cited above, is the source of most of the analysis of the outbreak presented in this section. It is worth noting at this point that the superlative "Most Violent Tornado Outbreak of the Century" that forms part of this book's subtitle is based on the unsurpassed number of "violent" (F4 and F5) tornadoes during the outbreak. The outbreak established marks for the total number of tornadoes, the number of "killer tornadoes" (those causing fatalities: 48), the number of "significant tornadoes" (F2 and above: 95), and the cumulative length of tornado paths. No outbreak has come close to serving up tornadoes in as many states (the thirteenth state, New York, was dealt a minor blow in its northwestern corner.) Other outbreaks, however, have probably killed as many or more people, including an outbreak in April 1908 that is believed to have claimed at least 324 lives, and a March 1932 outbreak that killed 330. (Both outbreaks hit Alabama.) On consecutive days in April 1936, some 454 people were killed during an outbreak in "Dixie Tornado

_y, and the "Tri-State Tornado" of 1925 (see p. 68), long regarded as a single tornado, and the deadliest tornado event of the century, has come to be regarded as an outbreak. For what it may be worth, most sources (including NOAA) still concur with Grazulis that "The worst outbreak in recorded history . . . occurred on April 3–4, 1974" (*Significant Tornadoes, Vol. I*, p. 34).

245. *Limestone County, which had the distinction*: Fujita ranked "First Tanner," which devastated Lawrence County, southwest of Limestone, before hitting Lawson's Trailer Park, as an F5; and "Second Tanner," which destroyed the houses of Walter McGlocklin, Annias Green, Don Lauderdale, Frank Orr, and others, and struck Donnie Powers and Felica Golden in their car, as an F4. Certainly, "Second Tanner" did far more damage in Limestone County. It may be that in his aerial survey Fujita conflated the paths of the two tornadoes, which were so close at times that they overlapped. Grazulis, in *Significant Tornadoes, Vol. II*, writes, "Nearly 1,000 buildings were destroyed by these two tornadoes, but no effort was made to determine the exact number of buildings destroyed by the individual tornadoes" (p. 554).

246. *"The destruction, the devastation"*: Newsweek, April 15, 1974.

246. *"Like vultures"*: Dayton Daily News, April 15, 1974.

246. *"I feel heartsick"*: Laffoon, *Tornado*, p. 126. I'm grateful, too, to the public information officers at the 178th Fighter Wing of the Ohio Air National Guard for allowing me to examine their records of the incident; and to Charles Beason and Roger Wildoner for sharing their memories with me.

247. *"It's the worst disaster I've ever seen"*: Xenia Daily Gazette, April 10, 1974.

247. *"You will make it as well as Henry Aaron"*: Athens News Courier, April 10, 1974.

255. *A self-congratulatory federal government report*: NOAA, *National Disaster Survey Report 74–1*, p. 31.

256. *"did concede that the amount of radioactivity"*: Athens News Courier, March 25, 1975.

261. *Eastern Airlines Flight 66*: New York Times, June 25, 1975.

261. *Indeed, Flight 66*: An analysis of the accident is included in Shari Stamford Krause, *Airline Safety: Accident Investigations, Analyses, & Investigations*, p. 207–220.

262. *"rare downbursts"*: see Fujita, *Memoirs*, p. 105–107; and Fujita, *The Downburst: Microburst and Macroburst.*

262. *"The criticism led to"*: Fujita, *Memoirs*, p. 107; his remarks on Wegener are on p. 103–104.

262. "professional jealousy": Ibid., p. 110.

262. "one of the major, rapid payoff, success stories": James W. Wilson and Roger M. Wakimoto, "The Discovery of the Downburst: T.T. Fujita's Contribution," in *Bulletin of the American Meteorological Society*, January 2001, p. 49–62. When Fujita retired from Chicago's faculty, in 1990, the *New York Times* marked the event by noting, "Two years from now, the Federal Aviation Administration will set up Doppler radar devices at airports nationwide to detect the kind of air movement that can diminish a plane's ability to fly—a move that results in large part from Professor Fujita's work on air patterns called downbursts and microbursts" (July 1, 1990).

263. *It cost $113.56*: The printing cost of Fujita's *Memoirs* is noted on Kazuya Fujita's website, *www.msu.edu/~fujita/tornado/smrp252/archives*, along with a good deal of interesting material on his father.

263. *"Although I regret"*: Fujita, *Memoirs*, p. iii.

264. *"Anything that moves"*: New York Times, July 1, 1990.

SELECT BIBLIOGRAPHY

The following books helped to form the backdrop of my education in meteorology, the '70's, Alabama, and more or less related matters. In cases in which books on this list were the source of material in the text, they are cited in the Notes, along with magazines, newspapers, journals, and web sites not included here.

Aaron, Henry, with Lonnie Wheeler. *I Had a Hammer: The Hank Aaron Story.* New York: HarperCollins, 1991.

Abbey, Robert F., and Kishor C. Mehta, co-chairmen, and Richard E. Peterson, ed. *Proceedings of the Symposium on Tornadoes: Assessment of Knowledge and Implications for Man, June 22-24, 1976.* Texas Tech University: Lubbock, TX: 1976.

Akin, Wallace. *The Forgotten Storm: The Great Tri-State Tornado of 1925.* Guilford, CT: The Lyons Press, 2002.

Allaby, Michael. *Tornadoes.* New York: Facts on File, 1997.

April 3, 1974: Tornado! Louisville, KY: The Courier-Journal and The Louisville Times, 1974.

Axford, Faye Acton, ed. *"To Lochaber Na Mair": Southerners View the Civil War.* Athens, AL: Athens Publishing Company, 1986.

Blanchot, Maurice. *The Writing of the Disaster,* trans. Ann Smock. Lincoln, NE: University of Nebraska Press, 1986.

Bluestein, Howard B. *Tornado Alley: Monster Storms of the Great Plains.* New York: Oxford University Press, 1999.

Boone, C.F., publisher. *April 3, 1974: The Alabama Tornadoes.* Lubbock, TX: C.F. Boone, 1974.

Bradford, Marlene. *Scanning the Skies: A History of Tornado Forecasting.* Norman, OK: University of Oklahoma Press, 2001.

Bibliography

Brown, Slater. *World of the Wind.* New York: Bobbs-Merrill, 1961.

Burroughs, William J., Bob Crowder, Ted Robertson, Eleanor Vallier-Talbot and Richard Whitaker. *The Nature Company Guides: Weather.* New York: Time-Life Books, 1996.

Burt, Christopher C. *Extreme Weather: A Guide and Record Book.* New York: Norton, 2004.

Butler, William S., ed. *Tornado: A Look Back at Louisville's Dark Day, April 3, 1974.* Louisville, KY: Butler Books, 2004.

Calder, Nigel. *The Weather Machine.* New York: The Viking Press, 1974.

Chaboud, Rene. *Weather: Drama of the Heavens.* New York: Harry N. Abrams, 1996.

Collier's Encyclopedia 1975 Year Book, Covering the Year 1974. New York: Macmillan Educational Corporation, 1975.

Darton, Eric. *Divided We Stand: A Biography of New York's World Trade Center.* New York: Basic Books, 1999.

Davidson, Keay. *Twister: The Science of Tornadoes and the Making of an Adventure Movie.* New York: Pocket Books, 1996.

Davis, Susan Lawrence. *Authentic History Ku Klux Klan, 1865-1877.* New York: American Library Service, 1924.

DeBlieu, Jan. *Wind: How the Flow of Air Has Shaped Life, Myth, and the Land.* New York: Mariner Books, 1998.

De Villiers, Marq. *Windswept: The Story of Wind and Weather.* New York: Walker and Company, 2006.

Dunnavant, Robert, Jr. *Antique Athens and Limestone County, Alabama: A Photographic Journey, 1809-1949.* Athens, AL: Pea Ridge Press, 1994.

——— *Historic Limestone County.* Athens, AL: Pea Ridge Press, 1993.

Edinger, James G. *Watching For the Wind: The Seen and Unseen Influences on Local Weather.* Garden City, NY: Anchor Books, 1967.

Edoin, Hoito. *The Night Tokyo Burned: The Incendiary Campaign Against Japan, March-August, 1945.* New York: St. Martin's, 1987.

Finley, John P. *Report of the Tornadoes of May 29 and 30, 1879, in Kansas, Nebraska, Missouri, and Iowa.* Washington, DC: Professional Papers of the Signal Service No. 4, 1881.

Flora, Snowden D. *Tornadoes of the United States,* revised. Norman, OK: University of of Oklahoma Press, 1954.

Frady, Marshall. *Wallace.* New York: Random House, 1996.

Frazier, Kendrick. *The Violent Face of Nature.* New York: William Morrow, 1979.

Bibliography

Fujita, Tetsuya Theodore. *The Downburst: Microburst and Macroburst.* Chicago: SMRP Research Paper 210, 1985.

—— *Memoirs of An Effort to Unlock the Mystery of Severe Storms During the 50 Years, 1942-1992.* Chicago: Wind Research Laboratory, 1992.

—— *U.S. Tornadoes, Part One: 70-Year Statistics.* Chicago: SMRP Research Paper 217, 1987.

Fulton, Charlotte, with Kelly Kazek. *Etched in Limestone, Vol. 1: Images and Anecdotes of Old Limestone County.* Athens, AL: The Athens News-Courier, 2002.

—— *Etched in Limestone, Vol. 2: Living and Learning in Old Limestone County.* Athens, AL: The Athens News-Courier, 2003.

Gilbert, Dick. *Just My Luck! An Autobiography of Dick Gilbert, WHAS Radio 'Traffic Tracker.'* Louisville, KY: The Gilbert Foundation, 2001.

Grazulis, Thomas P. *Significant Tornadoes, 1880-1989. Volume I: Discussion and Analysis.* St. Johnsbury, VT: Environmental Films, 1991.

—— *Significant Tornadoes, 1880-1989. Volume II: A Chronology of Events.* St. Johnsbury, VT: Environmental Films, 1990.

—— *The Tornado: Nature's Ultimate Windstorm.* Norman, OK: University of Oklahoma Press, 2001.

Hamilton, Virginia Van der Veer. *Alabama: A History.* New York: Norton, 1984.

Hearst, Patricia Campbell, with Alvin Moscow. *Every Secret Thing.* Garden City, NY: Doubleday & Company, 1982.

The Heritage of Limestone County, Alabama. Clanton, AL: Heritage Publishing Consultants, Inc., 1998.

Historic Documents of 1974. Congressional Quarterly. Washington, DC: 1975.

Jordan, Charles, and Teofista A. Jordan, Eds. *April 3, 1974: A Night To Remember.* Moulton, AL: Southern Printing, 1987.

Kahn, Ashley, Holly George-Warren and Shawn Dahl, eds. *Rolling Stone: The Seventies.* New York: Rolling Stone Press, 1998.

Kessler, Edwin, ed. *The Thunderstorm in Human Affairs, Volume 1, Second Edition.* Norman, OK: University of Oklahoma Press, 1983.

Killen, Andreas. *1973 Nervous Breakdown: Watergate, Warhol, and the Birth of Post-Sixties America.* New York: Bloomsbury, 2006.

Bibliography

Krause, Shari Stamford. *Aircraft Safety: Accident Investigations, Analyses, and Applications.* New York: McGraw-Hill, 1996.

Laffoon, Polk. *Tornado: The Killer Tornado that Blasted Xenia, Ohio, In April 1974.* New York: Harper & Row, 1975.

Larson, Erik. *Isaac's Storm: A Man, A Time, and the Deadliest Hurricane in History.* New York: Vintage Books, 2000.

Laskin, David. *Braving the Elements: The Stormy History of American Weather.* New York: Anchor Books, 1996.

Lindqvist, Sven. *A History of Bombing.* New York: The New Press, 2001.

Ludlum, David M. *The American Weather Book.* Boston: Houghton Mifflin, 1982.

———— *Early American Tornadoes, 1586-1870.* Boston: American Meteorological Society, 1970.

———— *National Audubon Society Field Guide to North American Weather.* New York: Alfred A. Knopf, 1991.

Lyons, Walter A. *The Handy Weather Answer Book.* New York: Visible Ink, 1997.

Moody, Raymond. *Life After Life.* Harrisburg, PA: Stackpole Books, 1976.

Murphree, Tom, and Mary K. Miller. *Watching Weather.* New York: Henry Holt, 1998.

Natural Disaster Survey Report 74-1: The Widespread Tornado Outbreak of April 3-4, 1974. National Oceanic and Atmospheric Administration. Rockville, MD: 1974.

The Official Associated Press Almanac 1975. Maplewood, NJ: Hammond Almanac, 1975.

Petit, Philippe. *On The High Wire,* trans. Paul Auster. New York: Random House, 1985.

————. *To Reach the Clouds: My High-Wire Walk Between the Twin Towers.* New York: North Point Press, 2002.

Pinder, Eric. *Tying Down the Wind: Adventures in the Worst Weather on Earth.* New York: Putnam, 2000.

Reader's Digest 1975 Almanac and Yearbook. Pleasantville, NY: The Reader's Digest Association, 1975.

Rogers, William Warren, Robert David Ward, Leah Rawls Atkins, and Wayne Flynt. *Alabama: The History of A Deep South State.* Tuscaloosa, AL: University of Alabama Press, 1994.

Rosenfield, Jeffrey. *Eye of the Storm: Inside the World's Deadliest Hurricanes, Tornadoes, and Blizzards.* New York: Plenum, 1999.

Schulman, Bruce J. *The Seventies: The Great Shift in American Culture, Society, and Politics*. New York: Da Capo, 2002.

Sontag, Susan. *Against Interpretation and Other Essays*. New York: Farrar, Straus & Giroux, 1967.

Stanton, Tom. *Hank Aaron and the Home Run that Changed America*. New York: William Morrow, 2004.

Svenvold, Mark. *Big Weather: Chasing Tornadoes in the Heart of America*. New York: Henry Holt, 2005.

Tanner, John Thomas. *A History of Athens and Incidentally of Limestone County, Alabama, 1825-1876,* eds. W. Stanley Hoole and Addie S. Hoole. University, AL: Confederate Publishing Company, no date.

The Thunderstorm: Report of The Thunderstorm Project. Horace R. Byers, Director, Roscoe R. Braham, Jr., Senior Analyst. U.S. Department of Commerce. Washington, DC: 1949.

Tolan, Sandy. *Me and Hank: A Boy and His Hero, Twenty-Five Years Later*. New York: The Free Press, 2000.

Tornado. Dayton, OH: The Journal Herald, 1974.

Wade, Nicholas, ed. *The New York Times Book of Natural Disasters*. Guilford, CT: The Lyons Press, 2001.

Walker, Robert Henry, Jr. *History of Limestone County*. Athens, AL: Limestone County Commission, 1973.

Weems, John Edward. *The Tornado*. College Station, TX: Texas A & M University Press, 1991 (reprint).

Werrell, Kenneth P. *Blankets of Fire: U.S. Bombers over Japan during World War II*. Washington, DC: Smithsonian Institution Press, 1996.

Whittow, John. *Disasters: The Anatomy of Environmental Hazards*. Athens, GA: The University of Georgia Press, 1979.

Williams, Horace Randall. *Weren't No Good Times: Personal Accounts of Slavery in Alabama*. Winston-Salem, NC: John F. Blair, 2004.

Williams, Jack. *USA Today: The Weather Book, 2nd Edition*. New York: Vintage, 1997.

Willis, J.M., ed. *Since April 3*. Brandenburg, KY: The Meade County Messenger, 1974.

Wolfenstein, Martha. *Disaster: A Psychological Essay*. Glencoe, IL: The Free Press, 1957.

Acknowledgments

I have many thanks to offer.

A dozen years ago, John Tayman and Mark Bryant encouraged me to extend myself as a writer by investigating the stories of ordinary people in remote places. They gave me a real-time education in journalism and were my best instructors. In 2003, they turned up suddenly and steered me toward the story of April 3, 1974. I am deeply grateful to them for their sustained generosity to me, and for their brilliance as magazine editors.

David McCormick, JillEllyn Riley, Rob Weisbach: thank you for your faith in this story and in me.

A grant from the Arts and Humanities Initiative at the University of Iowa helped finance some of my early research. The Iowa Writers' Workshop has been a home to me for a long time, and my colleagues—Jim, Cole, Dean—are my extended family. Most of *F5* was written at the Workshop. Connie Brothers, Deb West, and Jan Zenisek provided me with crucial, daily support and friendship.

A single conversation with Alice Truax in 2005 helped me to find my way to the eventual structure of this book: That, despite the fact that our meeting was interrupted by a car crashing into the diner where we were seated.

I have benefitted enormously from the help of two research assistants. Adam Clark was a patient and scrupulous instructor in meteorology. Austin Bunn, a gifted reporter and writer, had the unfortunate task of managing my loose threads. He compiled research for me, tracked down former associates of Tetsuya Fujita, and undertook the assignment of fact-checking my work, in particular reinterviewing people in Limestone County. He offered me valuable editorial advice,

Acknowledgments

and was a wonderful partner in thinking through problems that I encountered.

My close friends and trusted readers, Shannon Welch and Jon Thirkield: thank you. Jack O'Brien: thank you.

At the outset of my work, Thomas and Doris Grazulis were kind enough to meet with me at their home and offer wisdom on the subject of historic tornado research. Mr. Grazulis's work is a model of dedication and thoroughness.

Candy Medina in Louisville; Jane Willis in Brandenburg; Robert Stewart and Joy Warner in Xenia; the late Faye Acton Axford, Willie Green, Joe and Jo Ann Isom, Wes Isom, Don and Sheila Lauderdale, Bill Dunnavant, Buddy Evans, Spencer Black, Ralph Padgett, Paula Marbut, and countless others in Athens and Limestone: thank you for your time and your willingness to lend me materials.

The staff of the Limestone County Archives were unfailingly accommodating. Kelly Kazek of the *Athens News Courier* and Daphne Ellison of the Limestone County Emergency Management Agency provided scans of photographs. Charles Jordan shared many photographs from his collection. Simma Levine and Steven King assisted with obtaining permissions for the use of music lyrics. Many thanks to you all.

I am grateful, too, to members of the Executive Committee of the Limestone County Chapter of the NAACP, for helping to put me in touch with people who were able to speak about aspects of African-American life in Limestone, which has a rich, but virtually undocumented, history.

It's difficult for me to express my gratitude to the people whose stories became the center of this book. When I set out to investigate April 3, 1974, Limestone County was one of many places in which I stopped. I didn't know that it would figure as the location of the book until I found myself returning there again and again. Limestone struck me as unlike any other place I visited: a lost world and an ongoing world occupying the same site. I was moved by many of the people I met. I loved the rhythms of their speech, their self-effacement, their blend of reticence and forthcomingness, their occasional bluster, and their natural refusal to conform to stereotypes. The relationship between an interviewer and his subject is a complicated one. I lived with the voices of the people in this book for three years. To the many, many people I met who are not named in this book, and whose voices are not quoted: you helped bring this

306

Acknowledgments

world to life for me. To those who are named in this book: I hope I have begun to do you justice. You helped me to understand.

Understanding: It is the difficult challenge. I had to learn to understand that those who were lost that day three decades ago are still being searched for by the ones they left behind. "Disaster" stories are built on anonymous suffering and death; I had to learn that no such anonymity exists. Briefly then, by way of acknowledgment, one final tornado story: On April 13, 2006, as I was in the thick of writing *F5*, I came home in the evening with my wife, Emily, and our four-month-old son, Everett, to discover that a tornado was approaching our town. We retreated to our basement and listened to the radio. After a while, I ran upstairs to look at the radar on television. I watched hail fall on the street. Emily called me back downstairs. The noise of the storm changed from a battering rain to a sudden whine. It shouldn't have been necessary for me to be in a tornado to understand what Donnie Powers, Felica (Golden) Powers, and the families of Frank Orr, Marilyn McBay, Annias Green, and Walter McGlocklin went through. But it helped to impress on me the reality of that evening thirty-two years earlier. The funnel cut through the center of Iowa City, a few blocks from our house. There was plenty of damage to stare at the following day. I took pictures of it. Some of it is still there, as I write, nine months later. The tornado was an F2.

Emily, Everett: it is not just this book that would be impossible for me without you.

Permissions and Photo Credits

Photo Credits

Two tornadoes: Courtesy of Bulletin of the American Meteorological Society "Taking Cover as Second Tanner": Courtesy of Charles Jordan

Donnie and Felica photos: Courtesy of Donnie and Felica Powers

Orr family: Courtesy of Marilyn McBay

Green family: Courtesy of Willie Green

Sheriff Evans: Courtesy of M.W. Evans

Dr. Fujita: photo by Dale Wittner

Lawson's Trailer Park: photo by Charles Jordan Two Limestone damage pictures: from *April 3, 1974: The Alabama Tornadoes*, published by C.F. Boone

McGlocklin family photo: Courtesy of Walter McGlocklin

McGlocklin house and car photos: photos by Charles Jordan George Wallace: photo by Jim Tuten for the *Huntsville Times* Richard Nixon: from *April 3, 1974: The Alabama Tornadoes*, published by C.F. Boone

Map Credits

p. i map: Limestone County, Alabama, April 3, 1974. By David Atkinson, Handmade Maps.

p. 238 map: *Superoutbreak Tornadoes of April 3-4, 1974*. By T. Theodore Fujita. Courtesy of Southwest Collection/Special Collections Library, Texas Tech University, Lubbock, Texas.

Quoted material is used by permission as follows:

Memoirs of an Effort to Unlock the Mystery of Severe Storms During the 50 Years, 1942-1992, by T. Theodore Fujita. Copyright 1992 by T. Theodore Fujita. Published by the Wind Research Laboratory, University of Chicago. Used by permission of Kazuya Fujita.

I Had a Hammer by Hank Aaron and Lonnie Wheeler. Copyright 1991 by Henry Aaron and Lonnie Wheeler. Used by permission of HarperCollins Publishers.

Transcripts from broadcasts on WHAS-AM, Louisville, are used by permission of 84WHAS.

© 1971 *If*—written by David Gates—Sony/ATV Tunes LLC. All rights administered by Sony/ATV Music Publishing, 8 Music Square West, Nashville, TN 37203. All rights reserved. Used by permission.

"Born To Lose" by Ted Daffan, © 1943 by Peer International Corporation, Copyright Renewed. International Copyright Secured. Used by Permission. All Rights Reserved.

© 1972 *Pass Me By If You're Only Passing Through*—written by Hall Hillman by permission of Leahrae Music Co under license from CGM Partners. Used by permission, international copyright secured.

© 1974 *Seasons in the Sun*—written by Jacques Brel and Rod McKuen by permission of Societe Nouvelle des Editions Musicales Tutti under license from Warner Chappell Music. International Copyright Secured. Used by Permission.

© 1951 *Bown's Ferry Blues*—written by Alton & Delmore Rabon by permission of Unichappell Music under license from Alfred Publishing Co., and Vidor Publications. Used by Permission. International Copyright Secured.